Between Ocean and City

The Columbia History of Urban Life
Kenneth T. Jackson, General Editor

Between Ocean and City

The Transformation of Rockaway, New York

LAWRENCE KAPLAN & CAROL P. KAPLAN

Columbia University Press

New York

Columbia University Press

Publishers Since 1893

New York   Chichester, West Sussex

Copyright © 2003 Columbia University Press

All rights reserved

Library of Congress Cataloging-in-Publication Data

Kaplan, Lawrence.
    Between ocean and city : the transformation of Rockaway, New York /
Lawrence Kaplan and Carol P. Kaplan.
        p.   cm. — (The Columbia history of urban life)
    Includes bibliographical references and index.
    ISBN 0–231–12848–7 (cloth : alk. paper); 0–231–12849–5 (paper : alk. paper)
    1. Rockaway (New York, N.Y.) — History. 2. New York (N.Y.) — History.
3. City and town life — New York (State) — New York — History. I. Kaplan,
Carol P. II. Title. III. Series.

F129.R8 K37 2003
974.7'243—dc21
                                                                        2002034754

Columbia University Press books are printed on permanent and
durable acid-free paper.
Printed in the United States of America
c 10 9 8 7 6 5 4 3 2 1
p 10 9 8 7 6 5 4 3 2 1

To the memory of all those Rockaway residents who died in the World Trade Center disaster of 9/11/01, and to all those who died in the crash of American Airlines Flight 587

And to the memory of our parents:

Esther and Nathan Kaplan
Florence and Morris Pasternak

And losing track
of where I was coming from
with the amnesia of an immigrant
I traveled over
the extroverted face
of America

But no matter where I wandered
off the chart
I still would love to find again
that lost locality
Where I might catch once more
a Sunday subway for
some Far Rockaway of the heart

Lawrence Ferlinghetti, from *A Far Rockaway of the Heart*

Contents

Illustrations

Rockaway, New York

BROOKLYN

JAMAICA BAY

JAMAICA BAY WILDLIFE REFUGE

J.F.K. Int'l Airport

JAMAICA BAY

NASSAU COUNTY

Beach 9th

Central Ave.

FAR ROCKAWAY

B. 35th

EDGEMERE

ARVERNE

B. 73rd

Rockaway Beach Blvd.

HAMMELS

SEASIDE

Cross Bay Bridge

BROAD CHANNEL

Beach Channel Dr.

B. 98th

ROCKAWAY PARK

NEPONSIT

BELLE HARBOR

B. 149th

JACOB RIIS PARK

Marine Parkway Bridge

ROXBURY

FORT TILDEN

ROCKAWAY INLET

BREEZY POINT

ATLANTIC OCEAN

Flatbush Avenue

QUEENS

Rockaway

Roads
Ponds
Parks

N

0 — 2 Miles

Preface

In the course of researching and writing this book, we have incurred debts to many individuals and institutions. Knowledgeable people helped us by granting interviews, making suggestions, and challenging our assumptions. We feel fortunate in the relationships that were formed in the course of our investigations. In many ways, this book became a dialogue with all those who expanded our perspective. It is difficult to name everyone who played this role, but we would like to single out for appreciation Helen and William Rausnitz, Pat Brownell, Lovette Glasgow, Goldie Maple, Doris Moss, Sol Gorelick, Elaine Babian, Mary Ann Quaranta, Bertram Beck, Julius Edelstein, and Louis D. Winnick. Roger Starr called our attention to obscure references, assisted us in gaining access to files not readily available, and offered useful insights. We had good talks at the *Wave* office with its publisher, Leon S. Locke, and its current coeditor, Howard Schwach. Local historian Emil Lucev kindly shared documentary material with us. We understand that some people mentioned above will disagree with our book's conclusions. Unfortunately, not all of those we thank lived to see this manuscript published.

Valuable information came from interviews cited in the notes. Only a minority of those we approached in the course of our research refused to cooperate. Certain individuals with whom we spoke at length did not wish to be named, and we have respected their requests. We omitted specific attributions in those cases in which conversations with informed people tended to be of a general nature, since they were usually supplemented by printed materials.

Several librarians helped immeasurably, calling our attention to materials that would otherwise have been overlooked. We are particularly grateful to William Asadorian and John Hyslop at the Queens Borough Public Library, Kenneth Cobb at the Municipal Archives, Rob Dishon at Fiorello H. LaGuardia Community College, David Pfeiffer at the National Archives in College Park, MD, Frank Braconi and Marian Sameth of the Citizens Housing and Planning Council, Robert Bernstein and Laura Rosen of the MTA, Roger Harris of Fordham University, and Harold W. Oakhill at the Rockefeller Archive Center. Vincent Seyfried made his extensive collection of old photographs available, and Miguel Mercado came with us to Rockaway to add new ones. Rita Noorzad skillfully created a map of the Rockaways.

Many friends and colleagues encouraged this project from the start, too many to list. But mention must be made of Ernest Urvater, Judy and Mort Tiersten, Jeanne Chase, Robert Twombly, Marilyn Smolin, Lilly and Paul Rozansky, Herbert Hoffner, Jay Greenfield, Leonard Sloane, Neil Mullin, Norman Zipkin, Gerald Leberfeld, Ruth Ross, and Norman Brodbar. We extend our appreciation to all members of the Kaplan family, especially our daughters, Laura and Nina, and our son-in-law, Bill Tiersten. We are also grateful to all those friends who tolerated our multiyear obsession with the Rockaways.

The Institut d'Anglais-Charles V, Université Paris 7, and the Columbia University Seminar on the City allowed us to present earlier versions of material from the present book. Our reading group, including James Edwards, Alice and David Sprintzen, Ruth and Arnold Silverman, and Barbara Reinfeld, offered thoughtful advice.

This manuscript benefited from the critical suggestions made by anonymous readers for Columbia University Press, which we did not immediately appreciate when they were first offered. We want to thank Peter Dimock, a senior executive editor at the press, and assistant editor Anne Routon for facilitating the publication process, and Kenneth T. Jackson for first suggesting that we send the manuscript to Columbia. Thanks also to our copy editor, Michael Haskell. Our debt to Doris Friedensohn, who patiently read through each chapter of this book and labored to make its arguments clear and its prose readable, is incalculable. Because she preferred to read individual chapters on long plane journeys, we are grateful for her love of travel. Neither she nor any of the other people cited are responsible for any of the book's shortcomings.

This book has been a joint effort. One of the authors, Lawrence Kaplan, grew up in the Rockaways and maintains a close connection with numerous friends who shared his experiences there. Like most of them he has a tendency to romanticize the past, but as a professional historian he has endeavored to overcome it. The coauthor, Carol P. Kaplan, has a more detached perspective and collaborated in transforming what began as a kind of personal memoir into a more scholarly treatment.

Between Ocean and City

Introduction

The study that follows deals with the harsh transformation of an urban community in the decades immediately after the Second World War. Rockaway, New York, located in the southern part of New York City's borough of Queens, is a slender peninsula, the westernmost of the barrier beaches that reach from the eastern tip of Long Island to New York's harbor. It is also known as Rockaway Beach, or simply the Rockaways, a name derived from a Native American word meaning "sand place."[1] Outsiders sometimes refer to the whole peninsula as Far Rockaway, but this is the name of only the largest and most built-up of the smaller communities that compose the Rockaways.

During the later years of the twentieth century, Rockaway received little mention in New York's newspapers of record. Whenever a story did appear, usually on a back page, it invariably discussed something unpleasant. Younger people living in the metropolitan area today know little about the peninsula; at best, they might have vague negative impressions. Passengers in planes taking off from, or landing at, John F. Kennedy International Airport often fly over it but take no particular notice of the strip of land that juts out between the Atlantic Ocean and Jamaica Bay.

Earlier generations of New Yorkers, on the other hand, were well aware of Rockaway's existence and the role it played in the recreational life of the greater metropolitan region. Throughout the first half of the twentieth century, its beaches provided a major source of diversion and pleasure to New York's masses. As an ocean community, Rockaway Beach used to be a popular seaside resort. Millions of people flocked to its shores every summer to enjoy the ocean, the boardwalk, and the amusement parks that provided a million dollars worth of entertainment (as one standard advertisement boasted). Rockaway publicists pointed out that the area was less crowded than its major rival, Coney Island, and claimed that it offered superior comforts. According to former parks commissioner Robert Moses, who was in a position to know, Rockaway Beach was "the city's favorite shore resort."[2]

For the first half of the century, the small, but growing, year-round population of the Rockaways enjoyed a sense of cohesion rare in contemporary urban society. The middle- and lower-middle-class neighborhoods in which the white population, primarily Jewish and Irish, lived followed a familiar seasonal calendar. Summer visitors arrived with the end of the school year, and most permanent residents felt relieved when these aliens returned to their concrete-bound city blocks each Labor Day. In addition, the delimited outlines of the Rockaway peninsula brought about a clearly defined local consciousness. This communal identity remains alive today in the memories of those who attended Far Rockaway High School, until the 1970s the only public high school on the peninsula and the one that most students attended. A 1997 Far Rockaway High School reunion, to which all alumni were invited, attracted more than four thousand people. Alumni also make active use of the Far Rockaway High School Web site.

Although officially part of Queens, Rockaway is separated from the rest of its borough by the affluent Five Towns of Nassau County and from Brooklyn by Jamaica Bay. Mass transit did not arrive until June 1956, and the community's remoteness from the rest of New York City made it feel like a suburb within the city's boundaries. Distanced from the hustle and bustle of Manhattan, its young people had limited contact with outside influences, and many residents remained rather provincial.

Shortly after World War II, Rockaway's character began to change. By the early 1950s, the area began to lose its resort function, and within another decade, the formerly vigorous recreational aspect of the peninsula had practically disappeared. At the same time, the permanent population grew substantially, and ethnic, racial, and class differences became more pronounced. For a variety of complex reasons, which trumped the desirability of living near the ocean, many middle- and lower-middle-class white families moved away. Around the same time, large numbers of minorities, mainly poor African Americans, moved in.

New York experienced the same severe housing shortages, compounded by the migration north of southern blacks and Hispanics, that confronted other cities after World War II. Rockaway's isolation and open spaces tempted public officials to regard the area as a convenient place to relocate poor minorities out of the center of the city. Many of these new residents, recipients of public assistance, did not come to the Rockaways by choice; rather, municipal authorities directed them there. Government agencies simply accepted the restrictive and segregated practices that prevailed in other parts of the metropolitan area and made no attempt to challenge them. As the seasonal trade diminished, the local establishment mounted little opposition to the introduction of large numbers of poor families into Rockaway's vacant summer housing stock. The horribly inadequate accommodations never troubled the responsible parties.

At first the new residents were moved into the old bungalows and rooming houses once used by a transient tourist population. Barely tolerable during the hot months of the year, they proved to be unhealthy and became dangerous firetraps during the winter. In fact, poor families sent to Rockaway lived in some of the worst conditions in New York City. Over the years, a succession of urban renewal plans necessitated the relocation of the same families time after time into progressively worse housing.

Starting shortly after World War II, and continuing for more than two decades, public housing developments were built in the Rockaways that eventually came to be occupied largely by a welfare population. Many of the tenants came from outside the community, so that the low-income projects served to bring more poor families to the peninsula. Although Rockaway was home to only .05 percent of the total population of Queens, it soon contained over 50 percent of all the housing projects in the borough. Before long, a large number of group homes were established for released mental patients. Around the same time, nursing homes for the elderly were built along the shore, and soon the Rockaways had more of these facilities than any other part of greater New York. Rockaway residents frequently used the term "dumping" to describe the process by which New York City moved deprived, helpless, and troubled individuals and families to its community.

Yet Rockaway proved to be an inhospitable location for many of these new arrivals. The decline of the resort had eliminated summer employment, and the few small factories that existed gradually disappeared. The peninsula's distance from industrial and commercial areas made commuting cumbersome and relatively expensive for people who were already strained by poverty and related problems. Social services were notable for their absence. As the number of poor people and welfare cases increased, large portions of the peninsula began suffering from the ills associated with modern urban life. Crime and substance abuse rates increased. The figures for unemployment, infant mortality, infectious diseases, school dropouts, and, later, HIV/AIDS became among the highest in all of New York City.

Recognizing that the summer shacks that housed welfare families beside the ocean in the Rockaways could never offer a permanent solution, municipal authorities decided to tear them down. But no provision was made for the residents, and no plan existed for future land use. During the late 1960s and early 1970s, several thousand people were evicted from these shacks, and miles of beachfront property were leveled. Over time some construction appeared on the vast sandy acreage, but for more than thirty years it remained empty except for weeds. The former houses, shops, and playing fields were demolished. While such destruction was visited on other places in the United States, this area in the Rockaways was the largest of its kind. The abandoned property created a disfigured landscape, one that appeared especially unseemly lying just adjacent to the beach in this beautiful setting. Observers described the land as bombed out.

Suffering in the Rockaways was not uniform. For various reasons, including political influence and segregated housing policies, some of the communities in the western section avoided the difficulties that beset the major portion of the peninsula. Orthodox Jews, who set up separate schools and religious institutions, established a rapidly growing, tightly knit enclave, mainly in Far Rockaway. Some members of minority groups became politically active and demanded decent public schools and other services for themselves and their families. They were not always successful, but their efforts did bring about certain positive results. Their resiliency is one of the more positive aspects of our story.

Many present day Rockawayites, including minorities, report that they enjoy living on the peninsula, citing virtually the same advantages enjoyed by their predecessors, including proximity to the shore and a sense of community. Outside of Rockaway, however, the impression has persisted that the peninsula is an undesirable place to reside or even visit. Residents from the 1930s, 1940s, and 1950s consider themselves fortunate to have grown up and spent their formative years in an environment rendered idyllic by memory, but few of them have chosen to remain.[3] Throughout the United

States, even in the absence of drastic neighborhood change, the children of those who lived in older urban housing tended to relocate after World War II, preferring new single-family homes and suburban amenities. Government policies regarding housing, road construction, and mortgage loans definitely encouraged this trend, a process cogently described by Kenneth T. Jackson in his *Crabgrass Frontier*.[4]

Clearly, events in Rockaway during the early postwar years had counterparts in other sections of New York City and throughout the United States. Everywhere, middle-class urban areas became transformed by the influx of less affluent people who were escaping from poverty in the segregated south or places like Puerto Rico and Mexico. Drug-related crime undermined many communities in urban centers both large and small, including Rockaway. Describing the bleak reality of present-day Detroit in his prize-winning study, Thomas J. Sugrue saw the motor city "plagued by joblessness, concentrated poverty, physical decay, and racial isolation." For him, Detroit became a case study in what he calls the nation's "urban crisis."[5] In their own way, the Rockaways replicated the urban crisis Sugrue described. His depiction of the conditions in Detroit applied to large parts of Rockaway as well.

Scholars have pointed out that the causes of the urban crisis are many and vary from place to place. Racially determined residential patterns have often played a key role, as they did in both Detroit and Rockaway. Banks decreed the racial composition of the Boston communities of Roxbury, Dorchester, and Mattapan.[6] Detroit, like other Rust Belt cities of the Midwest, suffered a loss of jobs due to deindustrialization. In Homestead, Pennsylvania, many people lost work when local steel mills closed down; the town declined as a result. This pattern was repeated in other American cities.[7] To a certain extent, Rockaway also suffered from the decline of employment opportunities, but, with the exception of those who earned money from the summer trade, most employable persons who lived in Rockaway had always earned their living outside the peninsula.

In some areas, such as the Poletown section of Detroit, municipal authorities, desperate to create jobs and anxious to comply with industry demands, were willing to destroy a vital community.[8] In New York, the lives of ordinary people in the Bronx and Brooklyn were turned upside down by the decision to build highways through inhabited neighborhoods. This is one of the chief reasons why mention of New York's "Power Broker," Robert Moses, still evokes anger from those old enough to remember how his construction projects eliminated viable communities.[9] However, in the Rockaways Moses played a different role. He worked to build housing rather than to destroy it. He also strove to preserve and expand Rockaway as a resort and to make it accessible to working people.

While some municipal leaders around the country allowed their city centers to decline, choosing suburbs as the places where the affluent resided and eventually worked, New York opted for a vibrant center and deteriorating peripheries. Several neighborhoods in the outer boroughs succumbed to the urban crisis as more poor people gradually moved in. The South Bronx and the Brownsville neighborhood of Brooklyn have become symbols of such trends. Wendell Pritchett has demonstrated how urban redevelopment programs elsewhere in the city relocated large numbers of poor minority families to Brownsville tenements, leading to the community's deterioration.[10] This also took place in the Rockaways. But to add to the peninsula's difficulties, New York City's welfare department used the Rockaways as a site for families with special problems and needs—that is, for some of its most intractable cases. Moreover, services in the Rockaways were less than adequate to nurture and assist these new arrivals and their children. Although Brownsville contained some of the worst buildings in the city, few of them were as unpalatable as the former summer rooming houses and bungalows in Rockaway. To add insult to injury, impoverished people here found themselves shifted around every few years by government agencies. One could argue that the Rockaway poor received worse treatment than their counterparts in any other urban location outside the south.

In researching the causes of Rockaway's postwar transformation, we were forced to conclude that the most significant role was played by official decisions. This book will show how the liberal administrative state took the lead in determining Rockaway's fate. Responsibility therefore rests with political leaders and the administrators of city agencies who carried out their decisions, assisted by cooperative local landlords. In defense of these bureaucrats, apologists argue that solutions were needed for major problems that contemporary racist attitudes rendered almost insoluble: Where should the poorest of the poor be housed? What practical remedy existed to meet the needs of indigent minority families whom few neighborhoods in New York City were willing to accept?

Apparently the political power of a white majority population, who regarded intrusion by minorities into their communities as unacceptable, made it politically suicidal to go against such sentiments. As a result, agencies delivering social services, such as the Housing Authority and the welfare department, would only send minority families to already segregated areas or to deteriorating sections of the outer boroughs. As far as officials were concerned, transferring urban problems to isolated areas of New York City allowed them to remain politically popular by removing social problems from the gaze of the electorate. They had little regard for the consequences of their actions or the human suffering they caused. Although these opportunistic policies temporarily solved pressing issues, they failed in the long run. Additional social ills eventually developed that impacted the entire city, and there could be little hope of resolving them. When their efforts inevitably failed, the liberal establishment received the blame. Many reasons have been suggested for the decline of liberalism after midcentury, but the predictable results of welfare state compromises, such as the ones that affected Rockaway, must be given weight.

While this book was being completed, two catastrophic events brought the Rockaways to the attention of the general public: the attack on the World Trade Center and the crash of American Airlines Flight 587 two months later. More than seventy residents of the peninsula, mainly firefighters and police officers, but also people who worked at the World Trade Center, lost their lives on 9/11. This number surpasses that of any other community in the New York area. Two months later, on November 12, the shock of the plane crash in Rockaway that killed all 260 people on board and demolished houses on the ground, killing five residents, added to the trauma suffered by local residents. At least temporarily, this forgotten section of New York City came to public attention.

Rockaway and its story have been neglected for almost half a century. We hope that this book will lead to a better understanding of its recent history and the experiences of its inhabitants. Former residents of the peninsula have tended to focus on the harm done to their beloved community. On one level, to be sure, city authorities allowed a resort to be undermined, a natural treasure that had long been a valued resource for the city's masses. In reality, however, the crimes committed against the people who were sent there were far more offensive.

CHAPTER I

The Resort in Summer and Winter

Many of those with longstanding connections to Rockaway tend to pose the same question: how could such a valuable resource have been allowed to go to ruin? All over the globe, beachfront property is treasured. Yet in New York City, the resort once called the city's favorite playground, described by the *New York Times* as "the equivalent of some of the great beaches of the world,"[1] became a symbol of urban decline.

Of course, not everyone connected with the peninsula views its transformation as a disaster. People who do so tend to define "decline" as the disappearance of the original community and its replacement by another that closely resembles some of the poorest sections of New York City. But it could very well be argued that such a definition assumes a past rendered mythical by memory, representing a longing for lost experiences that ignores unpleasant realities. Researching the history of the Rockaways, one discovers that a great many senior citizens, usually Jewish or Irish, living in the metropolitan New York area or in retirement elsewhere, have a nostalgic Rockaway story to tell. Whether they spent summer weeks at a rented room or bungalow or traveled out for day trips, older generations recall the strong surf, a sunburn received on the white sandy beach, an outing at Rockaway's Playland, or meeting members of the opposite sex on the boardwalk. Not surprisingly, persons with the greatest sense of loss had been part of the small year-round white community. Although they no longer reside in this fabled paradise, they still praise Rockaway's golden age. African Americans who lived in the old Rockaway may have different stories, but theirs are rarely heard.[2]

Idealizing the places of one's childhood is a familiar phenomenon; however, it has particular meaning for people who experienced the rapid changes in urban America in the years following World War II. A sizeable literature focusing on this period, including memoirs and works of fiction, memorializes vanished neighborhoods and lifestyles. Some nonfiction authors, also of the nostalgic school, assign blame for events that allegedly need not have happened. Usually the villains are portrayed as coming from outside the community. For example, Robert Moses is said to have destroyed the vital Jewish East Tremont section of the Bronx almost single-handedly,[3] while urban development is seen as having eliminated a functioning lower-class Italian village in Boston's west end.[4] Other studies, scholarly and anecdotal, depict the ways in which urban life was undermined during this same period.[5] With these examples in mind, it would appear logical to conclude that the Rockaways were victimized by external forces.

People who believe that the fate of the Rockaways could have been avoided emphasize the advantages of this resort community. Turning the original question back on its head, they argue that the presence of a wonderful ocean beach and boardwalk should by rights have kept the area attractive to the resident middle class. Moreover, the peninsula's many tracts of available land could easily have lent themselves to development, as well as redevelopment, thereby attracting new middle-class residents. Given all its empty space, Rockaway was perfectly positioned to satisfy the desire for home ownership. Suburban patterns, which centered around owner-occupied, single-family dwellings in low-density settings, already existed on a small scale on the peninsula, and they might have been extended further without much difficulty. Low real estate taxes within the city limits offered an inducement for those wishing to buy property. In addition, the introduction of public transportation in the mid-1950s allowed for commuting to Manhattan by subway, a benefit not possible in other suburban areas. At the same time, more affluent residents of the peninsula could have made the more comfortable, though expensive and roundabout, trip on the Long Island Rail Road line that has always operated out of Far Rockaway. Surely, the suburban characteristics of the Rockaways might have helped to offset the outward migration of a middle-class population after World War II.

The sociologist Roger Waldinger, discussing urban population changes in New York, could have been describing Rockaway:

> Some of the demand for single-family houses could be satisfied within the boundaries of the five boroughs. Queens and Staten Island, in particular, had enough cheap, vacant land to support a massive wave of suburban style construction. Ultimately, the suburban push could be met only in underdeveloped communities within commuting distance of the city's principal concentrations of employment.[6]

Many old-timers recognize that the Rockaway peninsula has always possessed a certain suburban quality, a point made by *The WPA Guide to New York City* published in the 1930s.[7] The area's sparse year-round population, just under forty thousand permanent residents in the late 1930s, on "a spit of land" eleven miles long, gave it the feeling of a rural township. Traffic during the off-season was light compared with most other parts of New York City, so that children had little difficulty safely negotiating the empty streets with their bicycles and roller skates. At the same time, the abundant empty lots and summer parking areas offered ample play-space and ball fields. The separated one-, two-, and three-family homes provided a sense of openness that contrasted sharply with the apartment houses of the populous, congested boroughs of Manhattan, Brooklyn, and the Bronx, as well as sections of Queens. During the 1930s, 1940s, and early 1950s, residents left their doors unlocked. "Everyone knew everyone" and looked after each other's kids, not only on the immediate block, but on adjoining ones as well. Small local shops readily advanced credit and willingly made deliveries to home-bound customers. The numerous local houses of worship brought residents even closer together. For example, before it was destroyed by fire in May 2002, many former Jewish residents maintained a continuing sentimental attachment to, and support for, the isolated, barely standing synagogue, Derech Emunoh, in the Arverne section of Rockaway. Similarly, the Irish revere their beloved parish churches.

For a number of reasons, community feeling ran particularly strong on the peninsula. Unlike most parts of New York City, Rockaway possesses clearly defined borders. Thus, while it might be hard to determine where Bayside or Bensonhurst begin and end, no such difficulty has ever existed for Rockaway, which consists of a barrier beach connected to a tapering section of the Five Towns of Nassau County and separated from New York City by bodies of water. Moreover, the community has often felt either ignored or singled out for special negative treatment. Rockaway has often viewed itself as a colony, one ostensibly having a representative government but dependent on the distant city for basic services and without sufficient leverage to ward off destructive policies. This colonial metaphor has contributed to the residents' self-image as a community that is both set apart and under siege. In fact, on two occasions, in 1915 and 1917, the Rockaways attempted to secede from New York City, even getting as far as receiving affirmative votes from the New York State Legislature. This occurred less than twenty years after the peninsula was detached from the town of Hempstead and made part of the borough of Queens and the newly enlarged Greater New York.[8] At numerous points during the subsequent century, residents have speculated about how the community would have fared without the city's repeated unwelcome intrusions, and a tiny secessionist movement still exists.[9]

Rockaway's geographical separation and its sense of isolation created a fierce localism. The areas on the other side of the two bridges were known as "the mainland." Indeed, the presence of "invaders" every summer reinforced the attempt permanent residents made to maintain a separate identity, particularly after Labor Day when the beaches became deserted, "and nearly all the bungalows, shops, hotels and bathhouses along the boardwalk [were] closed, like theatres out of season."[10] Many residents believed that summer visitors were a different breed, more diverse, more urban, more street-wise, and more sophisticated than Rockaway natives, but lacking the special qualities that came from living all year long in this sparsely populated community.

Rockaway institutions have always retained their own character and traditions. Every Memorial Day a parade consisting of soldiers from nearby Fort Tilden, diverse veteran organizations, local parochial school students, and scout troops with their bands would march down a three-mile section of the area's oldest main boulevard. Rockaway real estate agencies specialized exclusively in peninsula holdings, while two private hospitals, staffed by local physicians, served Rockaway patients. Political patronage took various forms for the permanent residents. Rockaway politicians not only interceded with outside authorities on behalf of constituents, they also helped them find jobs in the expanded seasonal job market. At the Rockaway courthouse, built during the New Deal, political connections helped natives get traffic tickets "fixed."

A single public high school in Far Rockaway served the entire peninsula exclusively until 1973, when a second high school opened. Few parochial schools existed in these midcentury years, and exceptional Rockaway students rarely went to elite public high schools in other boroughs, undoubtedly because of the distance. As a result, Far Rockaway High School brought together students from all socioeconomic backgrounds, and it gave them a coherent sense of community that remained powerful decades after graduation. Alumni from those earlier years speak about the comfortable socializing that took place on teams, in clubs, and in fraternities and sororities, despite ethnic and class differences.

Local weekly papers, especially the *Rockaway Journal* and the *Wave*, which have existed for more than one hundred years, kept people informed about events on the peninsula. The two weeklies provided a Rockaway-centered view of the world. Their editorial positions tended to favor dominant business interests, whose advertisements kept these journals solvent, and their opinions usually reflected those of the Rockaway Chamber of Commerce. A major unifying influence in the Rockaways, the Chamber of Commerce had begun operating in 1925 and for decades remained an effective presence in the life of the community. It maintained an office with a paid staff, a rotating presidency, and a full time executive secretary—a position held for many years by George Wolpert, a shrewd and capable director who understood New York City power relations and prided himself on his seemingly close relationship with the kingpin, Robert Moses. A photograph of the two men huddled together appeared regularly in the *Rockaway Review*, the organization's house publication (see figure 3). By 1947, the chamber's membership roster contained "well-over 1500 business firms, property owners and residents," essentially the most influential people on the peninsula. Real estate companies were heavily represented. In fact, exaggerated claims were made that between 85 and 90 percent of all private real estate in Rockaway Beach was "held in whole or in part by members of the Chamber."[11]

Boasting that theirs was "the largest and most active Chamber of Commerce in the United States for a community the size of the Rockaways," the chamber's stated function was "to serve the best interests of all of the Rockaways." As proof of their effectiveness, the *Rockaway Review* frequently ran another photograph showing a chamber president standing with Fiorello H. LaGuardia as the mayor signed a special refund assessment bill returning some three million dollars to local property owners. This measure had passed largely due to the chamber's efforts.[12]

Each year, the *Review* provided space for articles by public figures and New York City administrators, asking that they report on how they had brought improvements to the peninsula. Approximately twenty officials regularly complied with such an accounting, including the mayor himself. The most literary of the annual statements was usually that of the New York City Commissioner of Parks, Robert Moses. An annual chamber dinner, held in an elegant local hotel, rewarded the one municipal official who had best advanced the Rockaway cause during the year. Those honored included public servants, mayors, borough presidents, and, in 1952, the distinguished commissioner of parks himself.

Surprisingly, in his influential biography of Robert Moses, Robert Caro has very little to say about his subject's relationship to the Rockaways. Yet, as the local Chamber of Commerce well appreciated, for approximately thirty years Moses played the single most important role in determining the fate of the peninsula. It fell naturally to a man of multiple accomplishments, who held, at the pinnacle of his power, twelve different state and municipal positions.[13] In addition, Moses had a special interest in and affection for the Rockaways, one that went back at least to the 1930s and continued well into his retirement. Especially after the parks department assumed responsibility for seashore maintenance just before the Second World War, he would proudly point out that the millions of daily summer visitors to Rockaway gave it the distinction of having "the largest beach usage of any of the public beaches in the world."[14] While the peninsular community may not always have been his primary consideration, it remained high on his list of priorities. Other projects, such as Lincoln Center, sometimes took precedence for the comissioner, superseding the interests of the Rockaways, but this rarely happened.[15]

Moses was a man of strong opinions, secure in his belief that he knew the best course of action. Ever arrogant, he never doubted that he was right. He is a paradoxical figure: an elitist who believed in serving the public good. His confidence enabled him to accomplish a great many of his goals. No one could disagree with the statement "that he got things done."[16] Indisputably, he lived in an era in which governments heavily supported construction of roads, public housing, and other public projects. His legacy includes 12 bridges, 35 highways, 658 playgrounds, and more than 2 million acres of parks.[17] As Alexander Garvin observed in his important book, *The Ameri-*

can City, "Moses acquired and developed more city parks and playgrounds than any municipal officer in any American city at any time."[18]

Moses was a doer with a vision. The quality that most impressed his biographer, Robert Caro, was his ability to see the big picture, to take in the whole city of New York. But while he could create, he could also destroy. Caro cites twenty instances in which he bulldozed neighborhoods, always claiming that he was serving some greater good.[19] Although Moses acted in the name of the people, he frequently treated individuals like pawns. His obsession with highways and roads destroyed numerous New York communities, and even more would have disappeared if he had not occasionally met with resistance.

When asked late in his life what accomplishment gave him the most pride, Moses responded, "That was easy, Jones Beach."[20] Many observers agree that this beach on southern Long Island is the finest man-made shore park in the United States. It embodied his ideal of a public recreational facility. The park included spacious sandy beaches and a well-maintained boardwalk with tasteful food emporia and clean changing facilities built a considerable distance from the ocean. It also contained a large swimming pool, playgrounds, grass and trees, ample space for sports of various kinds, a theatre for outdoor performances, and sizeable parking lots. Even the roads leading to the beach were constructed to resemble parkland: they were richly planted and devoid of the clutter found on most access highways. As a public environmentalist, Moses was ahead of his time.[21] He considered amusement parks, concession stands, and billboards a product of private greed and a defilement of nature, and he absolutely forbade them.

At an early stage in his career, Moses realized that only public authorities could protect Long Island barrier beaches from the selfish interests of property owners. With his Progressive-era sense of civic responsibility, he believed that natural places should be considered a public resource and not sectioned off with signs declaring "no trespassing." By the 1930s time was running out for public conservation, as available ocean frontage rapidly became preempted for private or commercial purposes. Free access to beaches and other shorefront recreational areas could be salvaged only through governmental action. By placing them under public control and then building roads to them, he intended to make seashore parklands available to the region's masses.

Moses valued the role of play in people's lives—not just any kind of play, but wholesome activities, "healthy outdoor recreation."[22] He ranked swimming, boating, and fishing as among the most appropriate sports for a water facility. The beachside parks he built offered playgrounds, ball fields, archery, roller skating rinks, handball, basketball, ping pong, and tennis and shuffle board courts. The stresses of modern existence, Moses believed, could best be relieved through proper use of leisure time. He once wrote, regarding another potential resort, that it would relieve the pressures of city life by providing "a recreational ground for the millions cramped in the brick and steel of civilization."[23] Moses the moralist disapproved of the carnival atmosphere of amusement parks. He viewed these passive entertainments as contrived, commercialized exploitations of mass bad taste. For him, amusement parks were evidence that a particular resort had lost its basic purpose and would soon turn into a "slum."[24] If Jones Beach on Long Island's south shore represented the fullest realization of Moses's ideal public use beach, he viewed the New York City beaches of the pre–World War II era as the opposite, corrupted by private misuse. Jones Beach presented a clean slate that Moses fashioned completely in accord with his own tastes. In a report presented to the Rockaway Chamber of Commerce some years later, he succinctly described the difficult task of creating a viable ocean front community in the older places:

> Such beaches as the Rockaways and those on Long Island and Coney Island lend themselves to summer exploitation, to honky tonk catchpenny amusement resorts, shacks built without reference to health, sanitation, safety and decent living. The better residential areas are threatened by spreading neighborhood blight. Finally after years of neglect ambitious real estate people buy up the ocean front from complacent politicians, build a boardwalk over high water and line it on the inside with junk. The City then has to buy back what the old townships once owned and what the original settlers fondly thought was inalienable, and so what was potentially a summer resort on salt water and the best year round residential community, lacking only convenient transportation, becomes in large part a slum, and finally a new generation of public officials faces the problems of rehabilitation of what should never have been allowed to deteriorate.[25]

Moses believed that Coney Island, which had never been properly planned, was a prime case in point. Its overused beaches and cluttered

boardwalks barely operated at a decent financial level, and they had begun
to deteriorate as a result. According to a 1937 report issued by the Department of Parks, Coney Island had three key problems: "overcrowding at the
public beach, inadequate play areas and lack of parking space." Rectifying
these difficulties would require such drastic changes, entailing the elimination of amusement areas as well as most concessions, that New York City
could not afford the cost, and no independent authority could be found to
issue the requisite bonds. The renovation plan proposed for Coney Island
at this time, Moses confessed, "is a modest one, which can meet only the
most urgent needs of the situation." In the case of Coney Island, Moses,
who has frequently been characterized as a man who did not care about the
masses, showed his generous, progressive face. It bothered him that these
"people of smallest means," who could not afford to go to other beaches,
had to endure inferior conditions. At the same time, he firmly believed in
outdoor recreation's importance to every citizen. Accordingly, he opposed
the imposition of any additional fees that might discourage use of the its
beaches.[26] After World War II, Moses became even more pessimistic about
Coney Island's future. In a story related by a real estate executive about an
appeal that he and other Coney Islanders made in the late 1940s for an in-
fusion of funds from the city, Moses's succinct reply left no doubt about his
position. He is reported to have responded, " I wouldn't give you two cents
for the property here."[27]

In Moses's estimation, Rockaway during the 1930s resembled Coney
Island in that a natural beach had been defiled and ran the risk of becoming
a "slum." But Rockaway had been less built-up and contained considerable
amounts of open space, which gave it the potential for improvement. The
cost, Moses argued, would be much lower than that required for Coney Island.[28] With its growing year-round population, which included some
wealthy neighborhoods, the Rockaways could better absorb change than
resort towns totally dependent on a declining amusement industry. Finally, because here, unlike Coney Island, he could extend the operations of his
various authorities, the development of the Rockaways appealed to him. It
offered an excellent opportunity to enhance his power.

The Rockaway peninsula Moses encountered in the 1930s, although
technically unified, included several semi-independent communities. On
the extreme western tip lay Breezy Point, a gated enclave with a smattering of bungalows that were used mainly during the summer. Breezy Point
residents did not like to consider themselves part of Rockaway proper. East

along the peninsula there was a small army base, Fort Tilden, and a dilapidated public beach, Jacob Riis Park, named for the turn-of-the-century
writer who advocated recreational opportunities for the poor. The affluent
towns of Neponsit and Belle Harbor bordered Riis Park. As a result of zoning restrictions engineered by influential citizens, they remained chiefly
residential. Strict parking regulations, coupled with an absence of hotels,
stores, or boardwalk, gave them an exclusivity that endures.

Rockaway Park's western border was located at Beach 126th Street,
close to the beginning of the boardwalk, and the community ended to the
east at the terminus of the Long Island Rail Road at B. 116th Street. The
neighborhood had a mixture of one- and two-family houses, well maintained hotels, and some rooming houses. These facilities were more expensive than those in the eastern part of the peninsula, which catered to
day-trippers as well as summer renters. Going east, the area from Seaside
(B. 115th–B. 94th) to Hammels (also known as Hammel, B. 93rd–B. 74th)
held a mixture of bungalows, rooming houses, and mid-sized hotels, most
built around the turn of the century, along with bars, carousels, and several amusement parks, including Playland. The beach blocks in Arverne (B.
74th–B. 59th) and Edgemere (B. 58th–B. 32nd) contained bungalows and
rooming houses, but few bars or amusement rides. Both districts, especially Arverne, had a wide area between ocean and bay and a relatively large
winter population. Far Rockaway (B. 31st to the Nassau line), the commercial hub of the community, with the greatest number of permanent residents, was geographically the widest of the Rockaway communities. The
street boundaries between sections and subsections were somewhat arbi-
trary. Holland stood between Seaside and Hammels, Somerville could be
found north of Arverne, Wavecrest lay east of Edgemere, and Bayswater
just northwest of Far Rockaway. Even Breezy Point had three separate di-
visions. In later years, an unofficial West Lawrence was proclaimed on the
Nassau border of Far Rockaway.

Transportation to and from the Rockaways and within the community itself left much to be desired. Two thoroughfares ran from east to west.
The narrow and ancient Rockaway Beach Boulevard (completed in 1886)
made its way through the crowded streets in the middle of what had originally been the amusement section. The more recently completed Beach
Channel Drive (1920s) ran closer to the northern end of the peninsula but
ended in the middle, and thus did not fully alleviate beach traffic. The Long
Island Rail Road operated one direct train line to Rockaway, which ran on

a wooden trestle built over Jamaica Bay. It was frequently disabled by small fires in the surrounding marshes. Upon entering the peninsula the train ran along a ground level roadbed, necessitating numerous grade crossings. The shortest route by car from Manhattan, Brooklyn, and a good part of Queens was Cross Bay Boulevard, a curvy causeway that was not wide enough to accommodate the increasing volume of summer traffic. Some labeled it "New York City's worst bottleneck."[29] Consequently, hot weekends in July and August saw colossal traffic jams. Worst of all, after getting across Cross Bay Bridge, with its inadequate movable span, drivers encountered a confluence of intersecting roads. Visitors who did not arrive early in the day found it extremely difficult to park. Many of the local streets were dead ends, causing gridlock and road rage.

Bodies of water on two sides made Rockaway cool and breezy in the summer, even though Jamaica Bay to the north, a dumping ground for raw sewage, had become terribly polluted.[30] The peninsula also had the advantage of a much larger expanse of ocean shorefront than other city beaches, as well as a lively surf. However, the ocean beach suffered from serious erosion as the natural movement of tides from east to west, combined with hurricanes and other storms, drove the sand further down the peninsula. By the mid-1930s, the deteriorating boardwalk, now too close to the sea and inundated with concession stands, bathhouses, and amusements, gave the area a dilapidated appearance.

The housing along the beach front, especially to the east of Rockaway Park, ranged from crowded bungalow colonies to rooming houses in varying condition. Repairs were scanty, since Depression-era landlords resisted spending the money necessary to bring their aging properties above minimum standards. Occupants shared toilet facilities and outdoor showers. Closely situated wood-frame rooming houses made the area vulnerable to fires. In fact, catastrophic fires punctuate Rockaway's history. Nonetheless, for reasons that are hard to appreciate today, thousands of renters (the summer population reached 225,000 in 1947) put up with inconvenience and lack of privacy and returned each year to the city's "favorite playground."[31]

Moses wanted to transform the Rockaways into a resort with a future. Thus, he set out to rehabilitate the entire peninsula. Part of the process involved bringing it up to date with what he conceived as the coming age of the automobile. In addition to improving a vast seaside park, he wished also to provide "a guide to those who seek to reclaim beaches man has spoiled, and to restore them at least measurably for the purposes to which they were intended by nature."[32] This immense undertaking required the resources of state, municipal, and federal agencies, along with imaginative financing from a number of public authorities that later came to be known as the Triborough Bridge and Tunnel Authority (TBTA). The extent of Moses's accomplishments in the peninsula, what he termed the "Rockaway Improvement," has not been given the recognition it deserves.[33]

To start the "Rockaway Improvement," Moses had the New York City Council transfer responsibility for public beaches from individual borough presidents to the Department of Parks and himself as its commissioner. He then completely renovated Jacob Riis Park so that it resembled, in miniature, his prized Jones Beach, with a spacious beach front, a pleasant walkway, ball fields, picnic grounds, a golf course, and playgrounds, all flanked by a seventy-acre parking lot. While the original plan also called for a swimming pool, that project was never completed. For access by car, Moses built the Marine Parkway Bridge which, through an extension of Flatbush Avenue, tied in with the Belt Parkway, just then being completed by the Parkway Authority under his auspices. For those requiring public transportation, Riis Park was reachable for the first time by newly chartered bus lines. At this time Moses also renovated the Cross Bay Bridge and the causeway leading up to it so that the Rockaways now had two modern bridges crossing Jamaica Bay. He constructed ramp roads to facilitate the smooth flow of traffic on and off these spans, with Beach Channel Drive on the north end extended all the way to the Marine Parkway Bridge, making the bridge completely accessible by bus or car even from Far Rockaway. For summer visitors, additional parking lots were provided in the resort areas of the peninsula, with more planned for the future.

If Moses had had his way he would have torn down all the unsightly housing bordering the beach throughout the entire length of the Rockaways so that the boardwalk could be pushed back and the beach widened. This constituted part of his scheme to extend a highway from the Marine Parkway Bridge all the way to the Atlantic Beach Bridge at the eastern tip of the peninsula. He envisioned building a road that would make its way out to the Hamptons, but this goal remained unrealized. Restrained by limited funding, Moses cleared away a mile and a half of what he called "the worst seaside slum in the City" (B. 73rd–B. 108th Streets), including amusement areas and concessions. In place of the "slum" he created a shore parkway with adjoining parks, playgrounds, handball and paddle ball courts, a roller skating rink, and a reconstructed boardwalk. These improvements were made in time for the World's Fair of 1939.

The Chamber of Commerce fully supported all of these undertakings. In fact, in December 1937, when the president of the organization prepared a list of priorities for the coming year, "cooperating with Commissioner Moses in the development of the Rockaway ocean front" was one of the highest.[34] Nevertheless, the organization's commitment to real estate interests made its leaders ever-vigilant about property owners receiving "fair and reasonable awards" for condemned land. Executive Secretary George Wolpert even tried to have Moses delay the start of condemnations until after the summer of 1938 so that landlords might collect one last round of summer rents. But the commissioner made short shrift of this request, bluntly characterizing it as "mostly pure bunk." Catching the chamber in the basic contradiction between its members' profits and the community's long-term need, he added, "We can't make this improvement consistently by doing favors for people."[35]

The most ambitious of all the Rockaway improvements designed by Moses, one which had universal approval, necessitated removing the numerous grade crossings that punctuated the bed of the Long Island Rail Road that ran east to west across most of the peninsula. He accomplished this by elevating the tracks and then placing a highway underneath, further facilitating the flow of traffic. The cost of this project, together with the elimination of a major bottleneck on Woodhaven Boulevard leading to the Rockaways, approached $50,000,000. It was an enormous sum, especially for the depression years, and a measure of the extensive influence Moses wielded at this time.[36] The bridges to Rockaway and the roads leading to them cost approximately $10,000,000. Moses used creative financing when he received governmental authorization to merge the Marine Parkway Authority with the Henry Hudson Parkway Authority. The new entity, known at that time as the New York City Parkway Authority, used the tolls on the Cross Bay Bridge, the Marine Parkway Bridge, and the Henry Hudson Bridge to back a fresh bond issue. This, in turn, helped to pay off old obligations as well as the immediate expenses incurred by the extensive construction costs. New York City provided $3,100,000 to pay for land condemned in Rockaway under eminent domain. The total sum raised for the whole Rockaway Improvement, including roads, bridges, parks, and shore renovations, plus the retirement of outstanding bonds, reached a figure of $22,100,000.[37]

The improvements made in the Rockaways during the late 1930s and early 1940s, including the elevation by 1942 of the Long Island Rail Road line (the "el"), despite wartime priorities, were designed to make the resort aspect of the peninsula "more popular and accessible" to the people of New York City. In Moses's conception, these advances in infrastructure would also encourage the expansion of a year-round population, which those with a broad perspective, like the Chamber of Commerce and Moses himself, knew to be inevitable.[38] Many more improvements were planned, and with the "Power Broker" fully in gear, the prospects for the future of the peninsula, as World War II began to intervene, seemed as sunny as a "beach day" in summer.

CHAPTER 2

Race and Real Estate

The ethnic groups that constituted the year-round population of the Rockaways during the 1930s and 1940s included Irish Americans, Jews, African Americans, and a smattering of others. An earlier white Protestant section of Far Rockaway had slowly dwindled during the twentieth century. Many of the Irish were drawn to an ocean community that resembled their original home in County Sligo on the Atlantic Ocean in northwestern Ireland. They had come before the turn of the century, to work first on the railroads and then in the amusement industry. They remained in the area where the rides, taverns, and fast food establishments that catered to the summer tourist trade clustered. Some operated hotels and rooming houses. Their section, Seaside, was affectionately known as "Irish Town" for at least half a century. Numerous bars with names like "Dublin House," "Blarney Castle," and "Sligo House" perpetuated the distinct Irish flavor of the neighborhood.[1] While Irish parishioners predominated in the many Catholic churches on the peninsula, they were joined by a substantial number of Italian Americans living near the bay in both Arverne and Edgemere.

The larger Jewish population followed a pattern characteristic of their experience in urban America. Wealthy, assimilated German Jews arrived first, followed by poor, eastern European immigrants. The more affluent Jewish residents lived in the smarter sections of the western peninsula, Neponsit and Belle Harbor, as well as in parts of Far Rockaway and Bayswater to the east. Working-class and lower-middle-class Jews resided in Hammels, Arverne, and Edgemere. They earned modest livings as shopkeepers and owners of small businesses or by commuting to jobs in other parts of New York City. A few of these families increased their income by renting rooms to summer visitors. Like the Irish, the more enterprising among them owned rooming houses or bungalows and charged relatively high rates during the peninsula's "golden age."

Old-timers who reminisce about the glory days tend to forget about the presence of an active German-American Bund in Far Rockaway, as well as about followers of the anti-Semitic radio priest Father Coughlin in Seaside during the late 1930s and early 1940s. Former residents also recall that certain teachers and other school personnel were hostile to African American and Jewish students. Police brutality toward minorities occurred freqently and was not effectively protested until after the Second World War.[2]

Largely hidden from view, invisible in the manner described by Ralph Ellison's novel *The Invisible Man*, were the African Americans. Although most of them arrived during the northern migration of the twentieth century, small numbers of black people had lived in Rockaway for hundreds of years; along with the English, they were among the region's earliest settlers. The Cornell family estate, established in the late seventeenth century and the first large homestead in Far Rockaway, used slave labor. (Cornell family members also helped to found the elite Ivy League university in upstate New York.) Almost from the very beginning of its resort history, Rockaway's summer businesses, including the amusement parks and hotels, employed poorly paid black workers for some of the more arduous jobs. Nonetheless, African Americans were almost never seen in white sections of town—on the wide span of beaches or boardwalks, in the shops, restaurants, amusement parks, and play areas, or on Central Avenue (Beach 20th St.), the main shopping street of the peninsula.

In truth, during the first half of the twentieth century Rockaway Beach practiced segregation on a large scale. Public accommodations such as restaurants, taverns, barber shops, and most of the movie theatres excluded black customers. The New Theatre, located in the heart of an African American section of town, compromised by reserving a part of its balcony for "colored." Popular restaurants, including some on Central Avenue, refused to serve blacks well into the 1950s. Bars proliferated in old Rockaway, but for years there was only one, "Tip Inn," that black people frequented. Surprisingly, considering the important role they played in urban education, parochial schools denied admission to African American children.

Residential segregation prevailed, especially in the western villages of the peninsula. African Americans lived mainly in two segregated enclaves: part of Hammels, between the railroad tracks and Rockaway Beach Boulevard, and in the Redfern area of Far Rockaway, which adjoined a poor section of Nassau County's Inwood. Statistics on the number of blacks vary. Today it is generally recognized that the official U.S. census undercounts minorities. In the mid-1940s the local Chamber of Commerce counted 2,500 African Americans as a rough estimate. But a survey just a few years later concluded that 2,000 black people lived in Redfern alone. Hammels had a somewhat smaller number, and a few other scattered pockets of African Americans existed, mainly in Arverne. Probably between 3,000 and 3,500 African Americans lived in the Rockaways of the World War II era, just under one-tenth of the total winter population. Summer brought no increase in their numbers, since black people did not come to this beach resort for a vacation.[3]

Few job opportunities for African American males existed, and these remained chiefly seasonal. Men with practical skills could only obtain work at low-paying jobs as "unskilled" laborers. In reality, they did carpentry, plumbing, electrical work, painting, and general repairs of properties. Yet the racist policies of unions, as well as strict "father and son" practices, denied them official credentials. Local civil service openings never became available to them, since most positions, including summer work for young people with the parks department, depended on family connections. Retailers, especially in white neighborhoods, refused to hire African Americans, except for positions which did not involve direct contact with white customers. In the late 1930s and early 1940s some black men managed to find work through New Deal agencies such as the WPA, but these positions were limited to the most unskilled and poorest paying jobs.[4] Nor did their job opportunities improve during the Second World War. Craig Wilder has shown that "black people made up less than 3 percent of the New York metropolitan-area defense workers, the lowest rate of any major defense production region."[5]

Several trends abetted the poor employment prospects of African Americans in the Rockaways and New York City in general. The manpower shortages of World War II provided a legitimate excuse for landlords to rely on Rockaway "handymen" (black artisans and laborers) for patchwork repairs. Similar low-wage "handyman" jobs existed in the thriving amusement industry but ended with the departure of the summer crowds. The enforced idleness black men endured during the winter in the Rockaways duplicated the life many of them had fled in the rural south, one of the most impoverished regions of the United States. Black women fared little better. With mechanized agriculture eliminating many menial jobs in the southern states, some African American women followed older relatives to Rockaway. Others were solicited either by employment agencies or individuals who drove south and persuaded young women with poor prospects to accompany them north for domestic work. In 1940, 77 percent of black women living in the borough of Queens worked in domestic service.[6]

Conditions for these young women in the Rockaways varied from barely tolerable to slave-like. Former domestics, interviewed for this study, have recounted how they had to work a minimum of six days a week, including evenings. One woman said that when she first started as a "live in," she was given only alternate Sundays off. However, a few hours every Sunday morning were granted to attend church services, which, in part, helps to explain the religiosity of this segment of the population. Once married, an African American woman tended to clean houses as a "daily domestic" for wages as low as twenty or twenty-five cents per hour, and sometimes as little as fifteen cents, with no security or benefits. Unlike the men, black women had little trouble finding such jobs. But for the most part domestic service, although steady, was a dead end, which had to be abandoned when sickness, injury, or old age intervened.[7]

Dishonest individuals brought many black teenage girls from the south to the peninsula by the carload. However, they were customarily turned out after the busy summer season, with no means of support and without any resources to return home. These vulnerable young women gravitated to the train station in Far Rockaway hoping for day jobs. The most desperate among them turned to prostitution. Mrs. Eleanor Hull, who ran her own Rockaway employment agency, understood the potentially exploitative nature of domestic service. Already known for her charitable works, Mrs. Hull conceived a plan to provide both immediate and long-term relief to these abandoned young women. In the fall of 1931, she brought together thirteen other like-minded African American women to form what eventually became the Women's Industrial Service League. Its mission was to provide assistance and a sense of community to young women alone and adrift in the Rockaways. Adopting the slogan "to save a girl," the organization's first activity consisted of providing the fares for unemployed servants who wished to return to the south. Those who preferred to stay on were offered assistance in finding employment and accommodations. Within a few years the League had raised enough money to purchase a large building in Redfern, which they used both as a dormitory and as an activities center.[8] The White Rose Working Girls' Home, established by Harlem women as early as 1897, provided a model for their Far Rockaway version of a settlement house.[9]

The fourteen founders of the Women's Industrial Service League served as a board of directors, with Mrs. Hull as the elected president. These volunteers raised money to pay off the mortgage and to support the various activities of the organization. Some taught crafts, and the finer products were sold, helping to cover the League's expenses. All the women took their religious beliefs seriously, doing charitable works and insisting on moral behavior for anyone using the League's premises. Residents could entertain guests only in the large downstairs room where socials were held. During World War II, black servicemen from out of town were invited to parties here. Mrs. Hull, now with an organization of determined women behind her, did her utmost to protect domestic service employees in the Rockaways. She even tried to get employers to pay social security taxes, an undertaking almost as hopeless then as it is today.

The League soon broadened its focus to include other issues affecting the black community. Its building was made available to civil rights organizations, such as the local NAACP, for meetings and fund raisers. Early on, members advocated for medical facilities as well as for the special health needs of black people living in Far Rockaway. They helped draw outside attention to the high incidence of tuberculosis in Redfern. The League made efforts to provide play space for neighborhood children and supported organized sports for both boys and girls. Some money was also set aside for college scholarships, so that others could receive an opportunity that had been denied to these remarkable founders. Their contribution, an early example of women's solidarity and the resourcefulness of black people, has remained an untold story in the history of Rockaway.

Housing was a major issue for the Women's Industrial Service League and the entire black community of the Rockaways. With rare exceptions, most African Americans lived in atrocious circumstances. The high incidence of TB was rightfully attributed to overcrowded living conditions. Repeatedly, observers likened what they saw in Rockaway's black neighborhoods to the abject poverty of "Tobacco Road" in the rural south. Diseases that were largely controlled or eliminated in the rest of the peninsula remained endemic to black neighborhoods. In the ghettos of Hammels and Redfern, life expectancy was considerably shorter than elsewhere.[10] Together, these communities had the highest rate of infant mortality in all of Queens.[11] Residential segregation ensured that black working people had no choice but to endure these conditions.

Surveys of Hammels and Redfern, conducted during the 1940s, concluded that these were some of "the worst slum areas in the country."[12] Redfern houses, described as "rat infested shanties," whose outdoor toilets and inadequate plumbing produced "disgraceful unsanitary conditions," came close to reproducing the worst of the rural south. The black section of Hammels had the dubious distinction of being the first part of the Rockaway peninsula to convert run-down summer establishments to year-round use. Wood-frame buildings in both communities often lacked central heating. In 53 percent of these structures there were no bathtubs, and 70 percent had no hot water. Since kitchen coal stoves were used for both cooking and hot water in these buildings, they required year-round operation. The risk of fire was exacerbated by the fact that the wooden houses stood close together, yet most lacked fire escapes. Housing code violations abounded, adding to the crumbling and desperate character of both Redfern and Hammels.[13] City inspectors continually ignored even the most glaring problems. Landlords, when pressed during the 1940s to justify the condition of their properties, blamed their failure to make repairs on wartime shortages of both materials and labor. As the Rockaways never had a shortage of black repairmen, even during wartime, it appears to have been cheaper for the landlords to bribe investigators than to spend the money necessary to make these homes livable and safe.[14]

While the white power structure ignored the needs of African Americans before World War II and tried to keep their presence hidden, the segregated black neighborhoods reduced the property values of the entire peninsula. With the exception of the exclusive and protected western sections, government appraisers started giving low ratings to Rockaway real estate. These ratings are known today, although their existence was long kept secret from the public. By 1933, after approximately one-half of the home mortgages in the country were in default, and private mortgage lending had virtually disappeared, the U.S. government entered the housing market. During the late 1930s, a New Deal agency, the Home Owners Loan Corporation (HOLC), undertook the sytematic appraisal of neigh-

borhoods throughout the country, street by street, to determine their suitability for possible federal loans.[15]

Sent by the agency to selected cities, investigators consulted with local
bankers, mortgage lenders, and real estate brokers before reaching conclusions about a specific locale's "desirability from a residential viewpoint."
Elaborate "security maps" were produced as part of a formal grading system, and neighborhoods were designated by colors, starting with green
(the highest), then blue, yellow, and red in descending order. Correspond-
ing numbers and a letter system (A,B,C,D) further clarified the evaluations. The agency employed certain standard criteria to determine grades.
An "A," rarely granted, was awarded to "new, well planned sections," definitely "on the up grade." "B" described areas which had recently "reached
their peak, should continue to be static for a number of years and remain
desirable places in which to live." On the Rockaway peninsula, only
Neponsit and Belle Harbor met the requirements for "B" status. Category
"C" proved to be the most nuanced and detailed, but generally designated
areas in decline, having "seen their better days." A clearly failing grade of
"D" indicated "those neighborhoods in which the deterioration taking
place in the 'C' areas [has] already happened." Sections of cities receiving
"D" were characterized by poorly maintained homes, vandalism, and sim-
ilar problems.

Scrutiny of these secret evaluations reveals that unabashed ethnic bias-
es, characteristic of the real estate practices of the time, played as important
a role as the condition of the buildings. The Irish neighborhood in the
Rockaways received a C-. All areas inhabited by blacks automatically received a D grade; the nature of the housing stock in these sections was not
even mentioned. The presence of Jews, considered then to be "elements"
nearly as "undesirable," hit a button that sent a neighborhood "lacking
homogeneity" into a lower range, usually a C or C-. Affluent Neponsit and
Belle Harbor probably received a B rather than an A because they were
largely Jewish and bordered areas with "heterogeneous" residents.[16] After
World War II, as prejudice against Jews lessened, this western end of the
Rockaway peninsula would become a prestigious address, attracting mil-
lionaires and politicians such as Mayors O'Dwyer and Beame.

Predictably, the identifiable African American areas of Far Rockaway
got a straight D. But a predominantly white section of Hammels, barely 12
percent "Negroes," received the same grade. The housing stock itself is
never described, but undoubtedly the presence of blacks, combined with

the nearby Jewish residents, accounts for the tract's negative evaluation. Other areas in Rockaway with a large Jewish presence never attained anything higher than a C. Most often they got tagged with a C-. Arverne, which one of the authors (L. K.) and his friends still remember with pride, was granted a C-. The evaluators had actually contemplated a D because of its "questionable" (i.e., Jewish) character. Interestingly, while not at all shy about mentioning that "Negroes" resided in such and such a place, thereby automatically bringing down property values, the appraisers euphemistically referred to Jews as "Austrians," "Hungarians," "Germans," and "Russians." (The author who grew up in Rockaway never met individuals who claimed these national identities.) Clearly, HOLC did not invent the evaluation of real estate based on racial and ethnic criteria, but its adoption of this practice ensured that these methods would be applied systematically throughout the country. More to the point, HOLC initiated "redlining" on a previously unprecedented scale, and ethnicity became a major consideration in appraising property.[17]

While the Rockaway Chamber of Commerce leaders may not have known about this specific HOLC report, they realized that banks had begun to reconsider granting mortgages and loans to certain communities in the peninsula. The findings of the HOLC strongly influenced Federal Housing Administration policies, which encouraged loans only to "good" sections. The FHA refused to insure places where minorities lived, as well as neighborhoods bordering ghettos.[18] Throughout the Depression, the lack of investment capital deterred private industry from carrying out any large-scale expansion of housing in the Rockaways, and the war that followed kept construction companies busy with military contracts. By the mid-1940s, more than a decade had elapsed during which little new building had taken place.

During the last phases of World War II, the Rockaway Chamber of Commerce began outlining future prospects for profitable postwar investments. It was universally acknowledged that the impending return of large numbers of servicemen would lead to a housing shortage throughout the country. The Rockaways possessed open expanses of land, a desirable location next to beaches, and proximity to the city. Local real estate interests saw the peninsula as a prime location for expansion. However, they believed that if Rockaway were to maximize its attractiveness to potential investors and remain economically viable, something would have to be done about the terrible conditions in Redfern and Hammels.[19] The first public official to recognize the need for housing reform in the Rockaways was Robert Moses.

In the 1930s, Moses had predicted the growth of a year-round population, and he had done his utmost in the prewar years to modernize the peninsula's infrastructure by constructing new roads and bridges. After the war, Moses's name would be associated with housing developments almost as much as with highways.[20] In a booklet he published in 1938, around the same time that his extensive Rockaway improvements were being completed, Moses provided detailed plans for a housing project running two miles, the length of Hammels and Seaside, to be built by private contractors behind his shore parkway. Although the proposal was shelved when the war began, it was brought to fruition some twenty years later.[21]

Even before the Rockaway real estate interests entered the picture, the Women's Industrial Service League seized the initiative by advocating adequate housing for the "unfortunates" in Redfern. By the late 1940s they had won over powerful forces. Always willing to join coalitions, the organization's second president, Mrs. Emily Capers Brown, formed an alliance with black ministers in order to conduct a survey of the conditions among African Americans in Redfern and then publicize the results. Calling attention to the high incidence of tuberculosis, still a frightening disease, they got the Queens TB and Health Association to launch a chest x-ray program. Mrs. Brown then led the way in establishing a Council for Health and Welfare designed to serve area needs, a major success for the time.[22]

It would take additional surveys by the New York City Housing Authority, the Housing and Building Department, and independent groups before the Rockaway Chamber of Commerce began advocating slum clearance in a serious manner. The last of these studies was conducted during the early 1940s under the auspices of the Rockaway Council for Neighborhood Unity, a reform organization led by the progressive Congregational minister Ellsworth Richardson. Previously, the chamber had given a lukewarm endorsement to low-income housing for the Rockaways. In 1940, the chamber's president supported "proper housing facilities" for people living in high-poverty tracts. However, he worried that the construction of a low-income project would bring more "outsiders" to the neighborhood. Without specifying who these people might be, it was clear from the article's context that he did not want additional African Americans moving into the community.[23]

During the next few years, every *Rockaway Review* list of postwar goals called for the extension of New York City transit to the peninsula. Nothing was said about housing the Rockaway poor. In December 1944, when the chamber learned that the New York City Housing Authority had surveyed the black section of Hammels with the intention of constructing a housing project there, it responded favorably. However, the contrast between the *Rockaway Review*'s headline, "Chamber Favors Local Housing Project," and the tepid news story that followed illustrates the organization's ambivalence. In 1945, it finally endorsed a low-income development, while expressing concern about the needs of shopkeepers in the vicinity.[24]

Throughout the United States, real estate interests and white homeowners actively fought against the construction of public housing in any area outside inner cities.[25] Why, then, did the Rockaway Chamber of Commerce act counter to this nationwide trend? Evidently, at this juncture the chamber needed to balance the requirements of different commercial forces operating in the Rockaways. It always gave primary consideration to real estate. Owners of summer properties, and others who catered to tourists, looked forward to lucrative seasons in the postwar years. They tended to favor the status quo. On the other hand, those involved in various aspects of construction stood to profit handsomely from new building projects.[26] Others, recognizing that the transition to a year-round community was inevitable, anticipated the expansion of business opportunities. They feared the negative impact on real estate values of depressed black neighborhoods and wished to do something about this looming problem. They knew that only the government possessed the necessary resources to rehabilitate depressed urban areas. It was most unlikely that private enterprise would ever invest in such undertakings. A similar argument justified locating public housing in Brownsville, Brooklyn, around this very time.[27] The chamber would have liked blacks to leave the peninsula altogether; because earlier housing projects accommodated many more whites than minorities, especially in mixed sections of the city, they might naturally have assumed that this would also happen in the Rockaways. In fact, the first Rockaway projects did have white majorities.

Initially, the Chamber of Commerce showed a willingness to support a low-rent project in either Hammels or Redfern, although the Housing Authority's field work seemed to indicate that the former location would have priority. For practical reasons, the chamber soon joined with the Housing Authority in emphasizing the need for housing in Hammels. This switch disappointed The Women's Industrial Service League, which had long advocated for Redfern.[28] In the end, however, the first of the publicly financed housing developments on the peninsula was placed neither in Hammels nor in Redfern, but in a previously uninhabited marshland section of Arverne.[29]

Government enterprises take a long time to materialize, and before any building commenced the housing shortage predicted by officials and real estate groups became critical. In New York City, the pressure to find accommodations for returning servicemen and their growing families reached such proportions that William O'Dwyer, before his swearing in as mayor in January 1945 (a ceremony, incidentally, that took place in Belle Harbor), set up an emergency committee on housing. Robert Moses was named chairman and charged with the task of producing immediate results. He had already been placed on the City Planning Commission by Mayor LaGuardia, and in 1946 O'Dwyer would appoint him the New York City Construction Coordinator, to be followed two years later by the chairmanship of the Mayor's Committee on Slum Clearance.[30] Thus, within a very short time, Moses would have more power to determine the fate of new housing than any other individual. Given his extraordinary prior efforts, members of the Rockaway Chamber of Commerce felt confident that he would now be in an even stronger position to advance the interests of their community.

There were realistic grounds for such optimism. In the fall of 1945, Moses, in his capacity as chair of emergency housing, conducted an inspection tour of the peninsula and consulted with some of the chamber's executives. He told them about his proposed remedy for the crisis in the Rockaways, and they immediately lent their support. His plan, intended only for the short run, would make use of summer residences for the many off-season months when they were normally vacant. Veterans would become renters shortly after Labor Day, the official conclusion of the summer season, and then vacate the premises just before Memorial Day, its usual beginning.

Ironically, Moses had previously expressed open contempt for much of the Rockaway summer dwellings: the wood-frame rooming houses, built around the turn of the century, and the stucco, utilitarian bungalows, which had arrived a decade or two later. But the city now faced an acute problem. From the start, Moses vigorously opposed the use of tents and prefabricated units for emergency housing. For him, the quickest solution appeared to be the winterizing of empty summer buildings, already fitted with electric wiring, rudimentary plumbing, and modest furnishings. Immediately available, with minimum cost to the government, Rockaway bungalows and rooming houses would provide an expedient resolution to New York City's most pressing problem. Rockaway would not be the only site for winter conversions: Coney Island and even Long Beach in nearby Nassau County were also mentioned. But Moses calculated that approximately eight thousand people could be accommodated on the Rockaway peninsula alone.[31] Rockaway landlords, supported by the chamber, were delighted with Moses's plan. With the city paying for improvements, owners stood to greatly increase the value of their properties, and they would collect rents all year long.

Certain technical and legal matters remained before these landlords would give final approval to the proposed arrangement.[32] First, the owners did not wish to be hampered by restrictions set by the Office of Price Administration (OPA). Summer rents had not been limited during the war, and they remained high throughout the period, promising to be still more profitable in the future. The 1945 season brought large numbers of summer visitors, leading to high hopes for future summers.[33] Landlords feared that the OPA would eliminate seasonal exemptions once proprietors started collecting rents for a full year. They hoped to charge standard rates for the eight off-season months and much higher ones during the summer. At first, Moses wanted these houses converted to year-long use at permanently fixed annual rents, but this strategy interested only those landlords who owned inferior properties in poor neighborhoods. Ever pragmatic, he agreed to the idea of dual rentals that the landlords and the chamber put forward. Property owners also feared that temporary renters would refuse to vacate premises once summer arrived, resulting in delays for the seasonal renters and legal costs for landlords in the event of evictions. At every stage of the negotiations, the Chamber of Commerce backed Moses's scheme to use summer housing while publicizing the reservations expressed by local real estate interests.[34] Because Moses believed his scheme to be the only viable one, he resolved these obstacles in his typically single-minded fashion, even though the OPA was at first quite resistant. He won the support of veterans' groups, appealed to Congress, and ultimately got the OPA to grant exemptions that permitted Rockaway summer rentals at market levels. The OPA's legal department even promised to help evict recalcitrant tenants at government expense.[35]

There remained one further hurdle before the Rockaway landlords would declare themselves satisfied. In November 1946, the *Rockaway Review* published an editorial in favor of changing state multiple-dwelling laws. The editorial claimed that buildings on the peninsula could help ease the housing shortage by accommodating more than one family in each structure. Single-family houses would be converted to two-, two- to three-, and so on. The editorial neglected to mention the benefit to landlords. "In this acute emergency," it read, "we feel that any partial solution to the shortage of housing" should be pursued. Once again the powers-that-be, this time the New York State Legislature, made special arrangements for the Rockaway situation.[36]

The history of Rockaway real estate provides ample evidence of the ways in which an unchallenged lobbying force can successfully influence governmental authorities. In the postwar period, the landlords triumphed over powerful forces, and their profits rolled in. Most of the large houses on the shore, constructed around the turn of the century, were intended to be holiday homes for affluent families; the Vanderbilts owned one of these properties in Arverne. As the rich began migrating to eastern Long Island, vacationing in places like the Hamptons, real estate speculators bought up their mansions and turned them into summer rooming houses. Throughout the 1920s and 1930s, conversions from single-family to multiple-occupancy buildings took place in areas east of the strictly zoned Belle Harbor and Neponsit. No legal approval seems to have been given to these operations, and they easily lent themselves to abuse. But after the Second World War, when New York City passed laws regulating multiple-occupancy dwellings, Rockaway rooming houses faced the prospect of a sudden demise.

At the point that the City Council passed restrictive laws, attorneys for the real estate interests identified an exception: the category "heretofore converted Class 'B'," which seems especially geared to Rockaway rooming houses. It made possible the continued use of the former single-family homes as multiple-occupancy dwellings on the grounds that they would be open for summers only. Years later, when the city fathers wished to stop the conversion of apartment buildings into rooming houses by prohibiting occupancy of the latter by children, Rockaway lobbyists once again obtained an exception for seasonal structures. This pattern of special dispensation would continue well into the 1960s. The Rockaway bungalows remained unregulated, since these "one-family houses" could be rented as landlords saw fit.[37]

Although the terrible postwar housing shortage brought these landlords together with Robert Moses, they knew that he did not necessarily put their interests first. Many of them still rankled at the ease with which he destroyed property while carrying out his Rockaway improvements during the 1930s and at his refusal to give them an additional summer's rent in 1938. Consequently, they worried about his future plans for the peninsula. Moreover, these property owners knew of his original scheme for veterans' housing. He had proposed that New York City condemn shorefront properties, temporarily rent them, and then turn them over to the parks department. Part of the land was to be leveled in order to provide space for public parking lots and other beachfront improvements. The chamber strongly opposed this approach, and, except for a handful of badly needed shore parking lots built in 1948, landlords kept the houses that were to be rented by the veterans. George Wolpert, executive secretary of the chamber, had actually written to Moses in September 1949, requesting that some of these lots be placed in areas of Edgemere where no summer houses existed, but Moses responded negatively.[38] Rockaway landlords would have been even more concerned if they had known his long-range plan for the Rockaways: to permanently "get rid of structures of this kind" (i.e., bungalows and rooming houses) all along the oceanfront.[39]

Had Moses succeeded with his plan to revamp the Rockaways during the 1940s, the community might have had a very different fate. However, the circumstances of the immediate postwar era did not permit the kinds of expensive undertakings he had envisioned. Moreover, a large segment of the Rockaway business community opposed the sacrifices that Moses's plans entailed. The Chamber of Commerce, whose influence on public officials at this time remained considerable, would never sacrifice the summer profits of the landlords, who remained some of the organization's most vocal constituents. Indeed, the chamber had readily supported the exceptions to the various restrictive housing laws desired by the landlords.[40]

Despite its stated purpose of serving the needs of the entire Rockaway community, as articulated in Moses's various plans, the chamber remained committed to the short-term interests of certain of its members. This latter group, chiefly owners of summer housing, focused on maximizing profits from aging properties. While Moses saw a future for Rockaway based on the destruction of these "shacks," the chamber refused to countenance such actions. On the one hand, its leaders agreed with the Power Broker about developing the Rockaways as a year-round community based on solid residences adjoining a well planned resort.[41] Ultimately, however, they acceded to the demands of Rockaway's landlords and realtors. Later events would make resolution of this duality of purpose even more difficult.

CHAPTER 3

The Trestle Burns and the Projects Begin

It would be comforting to attribute the fate of the Rockaways to natural forces. Nature has not always been kind to this southern Queens community: the storms, hurricanes, floods, and erosion that frequently occur have taken their toll. As a barrier beach, the peninsula absorbs nature's aggression while protecting the coastal city of New York. In addition, after the Second World War, New York's municipal authorities used the Rockaways as an outlet for pressures emerging in the more densely populated parts of the urban colossus. This did not always serve the best interests of the area, its residents, or the people sent to live there.

Chance inflicts especial harm on those who are least prepared for life's contingencies. The burning of the Jamaica Bay trestle on 7 May 1950, an event that would have enormous consequences for the Rockaways, serves as a case in point. The trestle carried trains from the Rockaways directly to Penn Station in Manhattan in approximately half an hour, the fastest route for those commuting to work. The Long Island Rail Road had not shown a profit on its Rockaway branch for years and, now facing bankruptcy, gave little indication that it wished to undertake the necessary repairs. For at least two decades prior to the 1950 fire, Chamber of Commerce spokesmen had regularly requested that the wooden trestle be replaced with a fire resistant one. They usually received a sympathetic hearing from the city fathers, including Robert Moses, but no actions were taken.[1] In addition, as early as the 1930s, public officials made repeated pledges that the city would extend rapid transit to the Rockaways, but nothing came of these assurances either.

For six years (1950–1956), no rail connection existed over Jamaica Bay. During this time the community suffered in innumerable ways, some obvious and therefore easy to calculate, others more indirect. The now more arduous trip to the city discouraged people from moving to the Rockaways and limited the number of summer renters, diminishing landlords' profits. It also deterred families from embarking on a day's outing, harming the concessionaires and amusement park operators. Attendance at the various Rockaway beaches, which hit a record forty-eight million during the summer of the trestle fire, fell precipitously in the following years. Seasonal rentals had already begun to decline in 1949, a pattern that continued in 1950 and accelerated throughout the decade. The summer population reached a high of 225,000 in 1947, but was down to 106,000 five years later.[2] Within a short period of time, Rockaway began to lose its status as a major summer resort. Although other factors may have contributed, the absence of a direct rail connection was critical.

The emergency created by the trestle fire of 1950 forced the city to reconsider the situation. The Chamber of Commerce had immediately responded to news of the fire by dashing off letters and telegrams to Mayor O'Dwyer, warning him of the "catastrophe" that had befallen the Rockaways.[3] However, at that moment the mayor had more pressing concerns: corruption charges culminated in his sudden resignation from office, and he was hurriedly appointed Ambassador to Mexico by President Harry S. Truman. Consequently, he did not give the need for a new trestle the prompt attention it deserved. His successor, Vincent Impellitteri, was quickly apprised of its importance by the man whose favor he knew to be crucial to his own success in office: Robert Moses. The latter urged the immediate appointment of a blue-ribbon commission to study the matter and make recommendations regarding the future of the Long Island Rail Road branch to the Rockaways. The new mayor took up this suggestion and chose Moses to chair the commission.

Robert Moses has always had the reputation of opposing public transportation and advocating the automobile. Thus, he might not have been expected to favor a mass-transit project to Rockaway, especially one that would compete with two separate toll facilities run by the Triborough Bridge and Tunnel Authority, the Marine Parkway and Cross Bay bridges. However, Moses had other agendas that intersected with the crisis of the trestle. Since the 1930s, he had actually been trying to work out a practical way to replace the privately run railroad spur to the peninsula. The Rockaway Improvement had proposed eliminating grade crossings and creating an elevated structure, and it was generally understood that this would facilitate the extension of the city's subway system. Moses himself wrote as early as 1939 that it was "inevitable that the Rockaway branch of the Long Island Rail Road will be acquired before long by the City of New York for rapid transit purposes."[4] The files of the Triborough Bridge and Tunnel Authority contain an extensive internal correspondence that reveals Moses's efforts to work out the costs of construction and the ongoing operating expenses. Shortly after the final trestle fire, he wrote to the *New York Times* that "we must anticipate an enormous increase both in year round residence and summer use, when the city takes over the Rockaway spur of the Long Island Rail Road and makes it part of the rapid transit system."[5]

In May 1951, the blue-ribbon commission unanimously recommended the purchase of the Long Island Rail Road branch, the rebuilding of the trestle, and the extension of the New York City subway system to the Rockaways, at an estimated cost of $40 million. Recognizing that fares would never replenish ongoing expenses, they suggested that an additional charge be levied in each direction. Moses wanted the masses to continue to have access to the Rockaways. Accordingly, the report stipulated that the amount should be "substantially lower than present railroad rates," because high fares are "certainly a major deterrent to widespread use of these unexcelled beaches and recreation facilities and effectively drive more low income families to Coney Island, which is badly overcrowded."[6] The final draft, accepted by the mayor and ultimately by the Board of Estimate, portrays the Power Broker as sympathetic to people's needs. In words that could come only from his pen, Moses unhesitatingly affirmed the extension of public transportation as a public good. The Rockaway community instantly expressed its appreciation. Executive Secretary Wolpert wrote to Moses, "your support of this proposal has won for you the everlasting gratitude of the residents and property owners of our area."[7]

The chamber had reason to be grateful to Moses. Except for the extra fare, a continuing irritant for residents until it was repealed in the mid-1970s, the committee's report gave the community all that it had lobbied for, including the proposed route of the extended subway line. Moses and his colleagues recommended using the former tracks of the Long Island Rail Road so that the Rockaway train would parallel Woodhaven Boule-

vard until the White Pot junction with Queens Boulevard. It would connect there with the already existing subway tracks set up to travel westward
into the heart of Queens and then on to Manhattan, almost as quick a trip
as that made previously by the LIRR.

Moses planned the line through areas of New York City more solidly
middle-class than the longer Brooklyn route ultimately chosen. The white
establishment of the Rockaways, represented by the Chamber of Commerce, had urged the Queens route not only because it was more direct but
because they opposed the new subway traveling through the heart of black
Bedford-Stuyvesant. However, even with Moses's support, the Board of
Estimate ruled against it. The reason for the decision was never explained.
Therefore, the long awaited arrival of the New York subway in June 1956,
while ceremoniously applauded, was disappointing to the business interests
represented by the Chamber of Commerce.

However imperfect the final details of the subway plan, the community had much to celebrate. The *Wave* saw its arrival in June 1956 as the
"symbol of a new era for the Rockaways."[8] Nonetheless, many observers
later regarded its completion as the turning point in the peninsula's transformation, in that it integrated the Rockaways more closely with the city,
ultimately leading to the white community's decline.[9] Unquestionably, the
coming of rapid transit encouraged the trend toward permanent residency
that had begun after World War II. The following year, the *Rockaway Review* announced that seventy-seven thousand people now resided year
round in the peninsula, an increase of almost 100 percent since 1941.[10] After 1956, housing construction boomed, reaching a figure of approximately
two thousand apartment house units and several hundred one- or two-family homes by 1960.[11]

Contrary to popular belief, Rockaway's improved accessibility actually encouraged white families to move into neighborhoods that were distant from the ghetto areas. The segregated pockets of poverty remained as
remote as ever from the more affluent sections. Neponsit and Belle Harbor on the western end and Bayswater and Far Rockaway toward the east
continued to be neighborhoods of choice for middle-class white families.
These districts saw vigorous home construction, and they commanded
some of the highest real estate prices in the New York area. More modest
two-family homes began appearing in the Somerville section of Arverne
as well.[12] During the 1950s, private developers put up a middle-income
apartment house complex fronting the ocean in Wavecrest. The largest

such development in Rockaway to date, it contained some 1,650 apartments. Plans were made in 1956 for a sizeable cooperative apartment house located between Arverne and Edgemere (Nordeck Apartments), finally completed with city and state assistance in 1960. By the end of the 1950s, the Lefrak organization had built eleven separate apartment houses, mainly in Far Rockaway.[13]

Robert Moses continued to have high hopes for "New York City's favorite resort." He conceived the Wavecrest Gardens development, and, around the same time that it was being built, he designed a highway (Seagirt Boulevard) to improve access from the peninsula to the recently renovated Atlantic Beach Bridge (another of his accomplishments). His ultimate plan, announced a few years after the war, envisioned the Nassau Expressway running north from this bridge all the way to the Belt Parkway and the Van Wyck Expressway, thus connecting eastern sections of the Rockaways with the existing network of roads encircling Queens, Brooklyn, and Nassau County.[14] A modified Nassau Expressway was completed many decades later.

The white migration to the peninsula in the late 1950s consisted, for the most part, of working-class and middle-class people. Mass transit, which made Rockaway a convenient and desirable place in which to live and raise children, was a critical factor in their decision to move. Housing in Arverne, Edgemere, and sections of Far Rockaway remained relatively cheap. Schools compared favorably with those in other areas of New York, especially in the parts of Brooklyn where most of the newcomers originated. In terms familiar to Rockaway old-timers, the postwar cohort praised the small-town character of the community, which nonetheless contained all the amenities of the city, including movie theatres and shopping. They appreciated the ocean and the boardwalk and reiterated the timeless belief in the curative nature of sea air.

Despite this growth in population, the subway, now a permanent aspect of the peninsula's landscape, failed to live up to expectations. Transit ridership remained low, and financial losses on the Rockaway branch exceeded predictions, even with the double fare.[15] The slow ride to the city, the infrequency of trains, and the declining quality of service counterbalanced the advantages of the long awaited rapid transit. Moreover, despite Rockaway's accessibility as a beach resort, summer visitors simply stopped coming.[16] Even more significantly, long before 1956 when the trestle was rebuilt and the link with mass transit established, parts of the Rockaways were being made into repositories for poor people on welfare.[17] Barely a decade after the war, the community contained three low-income housing projects, with the fourth and largest already well past the planning stage.

It has been largely forgotten that the original New Deal housing legislation, ostensibly for the poor, was designed to stimulate the economy by helping the building industry and creating jobs. For many years public funding richly subsidized these industries and the construction unions.[18] Construction costs in Rockaway for 1959 alone ran about $100 million, most of it government backed. As Mayor Wagner pointed out at the time, "This would be a fabulous sum for most cities in the United States."[19] The Rockaway business community's support of housing projects is understandable in light of the substantial benefits that accrued to influential construction and real estate firms as well as to local workers directly involved in the process.

The original reasoning of public housing advocates has today faded from consciousness. Many liberals, like New York's Senator Robert F. Wagner Sr., sought to improve the well-being of families who were displaced by economic downturns. Believing that inadequate housing conditions created deviant behavior, these reformers maintained that when the "deserving poor" were put in a decent environment with clean, well-ordered accommodations, they would respond in a socially beneficial manner. To assure these results, the authorities established a screening process, which included an inspection of references, to eliminate "undesirables." Excluded were criminals, people on welfare, and unwed mothers. Only intact families, prepared to pay their own way, would be allowed to live in these developments. If renters or their children interfered with their neighbors' quality of life, they would be asked to leave. As a consequence of this selection process, many of the early low-rent projects proved to be a great success. Their long lists of applicants provided evidence of the projects' positive image.[20] Indeed, the first government-sponsored project in the Rockaways, specifically earmarked for returning servicemen, received 2000 applications for only 418 apartments while it was still under construction.[21]

This favorable view of public housing developments continued unchallenged until well after World War II. Veterans' groups vied with each other to sponsor them. For the most part, the developments won the support of politicians and elected officials, except when low-income projects were proposed in white, middle-class residential neighborhoods. New Deal supporters and liberals in general accepted the premise that the government should be prepared to supply such basic human requirements as decent housing, health care, and education. Aside from the New Dealers, some people with a social engineering perspective believed that government intervention in the housing market was necessary to the continued health of urban societies. Robert Moses belongs in this latter category. A conservative in many respects, Moses nevertheless recognized the social cost of deteriorating neighborhoods to entire communities. For him, housing projects "clean up diseased areas of the city," thereby preventing contamination. This view was relevant to the Rockaway situation. In a 1945 letter to the *New York Sun*, Moses argued that if New York City failed to create the proper environment for living and business, "the town goes back."[22]

The Rockaway Chamber of Commerce, which had favored the general idea of government-supported housing since 1945, joined forces with the servicemen's organizations in January 1948 to advocate a veterans' project for the Rockaways, and they were not shy about claiming credit after it got under way.[23] More important, they helped to select the site. At first, the chamber favored a development in Hammels; later, it advocated "the now barren wasteland of Arverne," a desolate area far from any other housing tracts or shopping facilities.[24] Soon the construction of an Arverne veterans' project became a top priority for influential chamber leaders. They never satisfactorily explained either why they changed their choice of location or why the other projects were placed on temporary hold, considering the desperate conditions existing in Hammels and Redfern. We can speculate that well-connected members owned property in the area selected.

The chamber's attempt to explain their position in the April 1948 issue of the *Rockaway Review* was tortured at best. They argued that an Arverne project would benefit slum dwellers in the worst sections of the peninsula, but they never showed how this would work. In fact, while local servicemen's families were given preference, few if any people from either Hammels or Redfern gained entry into the Arverne project, which opened in 1950. A limited number of black veterans and their intact families were accepted, constituting around 10 percent of the total, thereby giving Arverne Houses the distinction of being an early integrated development. A high percentage of these African American tenants came from other areas of New York City, while many white veterans who moved into the development had grown up in the Rockaways. No one on public assistance was admitted. In 1955, the first available figures regarding ethnicity in the Arverne Houses listed a tenancy over 87 percent white and 12 percent black out of a total of 418 families.[25]

Two years later (1952) a second low-rent project appeared in Rockaway, this one in run-down Redfern. Existing conditions there, as the New York City housing chairman described it, "would put Tobacco Road to shame." Redfern, according to journalists and bureaucrats, remained "one of the worst slum areas within the entire city of New York."[26] Once again the Chamber of Commerce took full credit for the project, even making the exaggerated claim that it had been "initiated exclusively" through their efforts. Both the Commissioner of Housing for New York State, through whose agency Redfern Houses received its subsidies, and the chairman of the New York City Housing Authority granted the Rockaway establishment this public relations success. Each acknowledged the crucial role played by the chamber in making the case for low-income housing and then preparing the entire community to welcome the new projects.[27]

Many years after the construction of the Redfern Project, the second to be built on the peninsula, the Chamber of Commerce continued to advocate fervently for additional low-income housing projects for the peninsula. Why the chamber continued to play this role is not easy to determine. Again, contractors and realtors stood to make money. Reports in the *Rockaway Review* suggest that the chamber's leaders shared the widespread belief that government housing would eliminate pockets of poverty and enhance the economic health of their community; they knew that most of Rockaway's black population would be ineligible for apartments and would be forced to move elsewhere. Undoubtedly, landlords who owned dilapidated real estate benefited too, since they received market prices for houses that, once condemned, cost virtually nothing to maintain. Those who had political connections or could make special appeals to appraisers tended to realize prices above market value. The announcement that an area was to be cleared generally served as a signal to landlords to cease making repairs, and many ignored serious violations. Homes left without heat, electricity, or plumbing deteriorated in Redfern and elsewhere every time a slum clearance operation was announced. Slum lords continued to benefit from this process.[28]

In many respects, Redfern Houses, just like its sister development in Arverne, met with outstanding initial success. In both cases, sparkling, well maintained buildings with playgrounds for children seemed to promise a better life for the occupants. Low rents, below market rates, remained an attractive feature. Once more, there had been a huge application list, and tenants felt fortunate to obtain desperately needed housing at affordable prices. People who moved into the two projects appreciated their clean apartments with new fixtures, efficient plumbing, and safe wiring. Many families of veterans found that their similar life experiences led to easy connections and good neighborly relationships. As working poor, they met the New Deal criteria. Residents from these earlier times speak glowingly about how much they enjoyed living in both projects. Outsiders, even local school personnel, have commented on the camaraderie existing between project families. Neighbors carpooled, looked after each other's children, and did favors for one another, and the children maintained special relationships into adulthood.

Although Redfern Houses had not been set up specifically for veterans, they received preference, while other applicants were closely screened for suitability. But unlike Arverne Houses, it included a small number of welfare families: 8 percent of the tenants in 1955, three years after the project opened.[29] Redfern initially offered counseling services for its new tenants, some of whom needed assistance in adjusting to a changed situation. While these services were useful to the new residents, they did not continue very long and were not duplicated in some of the later housing developments built in the Rockaways.[30]

The majority of the initial occupants of Redfern Houses, almost 57 percent in 1955, were white and came from outside the area. A small number of Puerto Ricans, a group entirely new to the Far Rockaway section of the peninsula, also gained admission. There is no evidence that the Rockaway establishment, including chamber officials, felt any remorse about the paucity of minorities in the project. The overwhelming majority of African American inhabitants of Redfern did not meet the stringent criteria for admission. Leaders of the Women's Industrial Service League subsequently said that their failure to place families from this predominantly black neighborhood into the Redfern project was one of their biggest disappointments.[31]

And what of the Redfern residents who were displaced by the project? With few resources and low incomes, they could only afford apartments like those that had been destroyed. New York City still had a serious housing shortage, which was particularly severe for blacks. Despite their lack of choices, many of these long-time residents felt comfortable living on the peninsula and wished to remain. The only local area open to them in segregated Rockaway was the dilapidated section of Hammels, just north of Rockaway Beach Boulevard. The city officials who relocated families here, or encouraged its selection, showed callous indifference to its substandard accommodations. Almost a decade earlier, Robert Moses had described the now-available rooming houses as "old frame tenements."[32] The derisive term, "rookeries," was also used at this time to characterize these rundown buildings. Exposés had begun to appear in local newspapers, such as the February 1949 *Wave* story about rats in Hammels.[33] Some critics pointed out that part of this district had already been earmarked for urban renewal even as people were being moved there. Within a few years many relocated families would have to be shifted once again.[34]

The Hammels property owners were a greedy lot. Before World War II, they had converted some poorly constructed, wood-frame summer dwellings in bad condition for year-round use by poor black people. Many of the buildings stood barely a few feet apart, and others were attached. Those that did not front on the street were accessible only through narrow courts located on interior blocks. A few years after the war, landlords refashioned some additional houses to take in more occupants. This occurred by design rather than coincidence. Just as Redfern families were being moved into Hammels, the Rockaways were beginning to experience a steady decline in summer rentals, especially in areas adjoining black neighborhoods. In September 1949 the *Wave* editorialized on this disturbing trend:

> Last summer it became apparent that the "easy money" was not here in such quantities as it had been. The people who wanted to rent summer places were more choosy and in many cases said flatly that they no longer could afford the high rents. Noting this trend, a number of owners are changing their practice and are offering accommodations on an all year basis.[35]

The newspaper, presenting these recent conversions in a favorable manner, argued that the transition to year-round residences offered a solution to the New York City housing shortage.

Encouraged by officials eager to relocate people from Redfern, landlords and real estate agents with Hammels property concluded that considerable profit could be made from these poor families. Converting the "class B rooming houses" originally designed for the tourist trade to permanent use proved relatively inexpensive. They already possessed furniture from previous summer rentals so that installation of additional apartment units and furnishings, makeshift heating devices, and a minimum of insulation constituted the major cost. Moreover, declaring the rooms "furnished" justified their charging much higher rents. Each owner attempted to assemble as many apartments as possible in order to maximize the number of tenants. Landlords utilized attics that had formerly served for storage and cellars that were either damp from the frequent Rockaway floods or overheated by nearby furnaces (if the building happened to have a furnace). Occasionally they turned garages into living quarters. Most of these buildings, marginal when rented seasonally, deteriorated as new occupants strained the facilities. Building inspectors must have averted their eyes—or received bribes—to overlook such violations.

By the 1930s, a sizeable section of Hammels a block or two from the beach already consisted of substandard housing occupied primarily by African Americans. After the war, some additional buildings in the vicinity were converted for year-round use. But once poor black families from Redfern began arriving, the conversions snowballed. Landlords, knowing that seasonal rentals were no longer possible, faced an ethical dilemma. As owners of summer property, they had always cut corners to maintain a certain margin of profit, and their transient renters seemed willing to put up with inconvenience for a few months. Now these property holders had the opportunity to make even more money by squeezing poor people who were being relocated.

Exploitation was rampant in Hammels. As far as we know, none of the buildings were simply abandoned. Landlords who lacked the stomach for the new style of operation simply sold their holdings at a loss to real estate speculators, who made fast profits by buying up many of these structures. Most summer landlords simply held on to their property, often just a single house or bungalow, and easily rationalized their financial rewards. Before long, newspapers began referring to this section of Hammels as "slum town" and, in another familiar comparison, "Tobacco Road."[36] One article described a ten-room house occupied by around forty people, whose owner collected $500 per month rent, a huge sum at the time. Another piece profiled a family living in two tiny rooms and sharing a bathroom and kitchen with a half-dozen other families. Not surprisingly, health officials were alarmed by the growing rate of tuberculosis in Hammels, which was now said to be the highest in all of New York City.[37]

However, Hammels was destined for change. Since the end of 1949, the New York City Housing Authority had been planning a new low-income project on the site, the third to be built on the peninsula since the end of the war. The Chamber of Commerce was once more among its strongest advocates, along with Robert Moses, who wanted the development completed before the arrival of mass transit.[38] Some of the supporters of public housing in Hammels, who held positions of influence in the community, actually owned property in the area and therefore stood to gain when the city government purchased the land. J. Clarence Davies III, the son of a prominent city housing official who was a close associate of Mayor Wagner, makes the claim in his book on urban renewal that Assemblyman J. Lewis Fox was one of these local leaders.[39]

To clear the path for the new project, residents of the designated blocks in Hammels had to be removed. Many of them had lived in their present apartments for a few years at most, and in some cases even less. Small shopkeepers also suffered from the condemnation process. When their leases expired, they were left with nothing. Landlords stopped repairing decaying buildings even before official notice of eviction was given. While some received modest prices for their dilapidated property, those with connections obtained much more. The *Long Island Press* printed a charge by a local political leader that when the city acquired this land, "some property owners got as much as 350 percent more than the assessed valuation for their properties." The accusation was never substantiated, but it was never challenged either.[40]

Between 1951 and 1953, residents of the Hammels site were relocated to the south side of Rockaway Beach Boulevard, bordering the ocean, to bungalows and summer rooming houses that were hurriedly being readied for year-round occupancy. Before long, this area acquired the familiar distinction of "the worst slum" in New York City.[41] Poor African Americans suffered once again. In the Rockaways, knowledgeable observers regarded slum clearance as a euphemism for "Negro removal." Not surprisingly, in 1954, when Hammel Houses were completed with federal government subsidies, the people forced to relocate were ignored. Admission to public housing still required a screening process, and the overwhelming majority of needy local families were declared ineligible. The *Wave* claimed that about two-thirds of the new tenants came from outside the peninsula, and the percentage was probably even greater.[42] Among the newcomers, just under 40 percent were white, 49 percent black, and 12 percent Puerto Rican. The figure for families on public assistance reached 18.5 percent, somewhat higher than that for Redfern Houses, but many of these recipients were senior citizens.[43] Nevertheless, the higher number of clients on welfare does reveal an official awareness of this population's housing requirements, one that would have a lasting impact on the Rockaways in the decades to follow.

The new housing project offered clean, comfortable apartments and safe play spaces. One African American resident, a married woman, stated that it provided the first centrally heated apartment her family had ever rented in Rockaway. Yet Hammel Houses did not have quite the success of the two previous projects built on the peninsula. A greater disparity existed in the ages and ethnic composition of the tenants. The development housed a larger percentage of welfare clients, and a certain number had social problems. Occupants expressed more dissatisfaction with what they regarded as neglectful maintenance. But the chief complaint concerned the lack of security in the area.[44]

Many reformers had believed that, in addition to improving the lives of occupants, low-income housing would also provide an economic and social boost to the immediate surroundings. Chairman Philip J. Cruise of the New York City Housing Authority told the Chamber of Commerce in 1953, while Hammel Houses was nearing completion, that the families coming into the new units "help give a community vigor and keep it a living growing place," and in the process serve to "rejuvenate a neighborhood."[45] Unfortunately, the opposite occurred. As the nearby streets continued to deteriorate, partially as a result of the relocation process, the quality of life in the new buildings suffered accordingly. The rising crime rate in Hammels affected everybody, including those in the new project, forcing them to be just as conscious of personal safety as their neighbors outside. The elderly felt especially vulnerable. Such concerns had not existed for those living in the more isolated Arverne Houses. Even the Redfern project had less difficulty with neighborhood crime, mainly due to established community institutions, such as churches and service organizations, that tended to mitigate social disorder. By contrast, in the area surrounding the Hammels project, relocated people who were largely strangers to each other were forced into crowded, converted summer properties. They lacked the long-standing ties that contribute to social cohesiveness. In short, rather than the project helping the neighborhood, the neighborhood eventually undermined the success of the project.

Low-income developments in the Rockaways contributed to the expansion of residential decay because of the rules that prevented the absorption of displaced local residents. Instead of ending the dreadful conditions that had existed for decades, the projects served, indirectly, to expand them. In the short run, those who moved into the projects benefited from their improved accommodations. But those who filled up the even more crowded summer dwellings accelerated the process of deterioration. Nonetheless, the waiting lists for public low-income housing remained long, never lower than one hundred thousand applicants in New York City.[46] The Nordeck Apartments, a successful middle-income co-op begun in the mid-1950s and completed in 1960, was situated next to the Arverne and Edgemere low-income projects, suggesting that public housing in the Rockaways was not viewed negatively at the time.

Because the expansion of high-poverty tracts remained confined primarily to Hammels, most Rockaway residents failed to appreciate the precedents that were being established during the early 1950s. The Rockaway community had not prepared itself for either the increase in population or the socioeconomic transformation that resulted from the influx of new residents into the area. Problems arising in Hammels were greatly exacerbated by a huge expansion of its welfare population. Some of the people on public assistance were long-time residents of the Rockaways, while others were brought in from distant areas.[47] In the schools serving Hammels, classroom overcrowding became a major concern of educators and parents.[48] There were no public hospitals in the vicinity. Few jobs were being created, since businesses based on resort-related activities had already begun to disappear.

However, public officials and local leaders chose to ignore the changing reality and continued to advocate for more public housing developments as the panacea for Rockaway's ills. With the exception of the first one built in Arverne, which involved no relocation, the new low-income projects generated new social problems. Yet the proposed solution remained the same: build more projects. Just as Hammel Houses opened its doors in the summer of 1954, Housing Commissioner Cruise spoke about an even larger project for the peninsula that was in the planning stages.[49] Despite the community's lack of preparedness, he counted on local businessmen and politicians to support the enterprise, for, in this regard, the Rockaway elite was unique in the nation. True to form, the Chamber of Commerce gave its blessing to the fourth low-income housing development to be built in the Rockaways in just under ten years.

CHAPTER 4

Rockaway's Welfare

In Arthur Miller's play *The Price*, one of the main characters, a policeman, announces that he walks a beat in the Rockaways. Another character responds, "That's Siberia." Although Rockaway had become incorporated into the City of New York in 1898, during the first half of the twentieth century its residents felt that they lived apart from the city. Their conception of the peninsula possessed a certain truth during the winter months, when Rockaway's remoteness, spaciousness, and relatively small population made it feel like a small town. Indeed, this southeastern section of Queens remained far from the swirl of activity in midtown Manhattan and other parts of the city. Perhaps too, the neglect of Rockaway during the early decades served to reinforce the feeling that this barrier beach maintained a distinct way of life. Despite the earnest endeavors of its active Chamber of Commerce, municipal leaders—with the notable exception of Robert Moses—assigned the peninsula a low priority, regarding it as a kind of backwater, a distant place peripheral to the central city. One retired New York City commissioner had trouble remembering its location on the map, and asked if it were part of Brooklyn!

As a result of Rockaway's status, services of various kinds tended to be inferior to those enjoyed elsewhere. The timeliness of snow removal has traditionally been thought to indicate an area's relative importance to City Hall. During the early 1950s, when one of the authors commuted daily from the peninsula to Queens College in Flushing, he observed that snow was usually removed later from Rockaway than from the other parts of the borough. The February 1969 snow storm, which damaged the Lindsay administration because of delays in snow removal in Queens, proved disastrous in the Rockaways, where no plowing took place for days and all forms of transportation ground to a halt.[1]

Other signs of neglect reveal a similar pattern. For example, the Rockaways continued to have difficulty with floods and sewage. A large part of its drainage system had been constructed during the ninetheenth century; it was patched up by the WPA in the 1930s. Seepage of sand into the archaic network, plus the continuously rising water levels of Jamaica Bay due to extended runways from JFK (formerly Idlewild) airport, caused regular flooding. The backup of raw sewage into streets and homes occurred repeatedly over the years, especially in the poorer sections of the peninsula.[2] Despite the undeniable health hazards connected with faulty drainage, the municipal government employed a piecemeal approach to trouble spots rather than seeking to undertake the necessary and costly overhaul of the entire system. As if to symbolize its disdain for the community, the city closed down the local court house just a few months before the completion of the subway line. It took this action despite the area's growing population, and the shutdown caused great inconvenience. Rockaway residents needing to resolve legal matters now had to travel miles away to Jamaica or Kew Gardens. The latter, although part of Queens, was not easily reached by public transportation from the peninsula.[3]

The appearance of mass transit in June 1956, which did not alter official inattention to the Rockaways, resulted in increased contact between the city and the peninsula. The arrival of the subway coincided with the rise of public anxiety about social ills in certain parts of New York City; problems such as juvenile delinquency and illegitimacy were viewed as threats to society's well-being.[4] Before long. such tendencies were "discovered" on the peninsula, and local journalists made a connection between rapid transit and the sudden eruption of social ills. They blamed the subway for changing the quality of life in Rockaway for the worse, as it had brought this formerly remote barrier beach into more direct contact with urban America.

While mass transit undoubtedly helped to speed the transition from a shore resort to a year-round community, it should not be seen as a major force in altering the area's socioeconomic character. On the contrary, as observed in the previous chapter, a substantial amount of middle-class housing was built, and many working- and middle-class families moved to the Rockaways precisely because of the subway connection. In truth, responsibility for the onset of "urban problems" must be placed with city officials and the complicity of local real estate interests some years before the rapid transit system arrived, and even before the old wooden trestle burned down. The process began with a municipal government policy that set a precedent by providing converted summer bungalows and rooming houses for World War II veterans. It ended with the Rockaways coming to be seen as a repository for the poorest of the poor.

Ironically, the main force behind this process was the agency that had been inspired by the New Deal in the late 1930s and conceived as the protector of citizens in need: the New York City Department of Welfare. In many ways, the Social Security Act of 1935, which established Washington's role in the field of public assistance, has come to symbolize the humanitarian thrust of Roosevelt's domestic legislation. Three major types of social provision were included: national contributory old-age insurance, state-run unemployment insurance, and federally subsidized public assistance. The last feature was designed to support vulnerable, nonproductive groups, including the aged, the blind, the permanently and totally disabled, and children. Aid to Dependent Children, originally seen as a temporary measure, was intended to help impoverished families restore their sense of self-respect and their capacity for independent living and to improve opportunities for their children.

Before World War II, a disproportionate number of America's poor lived in the rural south, and the recipients of aid were overwhelmingly white. In fact, before 1940 only between 14 percent and 17 percent of families receiving Aid to Dependent Children (ADC) throughout the country were black.[5] After the war, African Americans migrated from the south to the north in large numbers. In addition, the Puerto Rican population of New York City swelled from just under .01 percent of the total in 1940 to more than 10 percent in 1970. In all, approximately one million poor blacks and Puerto Ricans moved to the city during the 1950s and 1960s.[6] This vast transformation took place in a metropolitan area already suffering from a tremendous shortage of affordable housing. At the same time, industries that had traditionally provided jobs for new immigrants to New York began leaving. Unemployment and underemployment soon became a permanent feature of urban life, seemingly immune to earlier schemes designed to end cyclical poverty. Rates of out-of-wedlock births increased, as did the number of female-headed households.[7]

In the late 1940s and early 1950s, popular attitudes toward public assistance changed. From its inception as an aid program for deserving widows with children, ADC came to be associated with "immoral women" who also happened to belong to minority groups. Instead of serving as a temporary safeguard allowing people to get back on their feet, ADC was now seen as perpetuating deviance, especially "illegitimacy."[8] Welfare bashing also tied in with a right-wing political agenda. By attacking a program connected with liberals, which was supposedly wasting taxpayers' money, politicians could appeal to voters who were increasingly out of sympathy with the "undeserving poor." Magazines with a national circulation, *Look* and *Reader's Digest* among others, promoted hostility toward public assistance by running stories about the large number of "chiselers" and "frauds" exploiting the system.[9] In New York City, newspapers, especially the *Daily News*, the *World-Telegram*, and the *Daily Mirror*, delighted in exposing "welfare cheats," thereby giving the impression that programs benefiting the poor had no merit and should be eliminated.[10]

The general conservative drift in the United States in the years after World War II made it politically desirable for welfare agencies to try to limit services and cut back on expenditures. Social service employees who showed too much sympathy for clients were more than discouraged; they were reassigned or even forced out of the profession. In New York City in 1948, Mayor O'Dwyer appointed Raymond M. Hilliard Commissioner of Welfare, with an express mandate to rid the department of left-wing personnel who were thought to be communists, trade unionists, or too strongly identified with the poor. McCarthyism in the welfare department "threw out the Commies," as Hilliard bragged in a *Saturday Evening Post* article, and it also eliminated scores of dedicated caseworkers, the so-called "wasters."[11]

Coinciding with his purges of the welfare department, Commissioner Hilliard began insisting on a tough approach to families receiving benefits. More than ever before, social investigators were instructed to focus on eligibility and to reduce services. Unannounced night visits by special agents became a regular occurrence. Any woman found to have a male companion was automatically dropped from the rolls along with her children, even in the absence of proof that these men supplied the client with money. Despite all of Hilliard's efforts, conservative critics continued their assaults on New York City's Department of Welfare, its policies, and the very practice of welfare itself.[12]

It is necessary to appreciate this background in order to understand the next phase of Rockaway's history. Welfare department policies, promulgated by Commissioner Hilliard, helped drive New York's social problems to the peninsula. Many of the department staff who carried out his instructions, and those of his successors, were chastened by the experience of McCarthyism. They realized that advocating too strongly for clients could lead to adverse consequences for themselves. As Daniel Walkowitz maintains in his recent book on middle-class identity, the 1950s marked "a growing social distance" that separated New York social workers from their clients, thereby affecting attitudes and practice. An added ingredient, Walkowitz maintains, was the divide opening between these social workers, predominantly white, and welfare recipients, who were increasingly people of color.[13]

The existence of this conservative political atmosphere helps to explain how the welfare department and its employees could carry out regressive policies in the Rockaways. Families on public assistance were steered into the resort community and were placed in housing that was not standard or even marginal, but rather dilapidated shacks that had become unsuitable for profitable summer rental. Obviously, the authorities had a problem: what to do with the influx of poor people migrating into a city that already had a housing shortage. Urban redevelopment projects in various parts of New York exacerbated the situation because many families in need of housing did not meet the admission requirements for the low-income projects being built at this time. As former Commissioner of Welfare James R. Dumpson explained, in emergency situations such as fires or sudden evictions, bad housing was the best option. He added that this choice was made only in those exceptional cases in which any roof over a family's head would be better than homelessness. In normal circumstances, he claimed, the welfare department had no formal obligation to house clients.[14]

Commissioner Dumpson's assertion that the welfare department did not routinely handle matters related to housing echoes what other former city officials have maintained. When Dr. Doris Moss conducted her investigations of Arverne during the early 1960s, a welfare department official in Jamaica, Queens, told her bluntly that the department was "not in the business of finding living quarters for its clients."[15] During our own investigations, it became almost impossible to discover anyone who would take responsibility for the large number of welfare families who wound up in the shacks of Rockaway. Retired municipal officials repeatedly blamed underlings in the bureaucratic structure, insisting that no senior official would ever become involved in such practices. Former advisors to mayors insisted that none of their superiors even knew of the conditions existing in the Rockaways. In fact, they asserted, once the situation was brought to their attention they sought immediate measures of amelioration. Administrators who worked for Mayors Wagner and Lindsay made nearly identical statements to this effect.

The evidence contradicts these claims. In 1949, as Commissioner Hilliard was purging the welfare department and reducing budgets, he informed the Chamber of Commerce that he was initiating a new policy in the Rockaways. Welfare clients would be placed in former summer houses, some for the winter months only and others on a year-round basis. The cornerstone of this policy had been established a few years earlier, when bungalows and beach rooming houses had been provided for veterans during the winter. Poor black families, some of whom received public assistance, were placed in these dwellings a little later, as first Redfern and then Hammels were cleared for low-income housing. However, the practice of bringing welfare clients onto the peninsula on a large scale was an entirely new development. Once inaugurated, it would persist for decades.

In presenting his plan to the Chamber of Commerce, Hilliard stated that the presence of people on welfare would enhance the Rockaway community. He subsequently argued that welfare checks would benefit local businesses. Hilliard acknowledged that his department selected areas (mainly in Hammels) "where the housing is of extremely poor quality." He provided examples of clients squeezed into narrow spaces with "two, three or four families often room[ing] together in one, two, three or four room apartments," and justified this on the grounds that it made possible the sharing of "high rentals." Cutting costs always seemed to be one of his chief motives, even when fourteen people occupied "a four room shack." He obviously found this "not the ideal solution," yet suitable for "beneficiaries" of public assistance.[16] He never mentioned that the majority of the people being herded together were young children, including infants.

In later years, Rockaway leaders and editorial writers, puzzled by "welfare dumping" in their midst, would call attention to such illogical aspects of the policy as the limited work opportunities in the peninsula, dwindling seasonal jobs, and the lengthy and expensive trip to outside employment centers. Undeniably, this beach resort was an inhospitable place for poor people who wished to escape the relief rolls. The *Wave* editorialized more than once on this same theme. "What we cannot understand," they wrote, "is how a department charged with the welfare of the people of the city, could send underprivileged people here and expect them to improve themselves."[17]

In his 1949 statement on the new policy, Hilliard explained that Rockaway had been chosen by the welfare department because the people who would be sent there were not really expected to find work. "It would be preferable," he said, "for those families with employable persons to live in areas more accessible to places of employment."[18] Hilliard did not spell out the details of his plan, but the implications were clear. For the most part, the department moved to the peninsula single parents with young children, as well as families with multiple problems who were extremely hard to place elsewhere. Released criminals, parolees, drug addicts, and alcoholics, regarded as unfit for mainstream work opportunities, were also assigned to the Rockaways.[19]

During the following year, Commissioner Hilliard elaborated upon welfare department policy in a second statement to the Rockaway business community. He noted that during the previous year, the number of peninsular locals receiving public assistance had expanded by 40 percent. This was no accident, since they had been sent to the Rockaways under his direction. Always cost-conscious, Hilliard pointed out that the urge to limit expenditures made it "sometimes necessary to house families with three and four small children in one room." The same motive lay behind the choice of furnished rooms, no matter how inadequate the furniture. Thus, for him, saving taxpayers money constituted an important justification for using the Rockaways to house needy families.[20] Hilliard hoped that these arrangements would be temporary, but clearly this matter remained out of his control. As the swell of people sent to the community rose from a few hundred to thousands, "temporary" proved to be a relative term. Many of the accommodations served as living quarters for families on welfare for between five and fifteen years, occasionally even longer. Contradicting those who claim that the welfare department "was not in the housing business," the commissioner mentioned scores of instances in which welfare centers took responsibility for finding Rockaway apartments for their clients.[21]

In his 1950 statement to the chamber, Commissioner Hilliard made sure to compliment Rockaway landlords for their willingness to rent rooms to welfare recipients. Apparently, owners of apartment houses in other parts of the city were less receptive. Twice Hilliard thanked local real estate interests for being "very cooperative in making these places available to us."[22] The landlords had provided a solution to a dilemma faced by his department by making space available for tenants ineligible for public housing and not easily placed in private rentals.

Almost all the clients moved out to the Rockaways were African American. Many, who had just arrived in New York City from the south, had no means of resisting being shipped off to an unfamiliar environment with substandard housing. Given the racially segregated housing patterns existing throughout New York, welfare officials preferred to place these newcomers in black areas like Hammels. Very few sections of the city provided a comparable opportunity, and those that did tended to be overcrowded. The adjoining Jewish areas to the east did not actively oppose the process of relocation; the residents who could afford to merely moved away.

Among all ethnic groups, Jews were regarded as least likely to oppose the entry, by government decree, of blacks into their neighborhoods. Brownsville, a largely Jewish section of Brooklyn, had already begun to experience this kind of peaceful transition.[23] By contrast, Chicago had what one scholar calls "communal riots" by members of white, non-Jewish ethnic groups to prevent integration after World War II. Similarly, the prevention of racial mixing in residential neighborhoods became a major theme in postwar Detroit. Jonathan Rieder has demonstrated that Italians opposed the arrival of blacks in Canarsie, a Brooklyn community, much more vigorously (and sometimes violently) than Jews. To the west of Hammels, in neighboring Seaside, the Irish population offered greater resistance than the Jews of Arverne and Edgemere to the placement of black tenants. During the 1950s, Seaside still maintained an active summer business, and owners of property there showed no eagerness to convert to year-round rentals. For the time being, this neighborhood remained white. All over the country the same pattern emerged. As a result, both real estate interests and governmental authorities encouraged minorities to move into Jewish neighborhoods in Boston, Chicago, Detroit, Los Angeles, and other cities. Even Harlem was a partially Jewish area during the late nineteenth century and early in the twentieth.[24]

In general, Rockaway had an inexhaustible supply of unused summer houses that could be quickly converted for welfare families. Places like Hammels had a receptive class of landlords, anxious to obtain easy profits. For city officials, the peninsula had the added advantage of being off the beaten track. Its rising crime rate and negative health statistics would attract relatively little attention from the mainstream media and could therefore be easily hidden.[25]

Rockaway's relative isolation, a major factor in its selection as a repository for problems the municipal government did not want to leave in the city's center, produced particular hardships for families receiving public assistance in the early 1950s. The paucity of job opportunities has already been noted. The absence of supermarkets in areas of poor housing resulted in food costs that were higher than in almost any other part of the city, a fact admitted by the welfare department. Doctors, who would normally make house calls, were reluctant to do so during the winter months. The nearest municipal health facility, Queens General Hospital, required one to two hours of travel and three separate bus changes. One can imagine the difficulty involved in bringing a sick child to this hospital from the Rockaway peninsula in bad weather. There were no dental clinics, mental health services, or drug rehabilitation centers. Even the welfare department acknowledged the inadequacy of recreational facilities for both children and adults.[26] The two welfare centers in Brooklyn that served Rockaway residents were at least an hour or more away by public transportation.

The lack of resources and services did not deter a welfare department bent on a warehouse approach to poverty. While the responsibility for the sordid practice of "dumping" ultimately rests with the various city administrations, in reality the mayors during the 1950s do not seem to have been directly involved. Apparently, chief executives deliberately removed themselves from the details of welfare department policies, thus maintaining "plausible deniability." Former Welfare Commissioner Henry L. McCarthy described how he learned early in his tenure that mayors "didn't want to be bothered." He reported to a deputy mayor, who invariably told him to do what he thought best. Accordingly, commissioners had considerable leeway, as long as they did not exceed budgets or create too much negative publicity.[27] McCarthy, who was in a position to know, believed that his predecessor, Hilliard, operated in a similar fashion. The extensive correspondence between mayors and welfare department higher-ups during the Democratic administrations after the war offers no indication that policy matters were ever openly discussed. All published evidence leads to the conclusion that procedures affecting the Rockaways were conceived and carried out within the confines of the welfare department.[28]

That a valuable beach area became a repository for poor people was no accident. City officials, like Commissioner Hilliard and his successors, had a plan for the community. Rockaway's spaciousness, available housing, and willing landlords provided the city with a solution to locating a welfare population in a tight housing market. The "plan," once set in motion, continued for years.[29] Individual mayors, who did nothing to stop the policy, must be held accountable.

Hilliard's expression of appreciation to the Rockaway landlords involved an element of disingenuousness. The real estate interests clearly benefited from the arrangement. Filling up failing houses with welfare clients proved to be extremely profitable, especially with payments guaranteed by the city. In fact, obsolete real estate could now be turned into gold. According to Roger Starr,

> the arrival of welfare tenants in an apartment house is a signal to all other tenants that that the owner has abandoned hope in the future of the building. . . . Once owners find that they have difficulty attracting tenants who pay their own rent, their future expectations are reduced to a very short span. There is no hope of a change for the better that will enable them to select tenants again and so their financial interest is reduced to spending as little money as possible while collecting rent.[30]

Property owners in the Rockaways accepted their role as the "landlords of last resort," housing the "tenants of last resort."[31] They hoped to recover whatever investments they had made "winterizing" their properties as soon as possible, and they did so without too much difficulty. In certain instances, "cooperating" landlords received subsidies from the city for the conversion process. Occasionally, social investigators received bribes to steer families into certain buildings. In at least one instance, a welfare department employee allegedly went into partnership with a Hammels landlord, purchasing a summer house for profit.[32] Local newspapers reported instances of other corrupt practices involving welfare investigators. One fraudulent scheme that came to light involved kickbacks to a caseworker from owners of moving companies and furniture stores.[33]

Clients' rents, which at the time were paid by the welfare department, reached sixty-five dollars per month per room, even for apartments without kitchens. The *Wave* reported that the city actually paid more for a single room for families in Hammels than was normally spent on a multiroom apartment, adding that substantial profits could be made "despite the fact that in many instances the accommodations were not suitable for all year round occupancy."[34] Although such a figure may be hard to evaluate with the passage of time, one contemporary report calculated that the same rooming houses which returned revenues of between $250 and $400 "during the four month summer season could [now] earn as much as $780 a year." But price comparisons have little practical meaning, for the days of summer rentals in Hammels had long since passed. Furthermore, whereas seasonal occupancy had involved at least minimal upkeep, no such expenditures were required for housing welfare clients for years at a time.

Racist real estate practices served to further influence developments in the Rockaways. In 1954, the welfare department paid "double the amount of rent for one room dwelling units" for black clients that they did for whites, a trend that continued for many years.[35] This belies the claim of Commissioner Hilliard and other welfare department spokespeople that they were saving taxpayers money by moving clients to the Rockaways. Critics frequently pointed out that some of the high rents paid by the city for welfare families in the Rockaways could just as easily have been spent on apartments located elsewhere. It is difficult to escape the conclusion that the placing of welfare recipients in this distant peninsula involved redlining (the racial profiling of areas) and protecting white preserves.

In Hammels during these years, landlords continued to hope that a public agency might decide to institute slum clearance, enhancing their property values still further. By the end of 1953, the rumors concerning Title I urban renewal for the area became more persistent.[36] The expectation of lucrative buyouts and immediate superprofits led speculators to purchase rooming houses and bungalows from those landlords not willing "to go welfare." No doubt these immediate business considerations, benefiting so many of its members, help to explain why the Rockaway Chamber of Commerce took so long to publicly criticize the influx of large numbers of welfare clients. At least three years elapsed after Hilliard's original policy statement in 1949 before adverse comments appeared in the *Rockaway Review* and the *Wave*. The *Rockaway Journal* first mentions the matter in March 1953.[37]

The absence of protest by influential local agencies apparently proved an important consideration in the welfare department's decision to begin steering cases to the peninsula. Despite their admission that Hammels accommodations were unsuitable, the department downplayed the suffering caused by their policy. Old frame structures of ten to twelve rooms housed as many as ten or twelve families. One toilet was considered sufficient for every seven bedrooms, and not all houses met even this minimum sanitary requirement.[38] Almost none of these structures contained bathtubs or indoor showers. Mothers bathed children in kitchen sinks. Adults had to wait for summer months to shower, and some were even forced to use the ocean for bathing. Kitchens were frequently shared; some had hot plates rather than stoves. Families occupying basement flats often had no direct access to bathroom facilities. A reporter discovered nineteen children living in one rooming house near the beach. In the same house five adults crowded into five basement cubicles, with no toilet in sight.[39] The *Wave* reported cases in which garages, lacking any sanitary facilities, accommodated families on public assistance. It also cited numerous examples of the welfare department placing clients in rooming houses that contained known building code violations.[40] Every so often, after stories about terrible living conditions appeared in the media, building inspectors would arrive and levy fines. However, these penalties often proved cheaper than the necessary repairs. For example, one account lists fines as ten dollars per violation.[41] Landlords simply added "slaps on the wrist" to the normal expenses connected with operating slum properties.

Early in 1954, approximately two thousand people were reported to reside in Hammels. Eighty percent received welfare and 75 percent were black. The remaining population, mainly Jewish, lived near the area's eastern boundaries.[42] City services of various kinds, which had never been very satisfactory, began to decline even further throughout the 1950s. Garbage collection, previously nonexistent during the winter in the resort era, never became adequate to deal with the expanding number of people. Observers frequently commented on "the littered streets, uncovered garbage cans, and vacant lots used as dumping grounds." Stories about the presence of rats appeared regularly.[43] Flooded roads and backed-up raw sewage were considered commonplace occurrences. Broken street lights, with glass scattered on sidewalks, and abandoned, rusted-out cars marked the terrain.

Before long, public health agencies, including the Queensboro TB and Health Association, the Jamaica District Health Center, and the New York City Department of Health, began expressing deep "concern about the general poor health picture" in the Rockaways, especially in Hammels. By the early 1950s, Rockaway had the highest rate of tuberculosis in all of Queens and the second highest rate of infant deaths. Health officials agreed that substandard housing was the most serious local community health problem. "Overcrowding, high rentals, unsanitary conditions had created unhygienic living conditions for the relief clients placed in the Rockaways." They warned that "isolation was impossible for known tuberculosis cases" found there.[44] In 1953, Health Department officials took the unusual step of criticizing another city department, maintaining that the Department of Welfare "was creating a serious problem for the [Hammels] community by concentrating large numbers of relief recipients in highly congested and blighted neighborhoods." The accusation had no effect. In fact, Welfare Commissioner Henry L. McCarthy resigned from a joint agency trying to improve health conditions in the Rockaways, stating that demands for amelioration could not be met at that time. In similar fashion, McCarthy declined requests to locate a welfare facility, or even a branch office, in the community.[45]

Overcrowded housing that contributed to disease also represented threats to safety. Fires had always been a feature of the Rockaway experience, especially in areas containing summer dwellings. Now this problem became worse. Families lived in frame houses lacking central heating, and makeshift heaters became the rule. The existing mulitiple-dwelling law did not require Rockaway rooming houses to have fire escapes, but it did stipulate sprinklers in halls and stairwells. This minimum provision was usually ignored.[46] Fires began to occur, threatening lives and compounding emergency relocation concerns.

In the spring of 1954, a story in the *Long Island Press* carried the headline: "City's Worst Firetraps Are in Rockaways." The account described Fire Commissioner Edward F. Cavanagh Jr.'s shocked reaction to conditions in Hammels and adjoining neighborhoods. He concluded that the most dangerous buildings in all of New York City are to be found "in the welter of teeming, wooden boarding houses along the Rockaway oceanfront." Evidently, fire inspectors had avoided the area. Standing in the middle of Hammels (Beach 79th Street), Cavanagh told reporters that if these wood-frame structures, some of which were built around the turn of the century and just a few feet apart from each other, ever started to burn, "they'll go up in a matter of minutes."[47] Despite this well publicized tour, the violations in the neighborhood continued to mount with every available building that was converted for welfare recipients. To be sure, the number of fires increased as well. The *Rockaway Review* reported that in 1956, just two years after the Fire Commissioner's visit, "fire losses soared to a new high."[48] Subsequently, articles appeared describing loss of life, frequently among children.

Even before the Health and Fire Departments spoke out about the dangers existing in the Rockaways, Robert Moses, in his capacity as City Construction Coordinator, became the first public figure to call attention to the situation. In the summer of 1952, while being honored by the Chamber of Commerce, Moses had once again referred to Rockaway as the "city's favorite shore resort." However, in a public statement issued a few weeks later, he noted that summer housing along New York City's shoreline had been converted into "firetraps." Ironically, it had been Moses himself, just after the war, who initiated the process of winter conversions he now deplored.[49] In his critical comments, he referred to Rockaway and Coney Island as "resort slums," an expression that entered mainstream vocabulary around this time.[50] Moses's remarks opened up the flood of negative publicity that Rockaway real estate interests had always hoped to avoid. Criticisms appeared in the media that, among other things, referred to the changing racial composition of the area. In his response to Moses's comments, the chamber's Executive Secretary Wolpert acknowledged the existence of firetraps and even provided facts and figures to demonstrate the validity of the charges. But he claimed that Rockaway was the innocent victim of a design perpetrated by the city through their Department of Welfare.[51]

Wolpert's answer constituted an open attack by the Chamber of Commerce on the New York City Department of Welfare. For its part, the *Wave* had started to condemn the "dumping" of clients into Hammels rookeries months earlier. As early as April 1952, an editorial appeared castigating "some money-mad landlords. . . packing their buildings with tenants who are compelled to live under deplorable conditions." A few months later, the editor refused to "remain silent while the good name" of the Rockaways "is threatened by greedy, grasping landlords who have no scruples." The following year, the paper posed a moral question: "How can some landlords continue to collect exorbitant rents for overcrowded, sub-standard housing?"[52]

The Chamber of Commerce, on the other hand, tended to be more considerate of their "cooperating" members when discussing the situation, choosing to place blame for the creation of slum conditions on the city itself. In this version, landlords were being tempted and led astray by welfare department representatives. Any offending landlords must have been outsiders, as Wolpert implied in a 1953 *Daily News* interview, when he charged that "sharp shooting speculators" were buying up the onetime boarding houses to extort huge profits.[53] Occasionally the *Rockaway Review* even presented the slum landlords' point of view, describing the troubles they had in dealing with tenants on relief, among which were the tenants' disrespect for property and the nuisance of "having to collect weekly rents."[54]

In their attempt to continue representing owners of Hammels rental properties, while at the same time trying to protect the community's image, the chamber fell between two stools. The organization's call for an end to "welfare dumping" exposed these conflicting aims, since the practice benefited the slumlords and the "speculators." Just a few months after the exchange with Robert Moses, a division occurred in the ranks of the chamber. A Hammels organization, called the Rockaway Beach Property Owners and Civic Association, now sought to lobby for their special needs. At one point in 1953, the group advocated evicting all renters who, in protesting against prevailing conditions, threatened a neighborhood-wide rent strike. Such an extreme maneuver, in addition to revealing the landlords' callousness, would certainly have resulted in unfavorable publicity for the entire community.[55]

This first split in the previously unified Rockaway business alliance led to others, and before the end of the decade a myriad of separate organizations were formed, each pursuing the specific interests of its constituents. Certain groups represented entire sections, like Neponsit and Belle Harbor, while others, such as the Wavecrest Civic Association and the Frank Avenue Association, advocated for smaller entities. Some tiny, single-issue organizations came and went overnight, while others had greater staying power. Given the pressures on the peninsula and the conflicting needs of different populations and classes, such democratic, grassroots energy was healthy. However, the fissures weakened the Chamber of Commerce—the one organization that had always been identified with the Rockaways—leaving the community in a weaker position when dealing with outside agencies. The homeowners' groups and neighborhood improvement associations that appeared in the Rockaways at this time replicated similar developments throughout the country. Their emergence gave organizational authority to property owners who mobilized against the intrusion of African Americans into their neighborhoods. They feared the willingness of governments to undermine property values, and they blamed blacks for their insecurity. For the most part, fighting integration became their raison d'être.[56] Seemingly in response, in the mid-1950s an NAACP branch in Inwood–Far Rockaway began to make its presence felt.

During the 1950s, the influence of the Chamber of Commerce declined unmistakably. When the chamber initially criticized welfare department practices in the summer of 1952, George Wolpert claimed that for the previous year he had been discreetly asking the new commissioner, Henry L. McCarthy, to stop assigning clients to the Rockaways and had received reassuring promises.[57] However, there is no published record of any exchanges, and if such requests were made they had no impact. In a June 1952 statement to the *Rockaway Review*, McCarthy specifically praised "a steady *increasing* number of landlords in the Rockaways [who] are cooperating with the Department of Welfare by renting their premises for yearly occupancy," hardly evidence of a change in policy.[58]

After the summer of 1952, although the trend continued unabated, city officials became more defensive when queried about bringing welfare families to the peninsula. In May of the following year, at a public meeting in Queens, McCarthy confessed that his department sought to find any available shelter for clients, including "run down housing." The city resorted to such remedies, he asserted, because of laws requiring them to do so; a headline in the *Wave* reported, "Law Forces the Welfare Department to Place Recipients in the Rockaways."[59] McCarthy's acknowledgment contradicted a statement made earlier that year to chamber executives that his department "definitely never looked for any places in Rockaway." Actually, during that same year the *Wave* printed a story providing examples of welfare department agents approaching landlords for the purpose of renting rooms to relief recipients.[60] The chamber's efforts to go public with the charge that the welfare department created slums in the Rockaways had no effect on policy.[61] Throughout the 1950s, the deterioration existing in Hammels continued to spread eastward until it reached B. 74th Street. (It stopped there because the next block, B. 73rd Street, served as the terminus for the shore parkway and still contained some fashionable homes.) During this decade the welfare department persistently denied that it specifically used the Rockaways to house clients, while at the same time locals presented evidence to the contrary. A 1958 *Wave* editorial reflected community frustration when it asked rhetorically, "Welfare Department Still

Sinning?"[62] The same year, in a desperate appeal to all responsible city authorities, the chamber's magazine began with an editorial that accused the department of "sending relief families here." The piece was entitled "Please No More Slums."[63] Whereas the chamber had once issued demands, it was now reduced to imploring. Unfortunately, this appeal came too late. A month before the editorial appeared, newspapers reported that the welfare department no longer cared to meet with members of the Rockaway Chamber of Commerce.[64]

Despite subsequent official disclaimers, we know that at least until 1954 the welfare department did in fact admit to housing clients in the Rockaways. When a 1958 petition protesting welfare department practices, sent to city officials by George Wolpert and fifty signatories, reached Deputy Commissioner James R. Dumpson's office, he maintained that the department staff "had been instructed not to solicit housing in the Rockaways since 1954."[65] Yet after that point, property owners still continued to claim that welfare department staff directly approached them for the purpose of soliciting rooms. Many of these instances were reported in local newspapers such as the *Wave*.[66] The evidence was sufficiently reliable to cause the borough president of Queens, in 1958, to call for a "re-study of the present procedures of the Department of Welfare which have resulted in the influx of welfare cases into the [Rockaway] area." He was particularly disturbed about the increasing population density of a neighborhood that lacked "required amenities."[67] However, no such investigation ever took place. During the 1950s, some social service field workers, who were horrified at the unacceptable living conditions of Rockaway clients, duly reported these violations. If the housing officer to whom they reported could not obtain redress, a notice would then be sent to the housing division of welfare's central office, which held final authority. Usually nothing happened, leading social workers to conclude that departmental leadership approved of existing arrangements in Hammels.[68]

Throughout this period, the welfare department was still considered a liberal agency created by the New Deal. Accordingly, it became the target of right-wing newspapers. In March 1954 the conservative *Long Island Press*, which covered Queens as well as Long Island, began a series dealing with poverty in the Rockaways. Referring to Hammels as "slum town" or "welfare town,"[69] the articles presented graphic descriptions, photographs, and stories about the suffering and poor health of individual families. These made a stronger impact on readers than statistics possibly could.

Other articles pointed out how much profit accrued to slumlords, who were generously compensated with taxpayers' money. The series left the impression that the welfare department actively created the kind of concentrated high-poverty areas it had been expected to alleviate. One particularly telling story described a disabled war veteran and his wife, who worked as a domestic. The couple lived in a dingy cellar cubicle with leaking pipes and broken plaster, surrounded by rubbish and forced to cook on "a dirt-encrusted public stove." This upsetting account concluded with the information that the unfortunate couple had been moved to their building by the welfare department.[70]

However, the conservative media mostly tended to portray welfare recipients in an unsympathetic light. For example, the *Long Island Press*, in its otherwise admirable series, fed racist impulses by showing photographs exclusively of black people. Other newspapers resorted to the old chestnut about the "undeserving poor" squandering welfare payments, supporting these generalizations with a few anecdotes. Thus, while the welfare department was accused on the one hand of creating slum conditions, it was blamed for coddling "frauds" and "chiselers" on the other. Public assistance had become increasingly unpopular among segments of the white population in New York City, including the Rockaways. Local newspapers chimed in with articles calling for better supervision of welfare funding in order to eliminate abuses, and they editorialized against present policies. One paper advocated legislation making receipt of payments more difficult, including instituting residence requirements of up to one year, a position advocated by conservative politicians at the time.[71]

The media's linking of crime, public assistance, and race contributed to the unfavorable image of social services and welfare recipients. As petty crime began to occur on the peninsula, chiefly in the Hammels section, it was reported more frequently in the local papers, especially the *Long Island Press* and the *Wave*. City officials had chosen the Rockaways as a repository for their most difficult cases, and these so-called "problem families" arrived in a new environment that lacked the social structure existing in more established neighborhoods. Specialized services that might have mitigated some of the worst results of such relocations did not exist, nor were any attempts made to provide them. The resulting social dysfunction was therefore not surprising. Occasionally an administrator would admit responsibility, but without any suggested remedy. In 1958, New York State Housing Commissioner Joseph P. McMurray spoke openly about "problem families" presently living in Rockaway and the "difficulty of housing them" anywhere else. "These are people who must be rehabilitated," Mc-Murray declared, because ignored and untreated, they will go on to "inhabit the slums of the future."[72] In the Rockaways such persons remained ignored and untreated. Ultimately, the quality of life for all residents, African American as well as white, was diminished.

District Attorney Frank O'Connor, an aspiring politician who participated in an inspection tour of Hammels in November 1958, expressed shock at what he saw. O'Connor referred to the neighborhood as "a jungle unfit for human habitation." Such racist terminology would not have been lost on his audience. Announcing that the only approach to this "blight on American civilization" was to "get tough," he had several "welfare cheats" arrested. Agents from his office made a quick inspection, which resulted in the condemnation of four buildings, while eighteen others were declared unsafe. In addition, the agents handed out a few hundred summonses for violations.[73] Dramatic episodes such as O'Connor's tour led to the conclusion that untold welfare abuses flourished, and that unless prodded by "no nonsense" officials, current leaders would do little to correct them. No appreciable improvements in conditions resulted from this well-publicized visit to the Rockaways. Nevertheless, O'Connor was later elected City Council President.

Politicians and the press called for the removal of clients from their present quarters. However, they offered no practical remedy to the problem of inadequate housing for the dependent poor. Other New York City neighborhoods, such as Brownsville and the South Bronx, had begun deteriorating around this time. Therefore, finding space for welfare families remained a difficult task. Deputy Commissioner Dumpson, who had accompanied O'Connor on his tour, termed such an operation "a huge job." As a last alternative he installed displaced clients in hotels, and he implemented this policy on a small scale in the Rockaways by creating a single-room-occupancy establishment on a main thoroughfare, B. 116th Street. Inevitably, the SRO, which entailed huge expenses, contributed to the decline of a popular shopping area.[74]

The welfare department solved the problem of housing minority families on public assistance by moving them as far from the center of the city as possible. It followed a similar approach in dealing with individuals and families who had multiple problems. The political purges of the department had resulted in the dismissal of many social workers who might have pressed for solutions considered "too expensive." For political and economic reasons, more humane social policies did not appeal to urban administrators in the 1950s. A decade later, Lyndon Johnson's Great Society agenda would offer a fresh campaign against poverty, at least until the Vietnam War intervened. But during the Truman–Eisenhower years, New York City officials charged with the well-being of the needy took the path of least resistance, exacerbating human distress and undermining a once viable community.

CHAPTER 5

Robert Moses and the End of a Resort

With its miles of sandy beaches, breezes that blow from bay and ocean, and proximity to the heart of New York City, Rockaway was destined to become a major resort. As early as 1833, a fashionable hotel opened in Far Rockaway, catering to the rich and famous. Several more were built during the following decades. At first, ferries served as the chief means of transportation from the mainland, leading to the construction of hotels along the bay. Before long, summer mansions also dotted both bay and ocean shores along with several yacht clubs. The completion of the Far Rockaway branches of the South Side Railroad in 1869, the Long Island Rail Road in 1872, and the extension of the Far Rockaway railroad terminus to Seaside led to a marked increase in summer visitors, including some with more modest incomes.

Soon the ocean side of the peninsula, with its heart in Seaside, dominated the tourist trade. Within a mile radius there were amusement parks boasting roller coasters and ferris wheels, game arcades, restaurants, fast food establishments, and numerous taverns. Bath houses sprung up to serve the day tourists. In summer, "the Rockaways acquire[d] the color, congestion and gaiety of Coney Island."[1] Grand hotels appeared up and down the peninsula in the last two decades of the nineteenth century. In 1881, "the biggest hotel in the world" opened its doors (and went bankrupt almost immediately). By the mid-1920s, a walkway paralleled practically the entire oceanfront, second in length only to the fabled boardwalk in Atlantic City, New Jersey. In 1925, the Cross Bay Bridge opened to traffic.

Starting in the second decade of the twentieth century, bungalow colonies multiplied, spreading from Rockaway Park to the shores of Far Rockaway. By this time the rich no longer summered in the Rockaways. They were replaced by lower-middle-class and working-class people, chiefly Irish and Jewish. Some years earlier, large mansions had been converted into rooming houses, with rentals available for the whole summer or for shorter periods. Seasonal hotels continued to flourish; more than one hundred existed even during the great depression. On weekends during these years, according to the *WPA Guide*, "as many as a million people throng[ed] the five mile long boardwalk, [to] lie on the white beaches, and swim in the surf."[2] During the late 1930s, the Rockaway Improvement left Rockaway's Playland as the peninsula's only amusement park.[3] A photograph taken of Playland in 1985 shows the roller coaster, the amusement park's most spectacular ride, in the process of being demolished. In the background one can make out high-rise apartment houses hugging the shoreline. The photograph captures the transformation of the peninsula from a beach resort to a year-round residential community (see figure 8). For many old-timers, Playland and its "million dollar midway," built at the turn of the century and located virtually in the peninsula's geographical center, symbolized the glory days of Rockaway Beach as a tourist mecca. Yet while the disappearance of the roller coaster seemed to mark the end of an era, Rockaway actually lost its resort function gradually, starting at least three decades earlier.

During the first summer without a direct rail connection (1950), approximately forty-eight million visitors, an all-time record, were counted at the Rockaway beaches.[4] The subsequent decline in both seasonal renters and day-trippers can be attributed in part to the loss of the railroad trestle. Summer rentals, which began decreasing before the trestle fire, dropped precipitously throughout the decade and continued to do so even after public transit arrived in 1956. Shortly thereafter, the numbers of day visitors followed the same pattern. The decline continued until Rockaway not only lost its position as "New York City's favorite beach resort," it ceased to be much of a resort at all. With the exception of a few beach enclaves, one at the subway's Beach 116th Street terminus and the others at either end of the peninsula, including a diminished Jacob Riis Park, the Rockaways had become almost exclusively a year-round community.

Why did the peninsula lose its appeal as a major summer resort after World War II? The term "resort" suggests artificial or natural attractions that appeal to visitors who seek entertainment, health, or recreation. Rock-away possessed an excellent sandy shore, one of the greatest public beaches in the world, with some eleven miles of seafront. The Chamber of Commerce liked to boast that in Rockaway the city employed "the largest lifeguard force in the world," 258 during the 1950s, to be exact.[5] In later years, surfboarders chose Rockaway Beach as the best location for the sport in the entire metropolitan area, and it received rave reviews from surfing magazines. The boardwalk, although not as famous as the one in Atlantic City, was almost as long. At a time when environmental concerns were beginning to enter the nation's consciousness, the combined ocean and bay setting permitted Rockaway to consistently receive the highest ratings for clean air from the Department of Air Pollution Control.[6] And of course, the peninsula was close to the populated sections of the city, reachable by car or by various forms of public transportation.

One theory about the decline of Rockaway Beach blames postwar lifestyle changes. According to this account, the movement of city families to the suburbs eliminated the urgent need to escape to the shore. Many of the new residential areas contained recreational amenities such as swimming pools, parks, ball fields, tennis courts, and golf courses, as well as activities for children that lay well within the reach of carpooling parents. For the middle class and the affluent who stayed behind, air conditioning made city living more tolerable in hot, humid weather. The quality of urban life in the summer was further enhanced by outdoor concerts and performances of various kinds. In addition, the number of day and sleep-away camps for children increased. Furthermore, after World War II the improved highway system and the mass ownership of automobiles encouraged greater mobility. Previously distant vacation spots were now within the range of family cars. Air fares became cheaper and flights more numerous, providing ordinary people with options previously available only to the elite. A new generation, whose elders might have been content with sea breezes on a crowded beach and a stroll on the boardwalk, now had more money, more leisure time, and new opportunities for travel. Other popular holiday spots close to the metropolitan New York area, such as the Catskill hotels, similarly lost their appeal to the postwar generation.[7]

Yet some beach resorts on the eastern seaboard continued to draw tourists. Cape Cod, for example, suffers from excessive popularity during the summer, resulting in congestion and depletion of fresh water supplies. Legal gambling has enabled Atlantic City to maintain elegant hotels, despite the proximity of a population living in poverty. Traffic jams fail to discourage weekend trips to many beach towns along the Jersey shore and in Maryland, where vacation homes range from modest to elegant. The same remains true of communities along the southern tip of Long Island, from Fire Island to the Hamptons, where property values continue to inflate.

Robert Moses believed that the public would never grow tired of ocean and beach recreation. In his capacity as parks commissioner, he liked to assure Rockaway audiences that "summer heat will always drive increasing hordes to the ocean."[8] A recent book on popular culture, *The Beach: The History of Paradise on Earth*, addresses the perennial attraction that beaches have held for mankind throughout the ages. The authors conclude that while people have related differently to the ocean over the centuries, they never seem to lose their fascination with the pleasures of the seashore.[9] For those who grew up in the Rockaways, or who visited because of a love of surf and sand, the book's main thesis strikes a responsive chord and resonates with Moses's beliefs. Why, then, did the peninsula decline as a resort?

As early as the 1930s, astute observers, including Moses and the Chamber of Commerce executive secretary George Wolpert, recognized that the permanent population of the Rockaways would inevitably increase. Nonetheless, they hoped that the area would be able to remain a resort as well. Starting in the 1950s, the peninsula did in fact become more of a year-round community. Around the same time, however, it began losing its recreational appeal. The usual explanation for this phenomenon emphasizes the high percentage of poor, minority families that came to live in Rockaway. Some argue that because many whites felt uncomfortable in the presence of blacks, it was inevitable that white tourists would cease to come to a place primarily occupied by people of color. This argument does not explain why Rockaway began losing its resort function even before African Americans began to constitute a significant portion of the total population. Black people living outside the community never seemed to think of the peninsula as a place to spend their vacations either, so that an increase in minority tourists could not have been a consideration. In 1950, the peak year for daily summer visitors, African Americans living in the Rockaways numbered 3,404, approximately the same as ten years earlier. At this point, figures for both day-trippers and summer renters began to plunge. By 1960 the number of blacks grew to 7,976, while the white population expanded from 47,646 to almost 60,000. Ten years later, 84,600 whites and 11,506 blacks lived in Rockaway year-round.[10]

At a time when the populations of most other urban areas throughout the country declined, the Rockaways bucked the trend by gaining inhabitants at an amazing rate. The *Rockaway Review* made the claim, at one point towards the end of the 1950s, that their community was growing faster than any other section of New York City.[11] If white families continued to move to the peninsula, in spite of the slow rise in the percentage of black residents, then we need an explanation other than racial prejudice for Rockaway's rapid failure as a resort, which began during this same period.

In July 1952, Robert Moses declared that much of Rockaway had become a "resort slum." He had predicted this outcome in the late 1930s, when he put together his extensive *Rockaway Improvement*, making known to associates his plan to eliminate all the shacks bordering the beach throughout the middle of the peninsula. As long as these outdated structures remained, Moses asserted, the potential for further residential blight existed. Before the war, he had hoped to start a publicly backed housing development for working- and middle-class people in Hammels and to encourage private contractors to follow his lead.[12] He believed that housing of this sort would facilitate Rockaway's transition to a desirable residential community. However, neither before nor during World War II did the opportunity for such construction present itself. Shortly after the war, Moses intended to tear down bungalows and rooming houses that had served as temporary veterans' accommodations. He hoped that this would inspire the developments he desired. During the late 1940s the New York City Department of Parks created a series of beachfront parking lots, destroying a handful of such buildings in the process. However, this effort made only a tiny dent.

It would take time and a major commitment of money to eliminate all the run-down summer housing in the Rockaways. Before that goal could be achieved, some of the slum-creating processes described in the previous chapter began to take place. In certain sections of the peninsula, especially in Hammels, property owners were unwilling to undertake the expense of renovating their holdings to make them attractive to a new generation of seasonal renters. Rather, landlords found it much more lucrative to "winterize" buildings in order to accommodate families on relief, who were sent by the city in growing numbers. As the welfare rentals spread, nearby houses lost their desirability. And as this area came to be neglected and identified with very poor black people, tourists began looking elsewhere for vacation rentals. Some were content to rent further eastward on the peninsula, but a welfare population eventually followed them there as well. The only practical solution to rookeries was to tear them down and start from scratch, building new resort facilities in their place. Yet no agency in the Rockaways was prepared to undertake such a remedy.

This is only part of the story of how Rockaway ceased to be a resort. All along, two separate approaches to keeping the area viable for tourism coexisted. One was associated with Robert Moses and the other with local business interests, represented by organizations such as the Chamber of Commerce. Both wished to preserve the resort aspect of Rockaway, but they disagreed about how to accomplish this goal. Most chamber members were interested in making quick returns from real estate investments, but some took a longer view. This latter group recognized that if a Rockaway resort were to survive, it would have to appeal to modern tastes. They appreciated the fact that the new generation of tourists had different requirements than their parents and would not tolerate the conditions that formerly accompanied summer rentals. Those coming of age after the war had more money to spend on vacations, and did not wish to contend with the inconvenience and lack of privacy inherent to bungalows and crowded rooming houses. Vacationers now expected modern hotels and motels, swimming pools, golf courses, and tennis courts. Families were more interested in eating out than their elders had been. Those who could afford the expense demanded good food, yet the peninsula never had a high-quality restaurant. Former residents invariably refer to the now defunct Weiss' Restaurant, just over the Cross Bay Bridge in Broad Channel, as an example of fine dining in Rockaway's "glory days." In reality, however, it was a lesser version of Nathan's in Coney Island, which specialized in hot dogs and hamburgers. Enterprising businessmen called for the construction of cabana and beach clubs like the ones successfully operating in Atlantic Beach and elsewhere. Some advocated a convention center, to be located near the ocean, as a potential money maker for the entire community. Well-planned, luxurious holiday accommodations were springing up all over the country. Why shouldn't Rockaway Beach follow this example?

Robert Moses is one answer. Throughout his long career, the Power Broker resisted the commercialization of any natural resources that he believed belonged to the masses as a birthright. Viewing Rockaway's ocean beaches as such a resource, he tried to rectify the damage previously done to public space by private interests and to protect and enhance what had been spared. These resources are "our most priceless heritage," he liked to remind the community's businessmen.[13] Moses regarded sea resorts as places of recreation, to be maintained for the public just like parks. This approach ruled out the creation of the kinds of private luxury establishments sought by Rockaway entrepreneurs.

Many east-coast beaches have long been reserved exclusively for town residents. On Cape Cod and eastern Long Island, only renters or owners of property can park at town beaches, and even they must purchase an expensive sticker. (Cape Cod's National Seashore beaches charge a daily parking fee and are open to all.) As long as Moses remained in power, he vetoed all measures that restricted public access. For example, the parking fees at Jacob Riis Park, and those at the other peninsula parking lots, were set very low. Because of his special affection for the Rockaways, Moses tried in many different ways—without success—to realize his own vision of public recreation.

The commercial interests were also thwarted. When Idlewild (later Kennedy) Airport was completed after the war, it was viewed locally as a golden opportunity for promoting the Rockaways as a resort. The largest of the three New York City air terminals was situated just across Jamaica Bay from the peninsula and could be reached easily by car or bus in less than half an hour. In 1948 the president of the Borough of Queens told the Chamber of Commerce that the airport "heralds [a] new Rockaway era." From the very beginning of its existence, many expected that Idlewild's presence would result in general prosperity for the entire community. As the *Rockaway Review* optimistically predicted, "There lurks the attractive possibility that the Rockaways, as the nearest seashore resort to the airport, may assume in a few years the position of an international summer vacation land."[14] Even after the noise of low-flying planes began to reach annoying proportions, the chamber advised its readers that "the advantages accruing to an alert populace could more than outweigh the debit side of the progress ledger."[15]

Improving access to the Rockaways from the airport became one of Moses's goals. As the airport neared completion, he modernized the Rockaway Turnpike, which ran along its eastern edge. But this proved to be only a start. Moses envisioned streamlining Rockaway roads such as Seagirt Boulevard, which led to the renovated Atlantic Beach Bridge. This bridge would connect with the New York City parkway system by means of a new entity, the Nassau Expressway, a modern, six-lane highway designed to replace the increasingly inadequate Rockaway Turnpike. Some of these plans were in the works as early as 1947.[16] In Rockaway itself, a number of large parking lots were built in Arverne and Edgemere right after the war. By 1950 there were seven in all, serving off-season as ball fields and basketball courts. Moses deliberately vetoed the installation of parking meters within the lots, since these would limit children's play space during the off-season.[17] Unfortunately, the alternative method of payment, the toll booth system, lent itself to corruption because it permitted attendants to siphon off a portion of the parks department's proceeds. Certain acquaintances of one of the authors helped pay their college expenses through this larcenous activity, while one old friend, later a respected lawyer, was relieved of his job by a complicit department supervisor because he refused to participate in the scam. The story later circulated that he got fired for honesty. But such activities remained remote from the commissioner's purview, as he had little to do with the daily operation of facilities once they were set in motion.

The parks department, under Moses's leadership, continued to spend substantial amounts of money on public open space, a practice that diminished considerably after he left office at the end of the 1950s.[18] During his tenure, Rockaway remained a prime locus for departmental expenditures, especially for the restoration of eroded beaches and the repair of broken-down boardwalks. In 1957 alone, Moses called for a seven-million-dollar oceanfront reclamation program, involving, among other things, more than forty stone jetties along the beach. Two years later, another major antierosion program was set in motion.[19] Around this time too, Moses extended the boardwalk in Wavecrest eastward another one-half mile until it reached B. 9th Street. Adjacent to this beachfront, he built O'Donohue Park, a facility containing ball fields, playgrounds, picnic areas, concession buildings, and parking lots. Although he set the project in motion much earlier, it was finally completed in 1961, one year after he left the parks department.[20]

Toward the end of his stewardship in parks and housing, the commissioner announced additional plans, some quite grandiose, for expanding parklands in the Rockaways. In one of the last of these, he attempted to fulfill his life-long dream of realizing Jamaica Bay's great potential. Moses made the rehabilitation of Jamaica Bay, once the site of fashionable hotels and yacht clubs, a priority as early as the 1930s. In the early twentieth century, its waters had supported a thriving shellfish industry. By 1920, industrial wastes, as well as the million tons of raw sewage pouring into it daily from housing in Flatlands, Canarsie, and the Rockaways, made shellfish unsafe to eat. There was talk of expanding Jamaica Bay's industrial capacity and creating a deep-water port. The city's sanitation commissioner even wanted to set up the next major garbage dump there.[21] Every one of the summer resort hotels on the bay side of the peninsula had disappeared by this time.

In 1938 Robert Moses intervened by submitting a report to Mayor LaGuardia entitled *The Future of Jamaica Bay*. Describing the waterway's environs as "the greatest natural resource we have," and "the greatest recreational resource remaining within the city limits," Moses linked its reclamation to the Rockaway Improvement then in progress.[22] He intended to create a giant marine park and recreational facility to accompany the enhanced beach facilities being developed in Rockaway proper. Labeling the projected sanitation dump a "civic nightmare," he managed to remove this proposal from serious consideration. Next, he called for the construction of sewage treatment plants to control and then to eliminate the existing pollution.

Moses believed that only by placing the bay under the control of the Department of Parks could it achieve its natural potential. He hoped that with the outlay of a modest sum of money, new opportunities for recreation could be created for the citizens of New York City. These would include swimming, boating, fishing, and sailing in a safe inland waterway. Demonstrating his appreciation for the bay's unique qualities, Moses inserted the following poetic passage into his position paper:

> Its wide skies, its long water reaches and low, grassy and mysterious-seeming islands make Cross Bay Boulevard (despite the shacks and hot dog stands which already too much disfigure it) an avenue into a strange corner of primitive romance of a kind one would hardly expect to come upon between Ozone Park and the Rockaways.[23]

In 1945, to be sure, the parks department eliminated the shacks and hot dog stands from all the land it had acquired.

As a Progressive, Robert Moses was a committed conservationist, an aspect of his career that has been minimized by his critics.[24] There is virtually nothing about ecology in Caro's biography. Yet throughout his life, Moses sought to restore natural environments that had been corrupted by thoughtless and profit-seeking interests. He made his ecological views known on several occasions when referring to the Rockaways. In 1958, he wrote in the *Rockaway Review*, "We have finally decided that man must work with nature if he wants anything usable left for his children."[25] In his 1938 plan for Jamaica Bay, Moses described how preserving it in a natural state for recreational purposes would parallel what he did at Jones Beach, where the islands and lands under water that lay north of the state park had been protected. By protecting the islands of Jamaica Bay, he hoped to ensure "that their unique beauty and charm may be unimpaired and their future preservation [would] never be in doubt."[26] Moreover, in his vision they had an advantage over Jones Beach in that they could also serve as a haven for wildlife. As early as 1945, the parks commissioner explained to the Rockaway Chamber of Commerce how the Audubon Society supported his wish to provide a sanctuary in the bay for migratory birds and "many unusual species" that can be seen "in their native habitat." Such an opportunity presented itself "nowhere else in the city."[27] A few years later (1948), he persuaded the Board of Estimate to establish, under the control of the parks department, the present wildlife preserve on the bay's marshlands. It was to be located just off one of the chief roads leading to the Rockaways.[28]

Moses engaged experts in wildlife conservation to offer suggestions on how best to plan the preserve. They reported back that fresh water ponds would be necessary for the area to attract wild birds, although that would be a costly endeavor. Demonstrating his ability "to get things done," the parks commissioner accomplished the job free of charge when a new trestle was built across the bay in 1956. Moses, of course, had been chairman of the committee recommending the trestle. He used his influential position to get the New York City Transit Authority to construct two dikes, making possible the requisite ponds.[29] By 1953 the wildlife center on the bay was fully operational. It was the largest such refuge in the United States wholly within the boundaries of a city. The *New York Times* lauded this outcome in an article a few years later with the headline, "Bird Life Revives on Jamaica Bay: New Sanctuary Is Thriving."[30] Moses was never shy about taking credit for his accomplishments. Toward the end of his career he spoke of how his improvements in the Rockaways and its environs had predated the environmental movement. These accomplishments, he bragged, provide "evidence that we were paying attention to ecology and environment long before the present Daniels had come to judgment."[31]

Ultimate protection for Jamaica Bay was obtained in 1972, when the federal government created the Gateway National Recreation Area. This measure officially stopped any further extension of JFK Airport into the bay itself. It arrived too late to completely eradicate pollution of the waters and make possible Moses's dream of creating a major park facility for the entire waterway. Nonetheless, he had rescued the bay from the sanitation department and its dump, and he had helped eliminate the worst of the sewage run-offs. Largely through his efforts, the bay is not nearly as contaminated as it was when he first became involved and can once again be used for limited water sport activities.[32]

Moses never surrendered his great dream for the bay. While conceiving the construction of a public housing project in Edgemere in 1960, he called for the creation of a water recreation center for the immediate area, using Jamaica Bay as the focal point. As "the newest and largest park on the Rockaway peninsula," it would include a marina, playgrounds, tennis courts, and an eighteen-hole golf course. Moses intended this bayside site to "care for the recreational needs of all ages in the housing [project] and surrounding neighborhoods."[33]

In all the low-income developments constructed in the Rockaways under his auspices, Moses included playground equipment and park facilities open to residents and people in the surrounding areas. For example, at Redfern, the parks department constructed a two-acre community playground that featured a grass-surfaced ball field, one that would enjoy extensive use.[34] While involved with a Title I undertaking in Hammels, Moses promised to obtain state funds to construct "an additional shore front park" on the ocean between B. 73rd and B. 55th Streets.[35] This project, as well as the large bayside park planned in Edgemere, never saw the light of day. However, the Edgemere low-income project, completed in 1960, included substantial play areas, playgrounds, baseball fields, and basketball and handball courts.[36]

At the end of 1960, Robert Moses relinquished all of his key city posts. Two years later he resigned from the chairmanship of the State Council of Parks. This effectively brought to a halt many projects that would have enhanced Rockaway as a resort. His departure eliminated the chief inspiration for public parks and recreation facilities in the New York area generally and the Rockaways in particular. None of his successors followed his lead, even when the need became obvious, and no other major public figure would ever be in such a unique position to transform this ocean community.

In time, storms and normal erosion washed away countless beaches, especially in the middle sections of the peninsula. Stretches of boardwalk were allowed to remain in disrepair. Concerns about pollution of the ocean at Rockaway began to surface. Even Jacob Riis Park, which continued to attract more day visitors than any other space in the Rockaways, seemed shoddy and run down compared with the public beaches Moses had designed for the rest of Long Island. His last elaborate park projects for the Rockaways never came to fruition. The projected Nassau Expressway did get built, but in such a compromised fashion that it indirectly created more traffic jams than it eliminated. The shopping malls, fast food restaurants, and gas stations that came to line the Rockaway Turnpike terminus of the Expressway served to delay traffic there as well. Moreover, the very presence of such commercialization represents the exact opposite of what Moses sought to accomplish. The thousands of tourists descending from Kennedy Airport never materialized. The airport provides job opportunities for residents, but it has not reestablished a resort in the peninsula.

Old Rockaway always contained a large number of hotels; indeed, at one time they ran into the hundreds. The two biggest parks department parking lots that Moses constructed in the 1940s replaced the burned out remnants of the gigantic Prince Hotel in Arverne and the colossal Lorraine Hotel in Edgemere. Fire and conversion to summer rentals eliminated almost all of the former luxury edifices once located adjacent to ocean beach areas or next to the bay. By the end of World War II, approximately ten genuine hotels remained in the entire peninsula, mainly in the west end. Only five stood between Seaside and Far Rockaway. Before long this number would shrink even further, and most of those remaining were antiquated.[37] Entrepreneurs connected with the Chamber of Commerce continued to argue that the peninsula could survive as a resort only by providing modern vacation accommodations, yet no new hotels or motels were ever built.

Moses would not have permitted the conversion of the Rockaways into the kind of resort that exercised private control over public spaces. In any case, however, proponents of development never figured out how to finance the undertakings they desired. Private money was found for housing developments, such as Wavecrest Gardens, completed in 1950, as well as the Lefrak buildings and other year-round structures that came later. But one searches the public record in vain for any hint or rumor that vacation housing in Rockaway was planned with private funding. There were two exceptions to this generalization, but these exceptions proved the rule.

In the spring of 1955, the Neponsit Beach Hospital, a TB facility on a spot facing the ocean, adjacent to Jacob Riis Park, ceased to operate. The facility occupied a fourteen-acre beachfront lot and was considered a "hot property." Local real estate interests immediately saw an opportunity for profitable investment in what had always been the wealthiest section of the peninsula. Along with Belle Harbor, Neponsit was regarded as "the most restricted zone in New York City," and perhaps on the entire east coast as well.[38] As a result, well-connected business people wished to see the hospital and its spacious grounds made available for speculation. Among them was an influential local politician, James J. Crisona, who later became the borough president of Queens.[39] There was some talk of converting the hospital into a hotel, but the prospective investors mainly sought to construct expensive single-family homes. When the matter came to his attention in May 1955, Moses contemptuously dismissed any commercial Neponsit venture as building "small shacks on postage stamp lots."[40]

In no uncertain terms, Moses let it be known that he wished to use the land in order to expand the facilities at Riis Park. He discovered that the parks department had once owned the property before granting it to the city's hospital division in 1911, and he now demanded that it be returned.[41] The president of the Rockaway Chamber of Commerce, realtor Irving N. Klein, along with representatives of other local business groups, tried to appeal to him. They made the self-serving argument that the city would benefit financially from the sale of this property and from property taxes in the future. But Moses exploded. He became so infuriated that he sent off a series of vituperative letters to the only chamber member whom he respected, executive secretary George Wolpert. In the first one, dated 9 June 1955, Moses wrote:

> The responsible residents and business interests of the Rockaways, as represented in your organization, must be increasingly vigilant in years to come to make sure that the quest for the "quick dollar" by an unscrupulous few, does not negate or reduce the benefits derived from public improvements.[42]

Rockaway businessmen persisted in their efforts and tried to influence other city officials. When they succeeded in winning over the city controller, Lawrence E. Gerosa, Moses reacted angrily. He dispatched a letter expressing his contempt for those "selfish and short sighted interests who have sought to cash in on every square foot of frontage on which they could lay their hands." He went on to say:

The fact of the matter is that Rockaway would be nothing without the publicly owned, protected and operated waterfront, particularly the beach and land fronting on the ocean. . . . Need I point out what it costs the city in condemnation to acquire a narrow strip of beach at Rockaway from precisely the same elements in the real estate business for whom you are pleading.[43]

The pragmatic Wolpert stepped in immediately. He called a meeting of the executive committee of the chamber and got them to reverse themselves unanimously. In an apologetic letter to the commissioner, with copies to the mayor and council members, they now urged that the city grant full approval to Moses's request.[44] However, this did not end the matter. The welfare department put in a claim for the old hospital building, asking that it be used as a residence for the elderly. This eventually led to a compromise settlement, with the parks department retaining the beach and grounds and the welfare department getting the hospital. Moses seems to have been content with the agreement, chiefly because one thousand additional feet had been added to the public beach.[45]

A similar incident occurred two years later, in 1957, when Moses was in the midst of negotiating a middle-income housing development in Seaside-Hammels.[46] Members of the chamber began advocating for the construction of private cabana clubs and hotels along the beach in this Title I area, despite the improbability of the federal government ever financing such a speculative venture. Heedless of their previous encounter with the Power Broker, they wrote letters about it to Moses, which is puzzling in view of his well-known opposition to privatizing ocean resorts. In a memo to an associate who was to answer the chamber president's personal request for hotels and cabanas, Moses revealed his feelings.

Please draft a very emphatic letter putting this jackass out of his misery. Let's make it good and hot and heavy and final. It's hard to believe that any one of experience who has lived around here would advocate anything as crazy as this.[47]

This seems to have been Moses's last word on the subject. He would never support the construction of hotels, beach clubs, or anything of that nature, and the community did not possess the resources to undertake such initiatives on its own. Although the matter continued to be revived every few years, it never went beyond the talking stage and remained a dead issue.

In many ways, the conflict between Moses and the business-oriented Chamber of Commerce represented a clash of philosophies. The parks commissioner had a sense of the public good and a commitment to environmental conservation that conflicted with the dominant materialism of American life. A product of the Progressive era, he began with the assumption that parklands belonged to all the people. As a public servant, he had the responsibility of protecting such resources and, where possible, developing them for the benefit of the masses. Commercial interests, some well-meaning, believed that they could combine public pleasure with private profit. Indeed, by creating luxury facilities they hoped to attract a class of people who would pay for their recreation and thereby perpetuate the resort character of the Rockaways. Yet such a business strategy necessarily limited the number of those "consumers of recreation" who would be able to benefit. Moreover, there always existed a risk that protection of the environment could not be guaranteed when profits remained the chief consideration.

Rockaway as a resort fell by the wayside, while other recreation areas that combined private gain with exclusivity succeeded. With its ancient housing structures, Rockaway was not able to make the transition to the less equitable, but more profitable, approach to modern leisure. Moses would have been content with a Rockaway that had attractive well-maintained beaches complemented by parks and play areas appealing to city dwellers on a day's outing. He envisioned the surrounding sections as consisting of solid, respectable housing units, providing comfortable and attractive living quarters for Rockaway's growing year-round population. Despite the forces working against him, he would devote considerable energy to the nearly impossible task of bringing his vision of the community's future to fruition.

CHAPTER 6

Storms over Title I

Rockaway's various neighborhoods have always reflected class, racial, and ethnic differences, and even with their population growth not much changed during the 1950s, Neponsit and Belle Harbor maintained their reputation as two of the most fashionable addresses in all of New York City. In parts of Far Rockaway, solidly middle-class people owned single-family homes. Seaside housed working- and lower-middle-class Irish Americans. Arverne and Edgemere had similar class characteristics but continued to be predominantly Jewish throughout the decade. Italian Americans joined the ethnic mix in Somerville. The majority of African Americans lived in Hammels, with another remnant on the periphery of the Redfern low-income project. When a black family tried to rent an apartment in Belle Harbor, telephoned threats of firebombing eventually drove them away.[1]

While Hammels spiraled into poverty, most residents of the peninsula remained unaware of conditions in what had become arguably the most dreadful ghetto in all of New York. Barely a mile in length, it did not immediately impact the other sections of Rockaway. Taking the shore parkway or Beach Channel Drive past the enclave, drivers could easily overlook the terrible blight. Hammels was the "Other America" portrayed by Michael Harrington in his groundbreaking book.[2] Most Rockaway residents surely registered its existence on a subliminal level but publicly ignored it.

Of course, some Rockaway citizens concerned themselves with this other America in their midst. Liberal white organizations like the Arverne branch of the American Jewish Congress and the First Congregational Church in the Holland section did what they could to improve the lives of the Rockaway poor. In addition, the health department became outspoken in addressing TB, a rate of infant mortality among the worst in the city, and a new but growing substance abuse problem. In the early 1950s, officials at the newly built Arverne Health Center (now the Joseph P. Addabo Family Health Center) called together an interracial group to address the terrible conditions in Hammels. They proposed forming an organization, the Rockaway Health Council, to serve as a clearinghouse and, ultimately, to advocate for the needs of Hammels. Focusing almost exclusively on health issues, the council tried—and failed—to get city agencies, especially the welfare department and local private hospitals, to establish a local welfare facility.[3] However, the members of this group did not allow the intransigence of the various municipal authorities to weaken their resolve. On the contrary, the lack of response they regularly encountered provided an education for them regarding the city bureaucracies' treatment of poor minorities. A number of future community activists in the Rockaways got their start in these first health campaigns.

In the early 1950s Hammels lacked the wherewithal to defend itself. This resulted in part from the disorganization of people who had been thrown together without sharing common backgrounds, lacking institutions that might serve as a base for protest activities. With the exception of the Mount Carmel Baptist Church in Arverne, under the leadership of Reverend Joseph H. May, the existing black churches had neither the experience nor the inclination to take on the local white establishment. They were even less prepared to tackle the New York City bureaucracy. Although New York remained Democratic until 1966, the overwhelming Democratic majority in Rockaway (usually posting a margin of victory between 4 to 1 and 5 to 1) brought little benefit to the residents of the peninsula.[4] This proved especially true for Hammels, where the local "Colored Democratic Association" (later changed to the Arverne & Hammels Democratic Association) was run by Leonard E. Scarbrough. Self-educated and shrewd, Scarbrough maintained a dominant position in his community. Having lived in Hammels since the 1920s, he understood the Rockaways and had a wide range of connections. He also had the distinction of being one of the few African Americans to own property in town; he was, in fact, a slumlord. In addition to his real estate holdings, he served as adviser and point man for white speculators and slum landlords who specialized in Hammels properties. Reportedly, Scarbrough was the chief money lender for local blacks unable to obtain credit elsewhere. He also exercised considerable power in the largest black church in the district, St. John's Baptist.

White politicians had no wish to involve themselves in the internal affairs of the Hammels ghetto, thus opening up an opportunity for one who could demonstrate to his constituents tangible evidence of influence. Scarbrough's leadership of the democratic association in Hammels gave him access to Democratic Party officials on the peninsula and made him a spokesman and negotiator for African Americans. He became the dispenser of whatever patronage was allotted to this district. Individuals who had trouble with the law would turn to him for assistance, to raise bail money, for example. His small political machine served an important social function and had counterparts in other northern cities at this time. Like all machine politicians, these minority leaders wished to perpetuate the status quo.[5]

After the end of World War II, the leadership of the Chamber of Commerce did turn their attention to developments in Hammels. However, their concern had less to do with the well-being of local inhabitants than with the neighborhood's impact on the Rockaway image. Negative publicity in the media was undermining property values. The chamber recognized that if the Rockaways were to become a "suburban metropolis" (a term in fashion at the time), the Hammels slums would have to be dealt with. These long-range economic considerations led chamber officials to begin criticizing welfare department practices. Subsequently, they condemned "cooperative landlords" and speculators whose goals tended to be at odds with "the general good of the community." For Rockaway to be attractive to an affluent clientele, it would have to duplicate conditions prevailing in other white suburban areas. At a minimum, the poor neighborhoods needed to be contained, and, optimally, a means had to be found to eliminate them totally, removing the black population in the process.[6]

Once again, a deus ex machina arrived for the Rockaways in the person of Robert Moses, New York City's Power Broker. While his motives may have been different from those of the Chamber of Commerce, he shared their essential goals. He wanted to eradicate the "slums" in what he still hoped could be a viable resort. Despite the charges of racism leveled by biographer Robert Caro and others, there is no evidence that Moses gave thought to the social or ethnic composition of either the people using the beach facilities or those who would live year-round in the Rockaways.[7]

The rapid transit extension that he had made possible brought anyone who could pay the subway fare to the beach. Moreover, the local elite would soon discover—to their dismay—that Moses's first choice of an urban renewal site was an exclusively white area.

Moses's concern with Rockaway's crumbling summer housing stock, and his desire to renovate it, predate the growth in the black population. Before any other official, he recognized the potential for blight created by the antiquated rooming houses and bungalows crowding Rockaway's oceanfront. His shore parkway, with its parks and recreational facilities, traverses the area. In the 1950s Moses had the chance to complete what he had only imagined some fifteen years earlier, before he reached the peak of his power. Beginning in 1949 and continuing for over a decade, his chairmanship of the city's Slum Clearance Committee gave him control over the federal Title I urban renewal program established in that year. Title I, in fact, would become his personal preserve. He helped in its original design as enacted by Congress, together with the original bill's main sponsor, his old classmate at Yale, Senator Robert Taft. Before long he would prove to be its most able facilitator.

The Title I program offered private builders a means of obtaining large parcels of city real estate at reduced cost. Moses installed Title I operations at his headquarters on Randalls Island and brought onto his staff the same people who helped him run the Triborough Bridge and Tunnel Authority. This team attracted more federal money to New York than to any other city in the nation. By the time he gave up his control of slum clearance in 1960, the city had over twenty major projects completed or under way, more than twice the number of any other urban area.[8] Title I projects in New York City took up much of Robert Moses's time and energy during the 1950s. Whether or not they had a positive impact remains controversial, and the mushrooming attacks on the program proved to be one of the factors that brought the Power Broker to heel. He later acknowledged that his involvement with housing was his least successful endeavor. Moses was criticized for concentrating Title I placements in Manhattan (three-quarters of the total) to the detriment of the outer boroughs.[9] Yet in 1951, barely two years after the program passed Congress, he had begun contemplating two Title I projects in Rockaway.

In March of that same year, Thomas J. Shanahan, the well connected banker whom Moses used to provide loans for Title I investors, wrote the following letter to George Wolpert:

I am wondering if you are familiar with Title I Housing Projects. The reason I write is that Bob Moses has dropped me a letter with the thought that it might be a good thing to look into Title I with the idea of a slum clearance proposition—as he termed it—in the Seaside slums at Rockaway Beach.[10]

Wolpert wrote back immediately, eagerly expressing interest, but nothing came of the proposal for two more years. In May 1953, Moses sent a memo to his chief assistant, William Lebwohl, in which he asked his opinion about Title I for the Rockaways. "The write-down would be very small," he added. A few months later, Wolpert learned that such plans were in the works, and he again expressed enthusiasm. On the other hand, he suggested that the section needing renewal even more than Seaside was Hammels, just to the east. "With its many relief cases. . . the area was rapidly becoming a worse slum area" than anywhere else in the peninsula.[11]

Thus began the long saga of Title I in the Rockaways, one that challenged the patience of the Power Broker. Moses devoted a section of his book, *Public Works: A Dangerous Trade*,[12] to the difficulties he encountered. At one point, when Queens Borough President James J. Crisona, who was also a Rockaway politician, attempted to delay the whole enterprise, Moses wrote a stinging letter. It said, in part, "This is a big town and there are a whole lot of vitally needed improvements which come ahead of any such wholesale rebuilding of the Rockaways."[13] The favorable outcome attests to Moses's steadfastness on behalf of the Rockaway peninsula.

Ironically, Moses's favorite Title I project, Lincoln Center for the Performing Arts, became the one that led to a decline in his power. Its costs went beyond the large sum of money spent on construction. During a period of about four years beginning in 1955, approximately five thousand families were relocated during the clearance process.[14] Displacements had occurred before in other places, including the Rockaways; however, politicians and the media suddenly began to question the price being paid in personal suffering. (A corruption scandal, which involved the New York City Bureau of Real Estate and Nassau Management Company, also reflected negatively on Moses.) Almost all of the tenants forced to move from the Lincoln Center site possessed few resources, and they were mainly African American or Puerto Rican. In view of the discriminatory real estate practices in New York City, it was extremely difficult to find them suitable replacement housing. Many people wound up paying higher rents for worse accommodations than those they had vacated, often in areas such as Brownsville and the South Bronx. Another relocation site for former residents of the Lincoln Center area was the far off rookeries of the Rockaways.[15]

Moses, therefore, must be held accountable for dislocating residents living in slum clearance neighborhoods and for dumping them into bad housing units located elsewhere in New York City, including Rockaway. He always realized that the relocation aspect of urban redevelopment was an impossible task, and he simply tried not to concern himself with it.[16] He either delegated responsibility to others or, when pressed, manufactured statistics purporting to show that the relocated tenants had actually improved their circumstances by being forced to move. Even after he retired, Moses asserted without proof that "98 percent of the ghetto folks we moved were given immeasurably better living places at unprecedented cost."[17] The Power Broker recognized that the best remedy would be to move a majority of displaced residents into low-income projects. However, the waiting list for public housing in New York City rarely fell below one hundred thousand applicants. Furthermore, even if the evicted tenants from renewal areas were given priority, most of them did not meet the eligibility requirements in effect throughout the 1950s. Inevitably, Moses regarded the suffering inflicted on impoverished families as a necessary price of progress.

In late 1953 Moses chose an area of Seaside, in the Rockaways, for a Title I middle-income project, and he had little trouble obtaining a developer. Although he described the site as "a dilapidated and run down area, constituting a fire and health hazard," an example of a "resort slum," it hardly met the established criteria for urban redevelopment.[18] However, as a beach resort Seaside remained "predominantly open land" and therefore posed few relocation problems. The small number of residents to be evicted, a total of 169 families, possessed the means to make rehousing manageable and inexpensive. Seaside had received a grade of C- from the HOLC in the late 1930's and had experienced no improvement since then. While far from elegant, it was not really an impoverished neighborhood. Its redevelopment should have been relatively easy.

Originally, Seaside was the heart of Rockaway's amusement area. Although only half a mile in length, it had more bars than the rest of the peninsula. The accommodations, chiefly seasonal, combined the resort's familiar frame buildings and summer cottages with a number of small hotels. Some permanent inhabitants lived in two- and three-family homes, but only around 10 percent of the district's structures remained occupied all year round. Owners of property and residents, predominantly Irish, had strong ties to their neighborhood churches and were quite satisfied with their current situation. Indeed, when Title I plans were announced, they felt that Seaside had been singled out by Moses for victimization not once but twice. In 1937 the "Rockaway Improvement" had taken a huge chunk out of its beachside features, including hotels, concession stands, and all of the carnival attractions that Moses contemptuously referred to as "a cheap amusement area."[19] Now, some fifteen years later, Moses seemed poised to finish the job of eliminating "Irish Town," just as he had destroyed the Jewish section of East Tremont in the Bronx, an Italian community in Sunset Park, Brooklyn, and black and Puerto Rican neighborhoods all over Manhattan. The main character in Alice McDermott's prize-winning novel about Irish Americans, *Charming Billy*, says at one point, "My wife enjoys the Rockaways, you see, or used to, anyway, before it changed."[20]

Wolpert's letter of 15 September 1953, which suggested that urban renewal belonged in Hammels rather than Seaside, marked the beginning of the difficulties that would plague Title I projects in the Rockaways. When official approval was announced in February of the next year, the Chamber of Commerce expressed its strong displeasure with the site chosen. The organization's leaders continued to make a case for Hammels as the truly rundown site; they regarded the removal of black people from the Rockaways, not the destruction of a white area, as the main purpose of a Title I project. They were joined in their lobbying efforts by the local Seaside Property Owners Association. These groups began holding meetings and produced petitions signed by hundreds of people that protested the unfairness of proceeding with slum clearance in a place that was "not a slum."[21] The Rockaway Beach Property Owners Association, representing Hammels real estate, began complaining at the same time because their area had *not* been chosen for clearance. These landlords preferred to sell their properties for high prices and avoid the difficulties involved in operating welfare housing. Thus, they too joined the lobbying to preserve Seaside and clear Hammels. Another group, formed in Arverne and Somerville, took a similar position.[22] Around the same time, in Hammels, the Colored Democratic Association protested against Title I construction in their neighborhood. Scarbrough, the club's spokesman, had his motivation for such a stance questioned on the grounds that he benefited economically from slum housing.[23] Regardless of the truth of this charge, earlier relocation experiences had not been favorable for Hammels residents. They would now stand to lose once again if middle-income projects were constructed in their midst.

The chamber made its own views clear. Despite the protests in Hammels, Wolpert wrote to Moses in March 1954 that "the entire community is anxious to have the area between B. 74 and B. 83 Streets [i.e., Hammels], from Rockaway Beach Boulevard to the oceanfront, cleaned up" because the peninsula "can never be properly developed unless we get rid of this slum and welfare condition."[24] The chamber continued to oppose the Seaside development, but they did not make the slightest dent in Moses's resolve. Moses almost never responded to community resistance to his plans, although he did bow to the rich and influential "barons of Long Island's North Shore" during the construction of the Northern State Parkway.[25] Concerning Seaside, regardless of the large number of letters and petitions complaining about his intentions for the Title I site, Moses refused to budge. Nevertheless, before long he did seem willing to entertain extending Title I to Hammels as well. The Chamber of Commerce, which had been urging selection of this site, tried to take credit for the decision, but the commissioner's own motive remains uncertain.

Why Moses went along with the second Title I undertaking can only be determined from internal evidence and by speculation. The extended area for redevelopment included sections where the shore parkway had been built in the late 1930s, thus facilitating the construction process. All the new buildings would be placed in the very parts of the peninsula in which Moses, years earlier, had wanted housing to be built. Moreover, the plans called for a new low-income development in the Rockaways that would enable displaced residents of Hammels to be rehoused in superior accommodations, thus providing the perfect solution to the relocation dilemma.[26] Eager to answer critics who claimed that he never gave consideration to people's needs, he would do his utmost to achieve this particular goal.[27]

The location of the proposed new low-income project became controversial. Solely on the basis of rumors, various civic organizations sprang into action. Most groups seemed to agree that further public housing was essential for the Rockaways, but none of them wanted such housing in their own backyard, "the NIMBY effect." Immediately after Moses announced his Title I plans, in March 1954, affluent Belle Harbor, as a preemptive measure against urban renewal, persuaded the New York City Planning

Commission to change the neighborhood's zoning regulations to permit only single-family homes. Throughout the early part of 1954, the civic groups squabbled.[28] Finally, in May, an official statement was issued announcing that the next project would be placed just off Mott Basin, adjoining the Far Rockaway district known as Bayswater. The Bayswater Civic Association protested that theirs was a nice middle-class section ("high type homes" is how Wolpert described them) which should not be subject to lowered property values. These homeowners were joined by the Chamber of Commerce, which came up with an alternative suggestion: a site near Somerville.[29] The civic association representing the latter did not appreciate the chamber's interceding at their expense. However, Somerville was mainly lower-middle and working class and possessed much less influence than Bayswater.[30]

On this issue, of minimal consequence to his overall plans, Moses supported the Rockaway establishment. Appearing at a Chamber of Commerce dinner in June, Moses's key aide, the housing authority chairman Philip J. Cruise, made two announcements that met with approval from those assembled. Title I developments would be built in both Seaside and Hammels, and new low-income housing would be placed between Somerville and Norton Basin. Cruise concluded with an upbeat prediction: "I think the Rockaways are on the threshold of an era of prosperity and progress that will exceed even the hopes of its most ardent boosters."[31]

Property owners in Seaside felt dissatisfied, but there was little that could be done for them. Each year they petitioned Moses, begging him to delay condemnations so that they could collect one more summer's rents.[32] For six consecutive years, until 1960, they got their wish, not because of the Power Broker's generosity, but as a result of the many delays that kept construction from proceeding. At the end of 1954, perhaps because of the controversies surrounding Title I in Rockaway, the first sponsor bowed out. It took more than two years to find a replacement.[33] In the meantime, landlords predictably stopped making repairs, and properties deteriorated still further. The long delays made conditions in Hammels worse than ever. Moreover, plans to redevelop the area did not prevent the welfare department from moving additional clients into the condemned buildings.[34]

In the fall of 1957, the U.S. government approved FHA mortgages for Seaside Title I, but refused to do the same for Hammels. Because the proposed structures in the latter would be located in close proximity to an existing low-income project, federal housing officials, demonstrating their bias against minorities, objected that apartments there could not command the same rents as in Seaside. Moses recognized that the only chance to salvage a federally financed middle-income development in Hammels was to seek tax abatement from New York City, thereby making it possible to reduce rents.[35] This solution contradicted a major objective that Moses had always set for Title I: to charge market rents that would serve to increase tax revenues for the city. However, he now agreed to put aside that aim for his larger vision of the Rockaways.

The Chamber of Commerce voiced strong opposition to tax abatement, mainly on the grounds that subsidized rents would result in "a lower class of people" (by which they meant minorities) moving into the area. Once again, Moses demonstrated far less concern with the ethnic background of residents than did the Rockaway leadership. He finally won them over to his position by making the simple argument that modest middle-income housing receiving tax abatement remained infinitely superior to the status quo. Given federal government stipulations, there was no other alternative.[36] Moses then had to convince the Board of Estimate to absorb the tax loss, a cost to the city of approximately twenty-one million dollars over a period of some twenty-five years, according to one estimate.[37] Considerable opposition emerged at this stage, starting with City Controller Lawrence Gerosa, who presumably objected to such an expense in a far-off section of Queens. However, Mayor Wagner seems to have brought Gerosa into line. Borough President Crisona managed to postpone construction for almost a year. He raised questions about costs and called for a new, comprehensive study of the peninsula by the Urban Renewal Board of New York City. Such an endeavor would have delayed Moses's project well into the future.[38] Crisona instigated this delaying tactic even though his former associates in the Chamber of Commerce, behaving now like typical converts, badgered him to back off. Why he became so oppositional has never been explained, although some speculate that he hated Moses after the rejection of the Neponsit hospital deal in 1955.[39]

An unwritten law in New York City politics, known as "borough courtesy," stipulated that the five borough presidents would not vote for a Board of Estimate public works measure if their colleague from the borough in question disapproved.[40] Crisona clearly disapproved, but the measure to grant tax exemption nevertheless passed at the very end of 1958. Moses had support from Mayor Wagner and the means to persuade the other borough presidents that their own constituents stood to lose if they voted contrary to his wishes.[41] In January 1959, when the City Planning Commission followed the Board of Estimate in granting approval, the project seemed ready to move ahead. However, this time another federal department, the Housing and Home Finance Agency, entered the picture. Property owners in Seaside and Hammels had been complaining that they had been victimized by speculators who took advantage of the delays and bought up land at reduced prices. Insuring these properties began to pose a problem for the small landlords, but it was less of a concern for the large real estate companies. Presumably, the speculators hoped that their superior resources would enable them to negotiate better deals with the authorities once the two sites received final condemnation notices. Accordingly, they hired well-connected Rockaway lawyers and politicians to represent their claims.[42] Because rumors began to circulate about inflated prices, federal housing officials demanded careful appraisals of each parcel of land before granting their approval. The Chamber of Commerce and various civic associations threatened lawsuits against the city in order to speed up condemnation, but they had little impact. However, his powerful connections in Washington enabled Moses to rush this cumbersome process through so that the project could advance to the next stage.[43]

By early November, a sponsor, Zukerman Brothers, took charge by making a payment for the entire area to be developed, yet difficulties continued to present themselves. The new owner chose an architectural firm considered undesirable by the city and a relocation company that had been criticized for its previous work. Despite Moses's defense of the latter, Zukerman Brothers agreed to drop the firm. This decision satisfied the city's Commissioner of Real Estate.[44] The size of the proposed buildings presented another problem. In the Rockaways, the roar of planes taking off and landing at Idlewild (later Kennedy) Airport had long constituted a nuisance that residents had learned to tolerate. However, the new housing presented the possibility of even greater airplane noise. The original prospectus for Title I called for buildings of eight stories. In 1960, the sponsors, presumably with Moses's consent, announced that they planned to double the size to sixteen stories, which would make them the tallest buildings on the peninsula. If this proposal were accepted, two possible consequences were anticipated. First, in order to avoid these buildings, planes would have to ascend more steeply, thereby creating more noise. Alternatively, they would fly over more affluent sections of the Rockaways, causing discomfort to areas previously spared. Civic associations held protest meetings, petitions were signed, and agencies as disparate as churches and hospitals were called upon to take a stand on the matter. In the end, the City Planning Commission recommended a compromise: a twelve-story maximum. The Board of Estimate accepted it, as did most people who had protested, thus ending what should have been the last of the controversies.[45]

However, another problem arose, perhaps the most intractable of the lot, which might be called "the case of the black church that moved." This particular episode lasted the longest and is the most difficult to unravel retrospectively. Almost nothing about the case was printed in either city or local newspapers. Most of the key participants are no longer alive, although some old-timers retain secondhand knowledge of events. To this day, innuendos continue to surface. Robert Moses provided a brief summary of the matter, and there is a slightly longer account in the book by J. Clarence Davies III.[46]

The main African American church in Hammels, St. John's Baptist, had long stood on Beach 81st Street, a few blocks away from a synagogue and a Roman Catholic church built adjacent to one another on B. 84th Street. The Baptist church had been condemned when the low-income housing project was designed. In 1953, it received approval from the Department of Buildings to construct a replacement on B. 82nd Street. Three years later, the new St. John's church opened its doors to parishioners. Unfortunately, the general area had been earmarked for urban renewal, and the Title I architect's plan, published some months later, called for the elimination of B. 82nd Street. The new church was to be demolished along with the slum buildings. St. Rose of Lima and Temple Israel, however, would be spared. Reverend J. A. Jackson of St. John's maintained that he had been given assurances that his church would be similarly preserved, but he had nothing in writing to substantiate his claim.

This singling out of the Baptist Church appeared to the African American citizens of the Rockaways to be a blatant case of discrimination, and a protest movement began. Leonard Scarbrough, one of the leaders of St. John's, initiated a letter-writing campaign, appealing to elected officials from President Eisenhower to his local congressman. Scarbrough then wrote to religious leaders and all those administrators—federal, state, and city—whom he believed to be connected with urban housing. Although he received sympathetic responses, it became clear that Moses and his planners would ultimately get their way, since Title I carried with it the power of eminent domain. In November 1958, after several prayer meetings, Reverend Jackson and the church's Board of Trustees, including Scarbrough, accepted a compromise agreement. St. John's would move to a new site some eight blocks away (B. 74th Street) and would be granted an undisclosed sum of money.

Although it seemed permanently resolved, the matter erupted again three years later when Reverend Jackson passed away and his successor, Reverend Robert Sitton, refused to go along with the settlement. In the meantime, Scarbrough's reputation had suffered as a result of certain statements that he had made regarding his own questionable real estate practices, including an admission that he employed block-busting techniques.[47] Concern also emerged among the new leadership of the church about the whereabouts of the money granted St. John's, and accusations were made against Scarbrough and his lawyer, Assemblyman J. Lewis Fox, a leading white politician. Scarbrough retaliated by trying to remove Sitton from his post. A court case ensued in order to straighten out the financial dispute, but it could not reach a satisfactory resolution. Rev. Sitton and Scarbrough continued to disagree about the relocation of the church.

Eventually, an agreement was reached, and St. John's Baptist Church moved to B. 74th Street. Rumors about payoffs linger, especially since Scarbrough's role was thought to contaminate the proceedings. Nevertheless, no proof of these charges has ever been provided. Members of Rockaway's African American community continue to believe that Reverend Sitton should never have agreed to preserve the white churches while allowing Hammels's largest congregation to be uprooted. Today, the two exempted houses of worship stand amidst pleasant, middle-class apartment buildings constructed more than three decades ago. Half a mile away and geographically isolated, St. John's Baptist Church reminds local blacks of their second-class citizenship.

It would be difficult to provide a totally accurate count of the many times Title I experienced setbacks in the Rockaways. For example, a February 1958 headline in the *Wave*, three years before building commenced, read: "Title I Housing Project Stalled for 6th Time." Robert Moses claimed at the groundbreaking ceremony, on 31 October 1961, that clearing away all obstacles had taken seven years, a process which "should have been finished under normal circumstances in two years."[48] While Moses and his staff resolved one problem after another—including complications involving the Lincoln Center project—with resourcefulness and endurance, the Power Broker's control over New York housing construction had begun to erode.

Robert Caro erroneously concludes that Moses ultimately surrendered his responsibilities in this field of his own free will.[49] In reality, by 1960 Mayor Robert F. Wagner had eased Moses out of a position of power over housing. Wagner never articulated his motives. Some have suggested personal animosities, but the bad publicity regarding Title I scandals, and the inequities of the relocation process, certainly played a role. Then, toward the end of the 1950s, Wagner began to break with party regulars and resurrect himself as a reform Democrat. Moses had always worked closely with the Tammany Hall wing of the party, which now became a liability. He also maintained a relationship with Democratic Party fund-raiser and campaign treasurer Thomas Shanahan, whose reputation never recovered from the revelation that Title I sponsors had been making deals with his Federation Bank and Trust Company. The final blow came in June 1959, when the *New York Times*, long a defender of Moses, began running a series of articles critical of Title I.[50]

In 1960, Moses was permitted to resign his dominant position in city housing gracefully. Before leaving he issued a final parting shot. Once he was gone, Moses warned, the Title I program in New York City would be terminated. Without his special "know how," it would become, as he said at the time, "a dead duck." He proved to be correct. The developments that had been started under his direction were completed, but with one exception, in Brooklyn, those in the proposal stage were dropped. As far as New York City was concerned, Title I housing was over and Robert Moses's impact on housing had become a thing of the past.[51]

In the Rockaways there still remained the final problem of relocating residents from the Hammels site. Of all the many difficulties that had arisen, the question of where the poor, black people of the neighborhood would live became the most sensitive.

CHAPTER 7

Where They Live

The main victims of city policies in the Rockaways were the poor, black residents of Hammels who were forced by outside agencies to live in squalor. Many of them had been moved repeatedly; families who had started in Redfern, or in some other section of New York City undergoing urban renewal, had been shifted to one neighborhood of Hammels only to be relocated a few years later into another—like pawns on a chess board. At the end of 1959, when the Hammels middle-income development reached the clearing-out stage, residents faced the prospect of being displaced once more, many for the third time in less than a decade. Before the new sponsor assumed ownership, or even set eyes on the site, the buildings' conditions had been allowed to deteriorate badly. The New York City Director of Real Estate, during a tour of the area in December, said: "Some of the most miserable buildings I've seen in my life are in the Rockaways."[1] Owners of property had no incentive to maintain their derelict holdings and every reason to cut back on expenditures, since Title I gave minimum "market value" even for properties that violated housing codes. In effect, the government rewarded the most negligent slumlords.

Once Zukerman Brothers took possession in November 1959, their goal was to remove the people living on the site as soon as possible. Inherent in New York's approach to Title I was the city's permission for sponsors to continue collecting rents without concern for living conditions. Among other advantages for the builders, inspectors no longer appeared at the site. During the first winter (1960), news reporters described houses with broken windows and rusted-out pipes, lacking heat, hot water, and functioning toilets. Whenever pressed about such horrors, Zukerman Brothers contended that the housing stock had been permitted to run down before they took over. Moreover, they pointed out, such places "had not been intended for winter use." Nothing was ever done to make conditions more tolerable; on the contrary, they were permitted to grow worse.[2] By allowing limitless deterioration, the sponsor encouraged families to vacate. They were harassed in other ways as well: Some rents were actually raised, while a number of tenants found their payments rejected, an action often followed by threats of eviction and lawsuits. Warnings appeared suddenly, with "premises condemned" notices posted on doors. On occasion, evictions were carried out at night.[3] Such heavy-handed techniques were used mainly toward the end of the relocation effort, when pressure built to meet construction schedules.

For the most part, Zukerman Brothers tried to give the appearance of following the official guidelines for relocating site residents. In Seaside, they actually carried out their duties conscientiously, hiring a relocation company to do the job under the supervision of the New York City Bureau of Real Estate. Title I regulations stipulated that only standard housing units were acceptable. As spelled out by the relocation company's manager, the new apartments "must have central steam heat and a central hot water system . . . and a fully enclosed toilet and bath within the apartment." Families that found new accommodations on their own were to receive bonuses ranging from $275 to $500, including moving expenses, but "only after the apartments are inspected by the Bureau of Real Estate and approved by them as meeting all the requirements for decent housing."[4] These bonuses did not apply to people on welfare.

The resettlement of the 169 families living in Seaside went smoothly. As contemporaries noted, the area did not really require slum clearance. Although many residents objected to their impending evictions up to the last moment, these white working- and lower-middle-class people had no difficulty making other arrangements, nor did their choice of a new neighborhood cause concern. Bureau of Real Estate standards were universally met. Indeed, 30 percent wound up in public housing, while 15 percent had the means to purchase the new cooperative apartments being built in their very neighborhood. The others did equally well: Owners of propert made up 25 percent of the total, and they were able to use the proceeds they received to purchase new homes. The remaining 30 percent obtained rental housing outside the Rockaways. Most of these families duly received bonuses for finding accommodations on their own.[5]

Hammels, one of the most distressed neighborhoods in New York City, was a different story. Contemporary newspapers often presented statistics with confidence, claiming that 95 percent of the population were African Americans and 80 percent of them received welfare.[6] How they arrived at these numbers is not at all clear because no one knows for sure how many individuals lived on the site; at various times different figures were offered. As the project got underway in November 1959, the Slum Clearance Committee mentioned 1,763 families. Less than two years later, both the *New York Post* and the *Long Island Press* agreed that there had originally been 1,223 families, a figure 30 percent lower. At the same time, the Bureau of Real Estate could come up with the records for only 967 families.[7] Exact numbers will never be known. Most likely, the largest one cited came closest to the truth. Davies, in his study of urban renewal, maintained that many families "moved without the assistance, or even awareness, of city authorities."[8] During the process of relocation, it was discovered that numerous apartments in the area contained unrelated persons who helped share expenses but were never tabulated. Without contractual arrangements, these subtenants possessed no rights under federal law.[9]

As soon as rumors of the Title I project began circulating, some families, disgusted with their treatment, began simply leaving on their own. Often residents never knew about their right to receive decent housing. The sponsors easily exploited them because they wanted them gone. Operating independently of the relocation company, some slum landlords gave commissions to brokers who supplied them with renters. It has been rumored that Leonard Scarbrough played such a role. Those receiving welfare, and therefore not eligible for bonuses, had little incentive to make use of official channels, which they tended to distrust.[10] Clearing residents from the Hammels site started early in 1960, and took about a year and a half to complete—a relatively short time compared to other Title I projects, especially ones in Manhattan. Bureau of Real Estate personnel made a perfunctory effort to supervise, but they do not seem to have challenged company agents responsible for relocation. The real problem, from the very beginning, was finding new apartments for the expelled occupants. Its resolution set off a divisive struggle.

Many of the Hammels people preferred to move somewhere else in the Rockaways. Despite previous experiences with bad housing, they wished to remain in a similar type of community. Among the advantages of seaside living, they frequently mentioned the availability of fishing as a recreation for men and a source of food for poor families. However, accommodations that met Title I standards did not exist in areas reserved for minorities. When residents sought the assistance of the relocation company, they found themselves sent to Brooklyn (especially Brownsville) or other parts of Queens.[11] It was generally believed that once people were forced to leave the peninsula they never returned. Thus, many tried to find Rockaway apartments on their own. They preferred not to have anything to do with an agency that took racially divided neighborhood patterns for granted and did not have their best interests at heart.[12]

Because Robert Moses had faced criticism for the hardships created by urban renewal, he saw Title I in Rockaway as a way to redeem himself by providing wholesome living arrangements for poor people displaced by slum clearance. From the outset of the Title I program in New York City, he wished to link market-rate luxury and middle-income housing with public low-income housing.[13] Unlike Manhattan, where land was at a premium, the Rockaway peninsula contained plenty of available space. A low-income project in Edgemere, built in a vacant spot that sat just a few miles away from the two middle-income developments under way in Hammels and Seaside, offered a unique opportunity. The largest public housing development ever built in the Rockaways, it could absorb a significant portion of those displaced. Moses had high hopes for Edgemere Houses, scheduled for completion in 1960. He invited the mayor and governor to participate in the October 1958 groundbreaking ceremony and encouraged them to use the occasion to review all the state and city accomplishments in "the general rehabilitation of this area." In his own speech, waxing eloquent, Moses declared that the Rockaways were becoming a "new village."[14]

Although Moses's personal files indicate that he was aware of the strict admissions requirements that could undercut his intentions for the new project, he must have believed that he would be able to stretch the rules to accommodate the Hammels poor. In fact, the MTA files contain letters and memos written to associates on the Slum Clearance Committee, housing officials, and others; the notes make clear his desire to place relocated families in the nearby project. He informed Governor Harriman of his intentions in a November 1957 letter. Another document, an internal memo dated July 1958, reported to Moses that the chairman of the New York City

Housing Authority was fully committed to the plan.[15] In his correspondence, Moses occasionally used the modifier "eligible" when referring to the displaced Hammels residents who would be assured a place in the Edgemere project. Evidently, he defined that word very broadly. In a letter written to the Managing Editor of the *New York Times* in March 1959, Moses maintained that "in the instance of Hammels over 42 percent of the present residents are preferential site tenants for the new low income public housing project only a few blocks away."[16] To the very end of his involvement, Moses continued to advocate this position. In December of that same year, at the commencement of demolition in Seaside and Hammels, he reiterated his intentions: "Upon completion of the new public housing next spring, the present residents of Hammels, for the most part relief and other low income families, can move into Edgemere Housing."[17]

Despite Moses's efforts and the expressed desires of hundreds of slum dwellers, only a small number of people from Hammels were accepted into Edgemere Houses. By April 1961, with over 70 percent of the area cleared, only fifty-eight African American families from the site had been relocated into public housing developments in the Rockaways.[18] Because we know that some of them went to other Rockaway projects, the number admitted to Edgemere shrinks still further.[19] In the end, of approximately fourteen hundred families occupying apartments in Edgemere Houses, around 12 percent were African Americans.[20] Many of these minority occupants came from outside the Rockaways and were brought in only at a late stage, after civil rights groups applied pressure. The unmistakable conclusion is that the results fell far short of the promises.

One obvious reason for the failure of Moses's plan is that when Edgemere Houses opened its doors in early 1961, he no longer had the power to affect admission policies. From the mid-1940s until 1958, he had directed both slum clearance and public housing. He lost control of the New York City Housing Authority in 1958 due to its reorganization. His resignation from Title I responsibilities two years later removed him from power in the housing arena. When the time came to deal with the selection of new tenants, Moses could not influence the process. In New York after 1960, there would be no further link between Title I and low-income projects. All previous vows made by Moses and other responsible officials pledging that preference would be given to those affected by slum clearance expired without effect.

At that point, the results were predictable. A high percentage of the Hammels poor did not meet project entrance requirements. Clearly, the rel-

atively large number of families with multiple problems who had been deliberately sent to the Rockaways by city agencies were found ineligible.
They included individuals with a criminal record, drug users, and families
in which even one member had a bad reputation in the community.[21] The
rules also barred unmarried couples and single-parent families. Caps were
put on the percentage of Edgemere Houses residents receiving welfare payments, and as allegedly over 80 percent of the displaced Hammels residents
fell into this category, most of them were directed elsewhere. In the late
1940s, tenant selection for all low-income projects had become centralized.
Perhaps for this reason, the overwhelming number of admissions to Edgemere Houses came from outside the Rockaways, a pattern similar to that
which had occurred in all previous projects erected on the peninsula.[22]

There are other reasons why so few displaced African Americans from
Hammels were admitted into the Edgemere project. Many eligible families
neglected to apply. Some did not believe that they could satisfy admission
standards, while others were ill informed. Nor did the relocation company
see fit to provide information or to offer assistance with the complicated application forms. Some people, having been forced to move in the past, no
longer possessed documents proving their eligibility and were refused because of technicalities.[23] In addition, those black organizations controlled
by Leonard Scarbrough did not encourage people to move out of the immediate area. Scarbrough had always opposed public housing, preferring
to have as many families as possible remain in buildings that he either managed or owned.[24] Some white families gained admission to Edgemere
Houses through their connections with local politicians. Well-run public
housing was still considered a bargain by working-class people who lived
on the peninsula. One man remembered when interviewed that a two-bed-
room apartment cost him only $89.50 per month when the project first
opened, compared to $130 for a similar place in Wavecrest Gardens.[25] In
these early days, access was certainly made easier for whites. Of the families initially granted occupancy, 1,158 were white, 228 were black, and 20
were Puerto Rican.[26]

The Rockaway establishment, eager to keep the peninsula as white as
possible, opposed the movement of blacks onto the peninsula and hoped
to get rid of those who already lived there. Title I provided an opportunity for the latter goal. Nevertheless, urban renewal also had the potential
to expand the Hammels high-poverty tract into other sections of the
Rockaways. Just to the east of the construction site, Arverne contained

the same type of summer housing that had been converted in Hammels a few years earlier, creating "the worst slums in all of New York City." Arverne's landlords were also concerned about a declining summer business. Rumors even circulated about speculators buying up property in Arverne.[27]

Awareness of the threat emerged early. In January 1956, the president of the Chamber of Commerce, in his annual message, had asked:

> Where will these people go when the Hammels site is demolished?
> If space is not found for them in adequate housing, won't they be forced to create new slums in other vulnerable areas?[28]

Throughout the late 1950s, local newspapers constantly warned the community about the new dangers. In response, in 1959 the chamber established a new committee "on planning and development" chaired by one of its most prestigious members, municipal court judge Abraham Margolies. This committee was charged with heading off the spread of "slums" in the Rockaways.[29] Most of the existing civic groups banded together, forming the Rockaway Council of Civic Associations. Its leader was a Bayswater community activist, Jules Michaelis. Energetic and vocal, Michaelis had earlier put New York City officials on notice that if the blight continued, "our neighborhood and everything we stand for will be lost."[30]

Toward the end of the decade, these organizations began stepping up their attacks on speculators and welfare department practices. Along with others from the community, Michaelis criticized the welfare department as "the biggest headache to the people in the Rockaways."[31] Spokespeople for the department continued to deny that they deliberately housed clients in the Rockaways, but no one in the community believed them. Even the manager of the Title I relocation company acknowledged that the "only flaw in the system is that the Welfare Department might send relief families to rooming houses in the peninsula."[32] Newspapers constantly reported instances of "welfare dumping" and claims by individual landlords that they had been approached by department representatives who offered inducements, including bonuses and finders fees, to convert their summer properties.[33] Eager to house clients, the welfare department generally ignored known violations cited by the health department. Guaranteed rents were paid even though "the violations had not been corrected," as the *Long Island Press* reported.[34]

Every so often, reports about particular buildings became sufficiently grievous that conditions had to be addressed. One of the most notorious cases, revealed by the local media in March 1961, concerned a beach house in Arverne. One hundred people, almost all on welfare, had to vacate it because the owner had no certificate of occupancy. Health and fire department officials reported that the structure contained "no bath or shower facilities; no private toilets and not enough communal toilets for tenants; defective and leaking ceilings, holes in the kitchen walls and floors and cellar ceilings; heavy roach and rodent infestations; no sprinkler system; exposed electrical wiring."[35] For reasons never explained, this inferior dwelling and others like it had been acceptable to the city's welfare department. If department representatives did not actually put all their clients in such places, by agreeing to pay rents they demonstrated their complicity. Only when conditions attracted negative media attention did they take action to correct the situation. After years of frustration, community leaders acknowledged their failure to prevent the welfare department from "dumping" clients in Rockaway hellholes.

The next line of defense against the spread of high-poverty tracts was to step up investigations of all run-down housing in Arverne. Local people frequently commented upon the leniency shown by building inspectors, who found it possible to approve wood-frame structures and bungalows containing violations.[36] Many residents conjectured that some inspectors received handsome under-the-table payments from landlords. They had good reason for their suspicions. Some years later during the Lindsay administration, Buildings Commissioner Charles Moerdler "found corruption deeply ingrained among his department's building inspectors."[37] To circumvent unreliable city inspectors, the planning and development committee of the Rockaway Chamber of Commerce began demanding "more careful inspections" of buildings before they became available for rentals. Even more effective than the chamber in gaining media attention was the Council of Civic Associations, whose chairman, Michaelis, was outspoken and quotable. Responding to mounting publicity about the Rockaway situation, the new borough president of Queens, John Clancy, appointed an eight member "Watchdog Committee" for the peninsula in February 1960. Two months later, pressure from the community led Clancy to name Michaelis as chairman. The committee's function, never precisely defined, seems to have been to coordinate various city departments for the purpose of calling their attention to individual cases of substandard housing. It would then report back to the borough president. Presumably, upon receipt of such information Clancy would initiate certain unspecified actions.[38]

Michaelis interpreted his mandate mainly as one of publicizing infractions, while persuading the city's building and fire department inspectors to enforce building codes. His committee called attention to particular houses known in the community for having violations. The stated goal of the new agency was to help deter the spread of summer housing conversions beyond Hammels. By insisting on strict enforcement, however, its unspoken purpose was to hinder any further relocation of African Americans to the Arverne area. Michaelis and his associates tried to have substandard buildings condemned rather than improved, thus leading to the eviction of "undesirable" tenants of color. Apparently, no attempt was made to inspect accommodations that housed whites. The real nature of Michaelis's mission was revealed in an interview given to a metropolitan newspaper:

> You have a mixture that comes from down south or from Puerto Rico who are ignorant. You put this element into any kind of building and they'd ruin it inside a year. You can't rehabilitate these people.[39]

A June 1961 article in the *New York Post* found "an element of truth" in the charge that "the total civic attitude points in the direction of efforts to get minority groups out of the area—that this is going to be a white community with a white beach."[40] A few months earlier, the *Rockaway Review* editorialized: "The slum that once was confined to Hammels has become cancerous and is spreading its ugly tentacles into other areas of the Rockaways." In a classic example of "blaming the victim," the Chamber of Commerce concluded that the people coming into neighborhoods such as Arverne *"appear content to live and raise their families under the most abominable condition imaginable."*[41] Those with a similar point of view supported the housing bill introduced into the City Council by Eric Treulich, who represented the peninsula. Proposed as early as 1958, and finally passed in 1962, the legislation attempted to prevent any further conversion of summer homes (i.e., bungalows and rooming houses) to year-round use. In the Rockaway context, the Treulich Bill was actually designed to prevent poor black people from moving into Arverne. This latent function of the law was recognized by various groups, including the Queens Federation of Churches, which opposed its passage.[42]

One of the first to call attention to this racist strategy was Leonard Scarbrough. In November 1960, as head of the Arverne and Hammels Democratic Association, he accused the Rockaway Chamber of Commerce of being "an anti-Negro organization." He specifically referred to their opposition to blacks moving into summer houses. In the same month, Scarbrough charged the "Watchdog Committee" and its leader, Michaelis, with conspiring to rid the Rockaways of its black population.[43] Although Scarbrough frequently expressed the actual sentiments of Rockaway African Americans, his effectiveness was compromised. Just the previous year (November 1959) he had boasted to the *New York Times* about using crude block-busting techniques in Hammels to drive out white people and stated that he planned to use the same methods in Arverne.[44] The outcry that resulted from Scarbrough's remarks led to an investigation of the Rockaway situation by the New York City Commission on Intergroup Relations.[45] Its particularly damning conclusions supported the view put forward by local civil rights groups:

(1) insufficient standard housing to absorb site tenants; (2) opposition by local "civic associations" to Negroes moving in; (3) inability of the organized sympathetic community to help; (4) questionable tactics on the part of the relocators in pressuring families to move, especially out of Hammels, though they wanted to stay; (5) real estate interests and "operators" taking advantage of the families' plight; (6) no agency taking the responsibility to help.[46]

Unfortunately, these findings were never made public and had no impact on events in the community.

Effective support for the civil rights of dispossessed African Americans came from the Rockaway Council for Relocation and Slum Prevention, founded during the fall of 1959. Composed of progressive-minded people from the community, both black and white, the council focused on housing as both a moral and a practical issue. The leaders stressed that families who wanted a decent life for themselves and their children had been made to suffer by racist policies. They constantly reiterated that "these are human beings, not just numbers," and tried to bring the Rockaway situation to public attention.[47]

The council's inspiration and leadership lay in the hands of two dedicated and resourceful advocates. The president and chief spokesman, Reverend Joseph H. May of the Mount Carmel Baptist Church in Arverne, was a southerner by birth and an infantry veteran of World War II. Educated at Union Theological Seminary in New York and apprenticed at Concord Church in Brooklyn, one of the foremost black Baptist institutions in the country, Reverend May was a charismatic figure. Although soft-spoken, his dignified bearing and passion for the underprivileged made him an inspirational figure. He won lasting respect from the African American community by his own example and by encouraging many others to get involved in social and political issues. Some whites feared him; it was May who helped organize a rent strike in the Hammels Title I site in 1953 to protest terrible housing conditions, a decade before such a strategy was employed in Harlem.[48] Helen Rausnitz, another leader of the council, handled most of the organizational matters. From a left-wing background, Rausnitz had been a political activist since her teenage years. Now a mother with three children, she became involved in their school's PTA, the American Jewish Congress, and the Rockaway Health Council. She shared Rev. May's commitment to social justice, and the two made an effective, dauntless team.[49]

Rockaway's African American community recognized from the beginning of the Hammels Title I program that "slum clearance" meant minority clearance. This served as a starting assumption for the leaders of the relocation council, who called attention to the way in which urban renewal "helps to create new slums."[50] Most of the active members knew quite early that blacks could not expect help or even sympathy from the Chamber of Commerce or the civic associations. Nonetheless, in the beginning the council tried to work with these organizations. They had more success cooperating with other local civil rights groups, mainly the Far Rockaway–Inwood branch of the NAACP, the Women's Industrial Service League, and like-minded clerics.

The Council for Relocation and Slum Prevention immediately protested conditions at the Hammels Title I site. First, they appealed to the sponsor, Zukerman Brothers, without much success. Then they reminded officials in the Bureau of Real Estate of their responsibility for tenants and subtenants, who had been totally neglected by the relocation agents. Their demands had particular relevance when two children in unheated buildings died of pneumonia during the winter of 1960–61. Some improvements followed this tragedy.[51] The council began referring to relocation as "evacuation." At the same time, Rev. May accused New York City of practicing "discrimination" in their housing policies by choosing overcrowded neighborhoods that lacked adequate accommodations.[52] He also called attention to the existence of segregated neighborhoods in the Rockaways, hitherto an unacknowledged reality. While highly critical of housing conditions for poor people in the Rockaways, as well as the city's slum-making policies, the council joined the Queens Federation of Churches in opposing the Treulich Bill. They recognized that the bill's sponsors wished to make it difficult for African Americans to remain in the Rockaways. They took the position that certain summer residences could be converted into standard homes, suitable for relocated black families—as long as inspectors insisted that such houses be fully repaired.[53]

May and his group wanted decent living conditions for all people in Rockaway. "Do we not have a moral obligation to our fellow man to help provide for adequate housing?" he asked in a letter published in the *Wave*.[54] In this spirit, the council took Robert Moses at his word by trying to open up Edgemere Houses for minorities. By the time they began their campaign, 70 percent of the project had already been filled, exclusively by whites. The council approached the matter in several ways. As a beginning, they organized protests and demonstrations. At one point the housing authority suspended all admissions to the project. When the process resumed, the authority sought out eligible minority candidates, encouraged by the council. Rev. May personally solicited applications from African Americans, sometimes actively recruiting families from outside the peninsula. The council then launched a publicity campaign informing Rockaway families about their eligibility and assisting applicants in completing their forms. They also held informal clinics, coaching people on the proper answers to give when they were interviewed.[55] Most of the minorities finally admitted to Edgemere Houses owed their success to the council's efforts.

It was common in the 1950s and 1960s for professional planners, architects, journalists, and influential writers, such as Jane Jacobs, to criticize low-income projects. Their main theme, that projects do not work, was stated most strongly by Nathan Glazer: "Public housing is the graveyard of good intentions."[56] Such conclusions may well have been merited by some of the housing developments in New York City and in the country at large, but they were not necessarily true of those in the Rockaways at that time. From the testimony of many people who lived there, Edgemere Houses and some of the other Rockaway projects worked well at the beginning. Interviews with people, both African American and white, who lived in Edgemere Houses during its early years lead one to admire this housing project's success. A modified integration pattern, which seems to have meant at least one black family on each floor, worked well. Elected building captains welcomed new tenants. Occupants felt positive about their new homes, and a camaraderie developed. The houses were new and clean, project management remained competent, and maintenance practices met high standards. An active community center served the Edgemere project and nearby housing developments. In addition to providing organized recreation for children and a social center for adults, at regular intervals it sponsored films, art shows, lectures, and political discussions.[57]

The militant Council for Relocation and Slum Prevention established itself as an important player in support of civil and human rights. The *Amsterdam News* began printing accounts of the Rockaways, using Rev. May's analysis of events.[58] As the organization gained in prominence, city politicians were forced to respond. In January 1961, Borough President Clancy appointed the two civil rights activists, May and Rausnitz, to his "Watchdog Committee." As might be expected, they differed with committee chairman Michaelis on policy and procedural matters. However, this did not prevent the latter from granting personal interviews and presenting himself as the committee's official spokesman.[59]

Racial issues in the Rockaways attracted press attention. In response, Mayor Wagner announced in September 1961 the formation of an Area Service Program (ASP) in Arverne, with J. Clarence Davies Jr., head of the city's Housing and Redevelopment Board, as its director. Wagner then set out his goal of halting the spread of "slum blight into Arverne." He added,

> We want to ensure that all dwellings in the area comply with various city codes. We want to prevent deterioration of the neighborhood and bring into the community an effective complement of social, educational and health services.[60]

The ASP set its parameters of operation between Beach 73rd St. and B. 58th St., south of the "el," with the aim of helping to stabilize the area. No less than eight city departments were called upon to coordinate their activities so that strict code enforcement would be carried out.[61]

Despite the ambitious purpose enunciated by the mayor, the ASP for Arverne did too little and arrived too late to have an impact on Rockaway developments. Referred to as a holding operation, it included such diverse bureaucratic entities as the welfare department, the health department, the police department and the Commission on Intergroup Relations. These city departments never succeeded in working together. Occasionally a slumlord received a big fine, a symbolic act that momentarily gave encouragement to the community.[62] More to the point, by the time the new agency began operating in the fall of 1961, Zukerman Brothers had virtually cleared the Hammels site. A few hard-to-place residents hung on until the end of the year, when the relocation company terminated operations.[63] Families forced to move had already found new places to live. Predictably, many of them wound up in the proliferating "rookeries" of Arverne. The additional services promised by the mayor took a long time to materialize and had no more impact on the immediate situation than the ASP. Similarly, the Treulich Bill, passed in 1962, arrived too late to influence the situation. It had even less of an effect than the mayor's special program. The litigious Rockaway landlords immediately tested the law in court, an effective tactic that served to bury the issue of house conversions indefinitely. The Treulich Bill's chief accomplishment was to further divide the Rockaway community.

The Area Service Project conflicted with the "Watchdog Committee," rendering the latter's work superfluous. In the end, neither endeavor succeeded. In March 1962, Michaelis called the service project "an out and out flop." He then resigned from the borough president's committee, claiming that the city "has done nothing at all" to prevent the growth of derelict housing in Arverne.[64] His colleague, Rev. May, who almost always disagreed with Michaelis, concurred with this conclusion. Months before, May told the *Amsterdam News* that Rockaway had "traded one slum home for another."[65] Throughout the community a consensus existed. In an editorial written after the committee began to dissolve, the *Wave* sadly noted that "in spite of all these efforts there is no noticeable improvement in Arverne." They added that "people close to the situation say it is getting worse."[66]

Everyone involved with the peninsula realized that Arverne had reproduced the Hammels pattern. The summer homes, former hotels, wood-frame rooming houses, and bungalows had been pressed into year-round use, sending another major New York neighborhood into serious distress. The immediate blame for such a tragic outcome has to be placed at the doorstep of those responsible for urban renewal in the Rockaways because they never devised any realistic plan for the relocation of site tenants. The Redfern project had contributed to the deterioration of Hammels, which suffered further when the low-income project was built there. Title I transferred human suffering and destitution to Arverne. A Rockaway newspaper related how the baton had been passed: "Thus the once glorious Arverne section was given the same title that had previously been tagged to Redfern and Hammels: the worst slum in the city of New York."[67] Rockaway's summer buildings languished. No longer used by seasonal renters, they were either abandoned or seized by the city as marginal housing for people on welfare. The blight continued to spread. If something drastic did not occur to halt the process, the downward spiral would inevitably continue.

CHAPTER 8

Trends of the Sixties

A remedy for the spreading blight in Rockaway did not come from the community but from Robert Moses. As early as 1958, he had let it be known informally that he contemplated an additional Title I proposal for the Arverne area.[1] In a public statement a year later, at a ceremony marking the demolition of the first buildings at the Seaside site, he directed his audience's attention to the shamefully ramshackle housing owned by rapacious landlords: "Thousands of huddled wooden shanties and disgraceful summer shacks, built without regard to health, fire hazard and proper zoning, cannot be replaced overnight."[2] Additional middle-income housing should be constructed in order to replace "the remaining disgraceful Rockaway slum areas," he maintained. His clearance plan represented part of a long-standing scheme to extend the Shore Parkway from the Marine Parkway Bridge all the way to the Atlantic Beach Bridge, connecting it with the Nassau Expressway and other Long Island highways. Since the 1930s, Moses had believed that a road and park alongside the ocean would protect the whole area from despoiling commercialization.[3] In 1961, with his proposal under discussion by city officials, Moses again used a ceremony, this time in Hammels, to spell out his scheme for Rockaway's future. The specific area he marked for development would expand from the current eastern boundary of Hammels's Title I site to include the adjoining section of Arverne (Beach 74th St. to B. 55th St). The frontage on the beach would be acquired with state funds, while the middle-income housing would be financed by both city and state programs. He wished to move rapidly, before Arverne acquired a large displaced population.[4]

Moses's commitment to the Rockaways had survived his loss of power over city housing. While building an extended Shore Parkway, along with beach protection and park additions, remained central to his plan, he hoped to eliminate the area's spreading deterioration as well. He never fully accepted the need to surrender the high rentals that would provide tax revenues for New York City, but his pragmatism led him to utilize the recently enacted Mitchell Lama state funding program, with its lower rents and reduced taxes, for the Hammels middle-income development. New York State had passed the Mitchell Lama law in 1956 in order to use tax-exempt state bonds to finance housing and reduce debt service. Most of the buildings constructed as part of the existing Title I project in the Rockaways had, in fact, been built under Mitchell Lama auspices. Moses prepared to make the same arrangement to construct middle-income housing further down the peninsula.[5]

By the end of 1961 Moses had worked out the undertaking in great detail and presented his designs to the responsible city officials. He even gave it a descriptive title:

> Proposal for Title I Partially Tax-Exempt Mitchell-Lama Housing, Together with Park and Parkway Improvements along the Rockaway Shorefront Between B. 74th Street and B. 53rd Street, with Widening of Rockaway Beach Boulevard and Relocating of Small Business Establishments to New Frontage Within the Redevelopment Area and an Extension of Shore Front Parkway Easterly to a Connection with Seagirt Boulevard.[6]

Moses also projected the financial arrangements with great precision, allocating most of the burden to federal and state governments. Rents, as well as the approximate number of commercial establishments and parking facilities, were calculated in advance, in accordance with Mitchell Lama guidelines.[7] Moses emphasized that the area to be razed consisted of poorly constructed ramshackle fire traps, whose eradication would be a boon to the Rockaways. The new housing would add to the peninsula's status as a year-round community, while also increasing its attractiveness as a resort. His plan gave priority to the lengthening of the Shore Parkway and protecting the adjoining beaches. New York City's costs would be kept to a minimum, with Albany and Washington assuming the greater part of the financial burden.[8]

As he had done with all previous Title I proposals, Moses immediately began recruiting construction companies. Abraham E. Kazan, president of United Housing Foundation, had worked with him on Penn Station South, Rochdale Village, and, later, Co-op City. Zukerman Brothers, who were involved in building Rockaway's first middle-income development, initially showed interest. Additionally, a firm directed by Fred DeMatteis of Nassau County expressed a willingness to undertake the new project. It was the DeMatteis company that eventually completed the middle-income development in Hammels when Zukerman Brothers' capital ran out.[9]

In December 1961 the commissioner of the New York State Division of Housing and Community Renewal wrote to Robert Moses, "We are interested in financing such a program if it can be carried forward." He added a qualification: his agency would "be happy to work it out with the appropriate city officials if there is some indication of their interest."[10] Aside from running the World's Fair, by 1961 Moses no longer held an official position in city government, although he remained Mayor Wagner's representative in negotiations related to federal and state arterial construction programs.[11] The Power Broker still dominated the Tri-Borough Bridge and Tunnel Authority (TBTA) and its huge resources, and he directed the New York State Council of Parks and the Long Island Parks Commission until December 1962. He also controlled the Temporary State Commission on Protection and Preservation of the Atlantic Shore Front, under whose auspices he set out to engineer the Rockaway venture.

But Moses's position of power in the city had changed drastically. His association with Tammany Hall had alienated both reformers and Mayor Wagner. Moreover, his authoritarian manner and arrogant personal style had lost him the support of key housing officials, such as James Felt and J. Clarence Davies Jr. The TBTA's lawyer, William S. Lebwohl, came away from an early meeting with Felt and Davies under the impression that they merely wished to delay the project, while further sessions with them demonstrated that they had very little interest "in doing anything."[12] Also totally at odds with Moses was Milton Mollen, who headed the New York City Housing Redevelopment Board after 1960.[13] In later years, Mollen recalled an encounter on Randalls Island, when he pressed Moses about the inconvenience to those families in Rockaway who lived in the path of the projected highway. According to Mollen, Moses showed no concern for displaced people, even those who had been forced to move because of earlier developments. "He left a legacy of distrust we're still dealing with," Mollen concluded.[14]

Despite the cool reception from city officials, Robert Moses believed he could get the support of the Board of Estimate. The cooperation of the borough president of Queens, John T. Clancy, would be essential, due to the tradition of "borough courtesy." "Pat Clancy is the key man," Lebwohl wrote to his boss in March 1962. Moses recognized as much even before receiving Lebwohl's memo. Starting in October 1961, he had set out to convince the borough president that his solution to the Rockaway decline was the only viable one.[15]

Moses used three arguments to persuade Clancy. Considering what eventually happened, the first two proved to be prophetic. In the first place, Moses asserted that his proposal "present[ed] a unique opportunity for a large scale rebuilding of Rockaway, the kind of thing the planners always talk about and almost never do." Second, it would be important to move quickly while federal and state funding was still available. Finally, Moses was quite willing to give the borough president credit for the results. Referring to some of the partial improvements on the peninsula in the recent past, he added, "Here is your chance to clean up the rest."[16] In August 1962, the borough president of Queens responded with his own plan. Clancy wanted New York City to designate the run-down areas of the Rockaways along the beach and freeway, between B. 74th and B. 30th Streets, an Urban Renewal District. This designation, he maintained, would not only attract the requisite public funding for housing, it would allow the shore preservation and highway construction sought by Moses.[17]

Moses disagreed. Funds for the highway, a park, and beach preservation were immediately available. Tearing down houses along the ocean up to four hundred feet behind the boardwalk as part of the process of building the road would jump-start slum clearance of the entire area from Arverne to Edgemere. Moses's experience had taught him that a call for an urban renewal program, including required surveys and studies, "will result in endless complications and delays and probably defeat the entire program."[18] He had opposed such an approach in 1958 when the former borough president, Crisona, recommended it, and he did his utmost to prevent it now. Before long, the disagreement between Moses and Clancy turned into an irreconcilable conflict. Their aims were not very different: the elimination of dilapidated buildings in the Rockaways, the construction of an improved road system, and the protection of the beach. However, Moses projected a two-stage approach because he did not foresee both operations receiving immediate backing. As he indicated to the Rockaway Chamber of Commerce, "the housing part of this program will inevitably follow the moving back of the boardwalk, the attack on erosion, arterial extension and park." They could not proceed concurrently.[19]

For his part, Clancy wished to undertake the needed housing, the park, and the parkway simultaneously, using an urban development format. Knowing Moses's obsession with road transportation, he may have feared that once funding for the shore parkway came through, less of an incentive would exist to go forward with the housing, which he regarded as primary. While the leaders of the chamber were confused by the differences between the adversaries, city officials sided with Clancy. A mere borough president's defiance of the Power Broker, with the support of his municipal colleagues, reveals how much influence Moses had lost in just a few years.

But Robert Moses was resourceful. By taking his case to Albany and presenting his project as a park and ecology issue, he managed to win over both houses of the state legislature. In the spring of 1963, a bill providing the necessary resources for the Rockaway shorefront improvement and the shore parkway received a majority vote. However, Governor Nelson Rockefeller, with his own ax to grind, vetoed the legislation. Moses's well-publicized resignation from all of his state posts the previous December had angered the governor. Now the Rockaways suffered.[20] Rockefeller's official justification for his veto, the bill's lack of cost estimates, did not ring true.

In the meantime, the Department of City Planning deliberated whether to designate Rockaway as an urban renewal district. At least eleven other impoverished city areas were similarly chosen for study. In the fall of 1963, the planning commission initiated an overall survey of the peninsula as if the Rockaways were an unknown entity, "to assess its needs, its resources and its potential, and to recommend appropriate action programs."[21] The following April, the planning commission issued a report, which focused on Arverne. It found a "rapid pace of deterioration" and an "obvious need to come to grips with the inadequate housing and the social and economic problems facing many of the minority families living here." Among other recommendations, the report called for "intensive work with these families living in the area . . . to insure that they receive maximum services and assistance and thus are better able to function in the community."[22] On 25 November 1964 Arverne was officially designated an Urban Renewal Area, making the ninety-block section of Arverne and Edgemere specified by Clancy eligible for U.S. government funding. The commission stated:

> A key challenge of the renewal program was to provide perma-nent, decent housing for families affected by clearance actions, with special attention to the needs of the many families displaced by previous renewal activity . . . [ensuring that] those families with social and economic difficulties be provided with intensified health, guidance, education and welfare services as part of the re-newal program.[23]

By the end of the Wagner administration just over a year later, nothing had happened in Rockaway to indicate that the Urban Renewal Area designa-tion had made the slightest impact on the community. The promised social services never appeared, and Arverne continued its steady deterioration. Robert Moses had been proven correct.

While the various studies were being carried out, hundreds of addi-tional poor families moved into the area. Relocation required people to shift from one dreadful neighborhood to another, resulting in steadily worsening living conditions. Families who had been relocated from Title I sites during the 1960s moved mainly to the Arverne beach blocks, into re-placement accommodations consisting of run-down bungalows and wood-frame buildings that were replicas of those destroyed elsewhere on the peninsula by urban renewal. As the *Rockaway Review* observed in 1963, rooming houses in Arverne that had had violations five years earlier still had them. Any building in the area free of infractions was "an exception," meaning that most residences were "operating without permission."[24] Even if landlords wanted to rectify deficiencies, they had little incentive to do so. It was becoming impossible to obtain loans or second mortgages, and in many instances insurance protection had been withdrawn. While in-dividually owned houses were subject to scrutiny by inspectors connected with the Arverne Area Service Program, the substantial holdings owned by speculators tended to be overlooked. Jules Michaelis later stated that he had resigned from the "Watchdog Committee" because corruption "made it impossible" to stop "the slums" spreading to Arverne and Edgemere.[25]

Increasingly, owners abandoned their buildings. Squatters occupied some, while others were boarded up awaiting destruction. "Structural fires" frequently caused inconvenience and occasionally injuries or even loss of life. At the same time, the small shops that had served the neighborhood and provided marginal employment disappeared, leading the Chamber of Commerce to label Arverne "a residential and commercial desert."[26] Services by public agencies failed to keep up with the growing numbers of poor people. Garbage pickup was inadequate. Heavy rains brought "floating sewage" that would never have been tolerated in other areas. Rats roamed the streets.[27] Nevertheless, the welfare department maintained its policy of working with "cooperating" landlords. By the middle of the decade, in Arverne and Edgemere approximately two thousand families subsisted on relief payments, the overwhelming majority of them living in oceanfront shanties. A Long Island newspaper released a study showing that the percentage of non-white families in the area whose annual income was less than $4,000 was almost 71 percent, compared to 53.5 percent in central Harlem. The percentage of dilapidated houses was more than five times as great as in Harlem (43.5 percent to 8 percent).[28]

To make matters worse, the Department of Welfare used the opening of Arverne to send an increased number of vulnerable families from other areas of the city to these newly converted summer shacks. According to Forest H. Whitney of the prestigious Community Service Society of Queens, "Arverne is the place where the Department has moved its problem families, many of whom are multi-problem with little energy to spend on themselves."[29] The New York Times wrote that "narcotics addicts, alcoholics, unwed mothers and others who could not meet eligibility for public housing, but who nonetheless needed to find a place to live" were sent to "the cheap bungalows" of the Rockaways.[30] This pattern persisted, even though unemployment on the peninsula remained three times as high as the rest of the city. Summer resort jobs had virtually disappeared. The few small factories, such as the Home Curtain Corporation and Chain Bike, which had once offered unskilled workers minimum-wage employment, closed up shop. The absence of a welfare center or a public hospital continued to create hardships.[31] In 1966 a welfare department satellite office was finally installed on B. 74th Street in a storefront facility that was soon to be torn down; the office proved barely adequate.

Despite the evidence that so many welfare recipients in the Arverne Urban Renewal Area lived in desperate straits, the myth persisted that the welfare department "coddled" clients. Another popular perception, that the poor were responsible for their own suffering, was reinforced by the department's desire to avoid responsibility. In denying their role, officials repeatedly maintained that welfare recipients exercised "freedom of choice" and opted to live in squalor. Thus, when pressed by reporters in 1966 to justify the use of broken-down summer rookeries, a spokesperson told the *New York Times* that the department's "clients picked their lodgings and gravitated toward Arverne because of its cheap rents."[32]

The consequences were predictable. Conditions that had earlier existed in Redfern and Hammels now prevailed in Arverne. Tuberculosis raged. Pregnant women lacked prenatal care, while young children never received necessary vaccinations. Rockaway came to surpass the rest of Queens in infant mortality. By the mid-1960s, African American infants had almost three times the rate of death as whites living in the same sections of the Rockaways. One former health worker claimed that blacks in Rockaway had "worse figures than the Third World." The peninsula also ranked among the highest in youths (aged twenty and under) diagnosed with venereal diseases.[33]

Drugs plagued the Rockaways in the 1960s and afterwards. Local police informed the *Wave* that two hundred drug arrests took place during 1971, while a fact-finding committee established by the Rockaway Health Council reported an average of one drug-related death per week in the teenage to young adult population between 1969 and 1971. During these years, the peninsula still did not possess any drug treatment centers. While the city fathers can be faulted for this lapse, the white-dominated civic associations opposed the establishment of such facilities because they wished to avoid the negative publicity that would result from acknowledging the existence of a drug problem.[34] As drugs escalated, so did crime. In January 1972, the *New York Times* ran an article under the headline, "Rockaway Residents Living in Fear of Muggers and Burglars." On the basis of interviews, the reporter concluded that both black and white families believed "there had been a sharp increase in crime and fear of crime." They felt that the streets of Arverne were less safe at night than ever before. Although more media attention tended to be given to white victims, the victimization rate for blacks in almost every serious crime category was considerably higher.[35]

All segments of the population believed that Arverne had a serious problem with juvenile delinquency, and these concerns were factually supported. In 1964, the juvenile offense rate for the Rockaways was 78.2 per thousand compared to 34.1 per thousand in Queens and 54.1 per thousand in all of New York City.[36] Locals commented on the lack of play streets and the inadequacy of the teen recreation centers on the peninsula. Most had no doubt that the quality of life in the community had declined during the last few years.[37] Yet the city offered no remedy. In Arverne and parts of Edgemere, especially where summer accommodations had been converted into year-round dwellings, personal insecurity became a fact of life. Houses were ransacked for anything that could be sold or pawned, especially second-hand plumbing equipment and pipes of various kinds. Drug addicts scavenged both occupied and abandoned buildings. Landlords blamed residents for these misdeeds, and were reluctant to replace items only to see them stolen once again. Inevitably, the poor suffered doubly; they were victimized and then blamed for their own misfortunes.

In the 1960s the Rockaways witnessed innovations in human services, but they were very different from anything the city planning commission had envisioned for areas undergoing urban renewal. Among the most prominent was the appearance of facilities for newly deinstitutionalized mental patients. Throughout New York State, such patients were sent into the community with little advance planning. Many of those released from Creedmore Hospital in Queens and Pilgrim State Hospital on Long Island wound up in Rockaway. Neighborhood settings ranged from private homes run by individual families to group homes "created out of old hotels." Facilities varied in quality, but those arrangements designed mainly for profit were particularly deficient. The owners of these facilities are believed to have bribed city officials. Some of these adult homes had over two hundred beds, often with three to a room. Many were overcrowded and had untrained staff that did not offer proper supervision. The requirements established by government agencies were rarely met. Corruption scandals surfaced on a regular basis.[38]

Neighbors complained about the bizarre behavior of patients and the negative impact on property values. Patients, lacking activities, hung around outside all the time. The district manager for the local community board reported that in order "to discourage the mentally ill from sitting on the benches in front of the Park Inn adult home, the benches were removed. Now the mentally ill stand in front of the Park Inn."[39] In Rockaway, the sudden presence of large numbers of mentally ill people seemed to many just another instance of government authorities pushing problems on a community that did not have the resources to cope. Nevertheless, by 1974 the peninsula contained 20 group homes, either in operation or in various stages of development, for a total of 3,957 beds.[40]

Because a large number of former mental patients were elderly and suffering from various forms of dementia, a need quickly arose for nursing homes. Private groups, operating strictly for profit, quickly sought to satisfy the need, utilizing land in Rockaway that was plentiful and cheap. In addition, all health facilities automatically received a property tax abatement of between 75 percent and 95 percent. The elderly who resided in the nursing homes generated very little business because they did not shop, and they strained the resources of the two private hospitals in the peninsula. The local establishment waged a campaign to limit the number of such institutions in the Rockaways. But in 1974 a court overturned all bans on the further construction of nursing homes, opening the door to private investors, who would now be restrained only by market forces.[41] By the 1990s, 6 percent of peninsula residents lived in nursing homes and health-related facilities. This was the highest level in all of New York City.[42]

African Americans, many of whom availed themselves of the new social service positions, made fewer complaints than other Rockaway residents about the presence of health facilities and group homes. For the first time, many held full-time jobs, paid into social security, and became eligible for medical and retirement benefits. In addition, foster-home care arrangements for the seriously and persistently mentally ill compensated providers generously, and black families tended to be more willing to open their homes.

During the 1960s, influenced by national developments, an African American voice began to be heard in Rockaway affairs. Local white leaders had rarely given thought to the needs of the black population, which had previously remained relatively passive. At best, there had been some meager distribution of patronage. The emergence of the militant Rockaway Council for Relocation and Slum Prevention came as a shock to the white establishment. Helen Rausnitz tells of the puzzled looks on the faces of local white leaders when she and Rev. May first stood up at meetings and called for the redress of the African American community's grievances. Eventually, May and a new generation of activists became combative in response to the racist attitudes they encountered. May, in particular, showed open contempt for the paternalistic attitudes of whites. He believed that blacks had rightful demands that should be answered immediately.[43]

The civil rights movement changed the national political climate. City governments in New York and throughout the country became more sensitive to minorities and even encouraged their participation in the War on

Poverty. In the mid-1960s, the Rockaway Community Corporation (RCC) was established as the chief antipoverty agency on the peninsula. The first official organization in the history of the Rockaways to be controlled by African Americans, it coordinated all poverty-oriented services for the area's low-income population. In an early successful activity, the RCC launched a publicity campaign to combat lead poisoning. It also prevented the closing of the local Legal Aid office.

Some of the most ambitious undertakings were directed at children, the most vulnerable segment of the Rockaway population. These included the opening of recreational facilities and the development of advocacy agencies. Paraprofessional positions were created for teachers' aides in schools and for family assistance personnel who visited families when children were experiencing difficulties. The Department of Health, Education, and Welfare contributed to the establishment of a public health facility in Arverne that provided medical and dental services for children. The terrible health conditions of Rockaway infants began to improve.[44] The nation's War on Poverty also addressed the specific needs of adults. It provided educational programs, which included preparation for high school equivalency tests and civil service exams and classes on the skills needed for operating business machines and dressmaking. The main beneficiaries of these programs appear to have been minority women.[45]

In the late 1960s, the local chapter of the NAACP became revitalized. Inspired by Lena Cook, first as a member and then as president, it joined the Council on Relocation and Slum Prevention in playing an active role in community affairs. Possessing impressive intelligence and energy, Ms. Cook had overcome early deprivations, including the absence of formal education that left her functionally illiterate until adulthood. Her warm personality and motherliness (she was affectionately known as "Mother Cook") drew others to her cause, and she even won respect from whites. Starting out as a member of the Women's Industrial Service League, Cook became a teacher's aide through a program funded by the War on Poverty. In this position she encouraged young people to take advantage of educational opportunities that had been denied to her. During the Vietnam War, she joined with white women in organizing demonstrations against U.S. involvement.[46] In an effort to gain more influence for minorities, NAACP members went door to door encouraging African Americans to register and vote. Under the organization's auspices, a day care center was established, and support was given to a Planned Parenthood office just over the Far Rockaway border in Nassau County. NAACP activists also raised funds to create badly needed recreation facilities for neighborhood young people, an enterprise that also provided them with jobs.[47]

The local chapter of the Urban League had a more narrow focus. Mainly concentrating on open housing, the league tried to integrate a few of the all-white neighborhoods of the peninsula. This proved frustrating, especially in Belle Harbor and Neponsit, where they had no success whatsoever. Later, in the middle-class Bayswater section of Far Rockaway, groups of white and black "testers" with identical housing requirements visited real estate agencies, and found themselves steered to quite different housing tracts. Eventually Bayswater did become integrated, although the ensuing "white flight" in the 1970s and 1980s significantly depleted its white population.[48]

Many Rockaway ministers became active in fighting for minority rights, including bringing War on Poverty funds to the Rockaways, but none had the impact of Reverend Joseph H. May. Despite his poor health, Rev. May was tireless and fearless in confronting the establishment. Black people in Rockaway had long complained about police brutality. In addressing this issue, May had the support of other black ministers and of liberal whites.[49] Encouraging minority participation, so that their increasing population on the peninsula could be converted into political influence, May worked on voter registration. He used his powers of persuasion to get black candidates to run for local office. Some activists got their start as poll watchers under his auspices. Throughout his life, education remained one of Rev. May's chief concerns. He appeared regularly at the City Council, the central Board of Education, and local school boards to advocate for his community. Some of his most important contributions came in the area of career training. Under his direction, the Mount Carmel Baptist Church established the first Youth Corps affiliate in the Rockaways. It taught young people skills that helped them get jobs with local agencies such as day care centers and public housing developments. His church also sponsored an after-school tutoring service and a Head Start Program. On occasion, he even visited local schools to advocate for individual children.[50]

Rev. May achieved his greatest success in the field of housing. One of the Council on Relocation and Slum Clearance's major aims was to place Rockaway's impoverished residents in decent homes. Its victory in opening up the Edgemere Houses for African Americans encouraged the organization to push for more housing projects. In 1961, when word began circulating that another low-income development was being proposed for the Rockaways, the white establishment showed its displeasure. At first civic groups representing "designated" areas expressed opposition, but soon practically every white organization—including the Chamber of Commerce, the Rockaway Council of Civic Associations, and local newspapers—joined in. Opponents of the plan argued that all four of the existing low-income projects had brought in people from outside the community and thus had indirectly served to create new "slums" in the area.[51]

As soon as it got wind of the city's proposal, the Council for Relocation and Slum Prevention gave enthusiastic support. Rev. May actually had a location in mind. He proposed replacing the forty-one broken-down buildings adjacent to his Mt. Carmel Baptist Church in Arverne with public housing for the people living on the site, many of whom were elderly. But the council encountered formidable resistance. Adding his voice to the antagonism of powerful local organizations, the borough president of Queens, John T. Clancy, came out strongly against the undertaking. However, Reverend May did not accept defeat easily. He encouraged officials of the Wagner administration to inspect the housing situation in Arverne. Deputy Mayor Julius Edelstein, a man with strong liberal convictions, came and was horrified by what he saw. As a member of the Housing Policy Board executive committee, he lobbied for the project.[52] Nonetheless, the borough president's opposition presented a seemingly insuperable obstacle.

Resolving the stalemate took more than a year and a half. A final showdown occurred at an open Board of Estimate hearing in October 1962, when Clancy once again voiced his disapproval. In a heated exchange, Rev. May accused the borough president of allying himself with "bigots who are doing their utmost to keep Negroes out of the Rockaways."[53] Strong accusations of racism had few precedents in such a setting, especially emanating from a distinguished minister. They caused a stir. In a closed meeting, the Board of Estimate voted to proceed. A compromise was reached when the city agreed to limit the new housing to "vest pocket" size, just 174 units. The understanding that Clancy would leave office in a month's time, and that his successor, Mario J. Cariello, did not oppose low-income projects in the Rockaways, also made the settlement possible.[54]

The Carleton Manor vest pocket development, completed in 1967, proved to be one of the most successful of all the projects built in the Rockaways. For one, it was placed next door to Rev. May's Church, and he made sure that many of his parishioners received preference in admission.

In addition, he was able to keep a close watch on its functioning by means of the Head Start program that he ran on its premises. The reduced scale—it was less than half the size of the next smallest project in Arverne—made Carleton Manor manageable. Many apartments were specially designed for senior citizens, while others contained just a few rooms, which ruled out large families.[55] Encouraged by the Carleton Manor model, the Council for Relocation and Slum Prevention once again argued for additional low-income housing in the Rockaways. Predictably, the white leadership resisted, asserting that Rockaway had done its share of absorbing New York City's problems. In fact, other vulnerable communities, such as the South Bronx and Brownsville, had been similarly used. Middle-class and affluent areas, on the other hand, always put up a strong resistance, as Mayor Lindsay was to learn later in Forest Hills. Privileged sections of the Rockaways, such as Neponsit and Belle Harbor, possessed similar political clout.

Although the Rockaway establishment did everything possible to prevent further low-income housing, governmental imperatives triumphed. Criticisms of minority relocation connected with the construction of some Manhattan projects led authorities to seek areas that had open spaces. In early 1963, it was reported that the city intended to build another housing development less than a mile away from the spot where two already existed in Arverne and Edgemere.[56] With federal funds available for such undertakings in the early 1960s, Mayor Wagner had requested that Borough President Cariello choose a site in Queens. Knowing that most communities vigorously opposed them, Cariello had vetoed three projected units within a two-year period.[57] But with pressure mounting, he gave his approval to the part of Queens that would cause him the least political damage. He justified his decision on the grounds that "public housing is a very important step in reclaiming Rockaway." The Council for Relocation and Slum Prevention applauded the borough president's promise that the new buildings would accept Rockaway families living in depressed areas.[58] Cariello's vow was reinforced by the city planning commission, which earlier had announced its intention of giving "top priority to 800 families uprooted because of the housing slum clearance."[59] In the end the project only contained 712 units.

It took a long time to complete what would be the last low-income project built on the peninsula. The land was not secured until August 1967, and construction did not commence for another two years. All along, Rev. May and the council urged the housing authorities to expedite the process.

In 1972, nearly a decade after plans were first announced, the Beach 41st Street Houses opened their doors. Despite the efforts of civil rights groups, few of the new residents were Rockaway locals. The project's completion came too late to accommodate those displaced by the Arverne Renewal Project.[60] Given the huge waiting list for public housing in New York and the desire to fill the buildings quickly, residents were selected (without screening) from Brooklyn and the Bronx. A large number of families who had previously been unable to meet admission requirements received apartments. Ironically, this last Rockaway low-income project became one of the first to develop a negative reputation.[61]

The population of the 41st Street Houses mirrored that of many of the low-income housing developments in Rockaway, reflecting transformations that were occurring nationally. Increasingly throughout the 1960s, families on welfare gained admission to public housing, while those whose yearly earnings exceeded a specified ceiling were encouraged to leave. Under the Brooke Amendment of 1969, public housing became practically free for the very poor, while those with salaries just above a prescribed limit paid market rates. Thus, working families tended to move out as their incomes increased and their rents rose. As buildings filled up with impoverished people who paid little or no rent, service personnel were eliminated, maintenance declined, and the buildings deteriorated.[62]

At the same time, court decisions made it increasingly difficult to screen new applicants or evict residents who disrupted the lives of their neighbors. An early study by the Citizens Housing and Planning Council of New York on the effect of "problem families" found that only a handful of such tenants in each building, or even one on a floor, would be enough to drive out people who could afford to leave.[63] Before long, the projects came to be regarded as accommodations of "last resort." After the mid-1960s, as low-income developments throughout the country came to be occupied mainly by minorities and became associated with antisocial behavior, they lost whatever popular support they once held.[64]

Rockaway's low-income projects exemplified the process during the 1970s. As the most problematic families from the inner city moved in, the housing suffered. Anecdotal evidence strongly suggests that tenants who caused problems in Manhattan projects were forced to choose between eviction and banishment to public housing in the Rockaways.[65] Queens borough presidents apparently knew that Rockaway's projects were being used for the dumping of difficult cases, but they failed to object.[66] Simeon

Golar, Mayor Lindsay's head of the Housing Authority, expressed the frustration of public officials when he asked: "What do you do with disruptive families in the projects? These are families with problems, and nobody wants to live with them."[67] Despite the awareness by public officials of the difficulties that would inevitably ensue, no extra funding was ever provided to deal with families in distress in Rockaway's low-income developments. No special services, not even extra security personnel, were ever introduced, despite the peninsula's having far fewer resources than comparable areas on the mainland. These policies ensured that public housing by the ocean could no longer hope to succeed.

In 1975, one hundred thousand people lived in Rockaway, while Queens had a population of two million. Yet Rockaway contained 57 percent of all the low-income housing located in the borough.[68] By the 1990s, between 45 percent and 50 percent of the residents in five of the six low-income developments in Rockaway were on welfare, and between 45 percent and 60 percent were single-parent families with children under eighteen. Barely 5 percent of families had two or more members employed outside the home.[69] The high concentration of projects reinforced antisocial patterns, including crime and drug dealing. It was believed that the majority of robberies on the peninsula were committed by local residents. Drug gangs operated with impunity.[70] Starting in the late 1960s, the projects came to be viewed negatively by the rest of the community. Many expressed the opinion that the presence of so much low-income housing cast a permanent pall on the Rockaways.

Yet not all low-income projects in New York City have been so problematic. There has always been a large waiting list for those seeking admission to public housing, and few vacancies exist. The list frequently numbers two hundred thousand families, even though the names of those not summoned are automatically removed after two years.[71] Screening, despite court decisions, has tended to be more stringent in New York than elsewhere, while maintenance, performed by union labor, has remained comparatively good. New York has seen no projects torn down, as in Newark, Chicago, and St. Louis. Many developments, such as First Houses on the Lower East Side, Williamsburg in Brooklyn, and Queensbridge in Queens, continue to function reasonably well. The U. S. Grant Houses in West Harlem, in close proximity to Columbia University, contain a high percentage of intact families.[72] Had city housing agencies decided to protect low-income developments in the Rockaways, they could have remained viable. Their decline was not inevitable. Rather, opportunistic and short-sighted public officials constructed a large number of units in a small area that was unprepared to meet the needs of tenants, and they failed to make provision for necessary supports. In fact, those few services that existed at the beginning were eventually eliminated. Callousness and cynicism then ensured that the situation would deteriorate.

As the Vietnam War began taking its toll on the domestic agenda, War on Poverty funds for the Rockaways began drying up. While a few programs were kept, including some in health and in the public schools, by 1968 several others in adult education and job training were unceremoniously cut. Even unsympathetic observers, such as the *Wave*, bemoaned the loss of programs that had managed to place deserving people in real jobs.[73] The conservative political drift of the following years ensured that these services were never restored, with predictably negative results for the poorer communities of New York. Rates of infant mortality and crime rose during the next few decades. We will never know how a lasting, determined campaign to eliminate poverty in the Rockaways would have turned out. What we do know is that its absence caused enormous suffering.

CHAPTER 9

The Whitest Neighborhood in New York

The tip of the Rockaway barrier beach lies west of the Marine Parkway Bridge traffic circle. Called Breezy Point, or sometimes just "the Point," it contains two other subcommunities, Rockaway Point and Roxbury. Despite the obvious geographical connection, its residents do not like to think of themselves as part of Rockaway.[1] Almost every media discussion of the Rockaways omits mention of the Breezy Point enclave, and there is a certain reality to the separateness of Breezy Point. Until the late nineteenth century, the area did not even exist. It was created by littoral drift which carried sand westward. Almost from the beginning of its existence as a bungalow colony, it was the only gated community on the peninsula and one of a small number in New York City. A gate lets outsiders know that they are not welcome. It would be safe to say that very few residents of Rockaway have ever set foot in this section or know much about it.

Breezy Point began as a tent city around the turn of the century. By the 1920s, bungalows for summer rental began appearing. During these early decades, it was separated from other parts of Rockaway by a Coast Guard station adjoining its northeast corner and by Fort Tilden on the southeast. Directly east were marshlands that, in the late 1930s, would become the refurbished Jacob Riis Park. By the 1950s a small number of permanent houses had been built, numbering around 400 out of approximately 2,700 dwellings.

The area, referred to by some locals as the "Irish Riviera," has always attracted an Irish American population. Minority groups have never been encouraged here, summer or winter. The families of the civil servants, police officers, fire fighters, and retirees who spend summers in Breezy Point have literally sought to keep the outside world at bay. This has not always been possible. During the 1960s, bizarre events occurred in this small community. They have been largely forgotten, which is unfortunate because they provide an instructive contrast to the fate that befell most of the Rockaway peninsula.

The first warning of things to come appeared in February 1960 in an article by the gossip columnist Walter Winchell. In his typical flip style, Winchell stated briefly that "the largest single tract of ocean beach front in the city of New York had been sold" to a developer. The tract he referred to was all of Breezy Point, not including Fort Tilden and the Coast Guard station, which had already been closed down. On 5 March 1960 the *New York Times* reported that the deal had been completed.[2] The news alarmed the 2,700 homeowners of Breezy Point because they did not own the land on which their houses stood; without exception, they leased their properties from a private company for only five or ten years at a time. Although arrangements differed, by 1968 none of the affected families would have had any claim on their homes. The land was sold out from under them.

The purchaser, the Atlantic Improvement Corporation, had grandiose plans for the Point that excluded its current inhabitants. Responding to a still-pressing shortage of middle-income housing in New York, the corporation announced the construction, without subsidies or tax abatement, of "a city within a city." Scores of buildings, varying in size from fifteen- and seventeen-story buildings to garden apartments, would be erected. The "new city" would contain schools, cabanas, restaurants, parks, houses of worship, shopping centers, libraries, and police and fire stations and would house approximately 220,000 people.[3] Everything about the venture was on a grand scale. The area encompassed three and one-quarter square miles (approximately eight hundred acres) and cost the corporation $17.5 million, paid in cash. Called "the largest price ever paid for a tract of land in the history of New York City," it was said to be "the nation's biggest private real estate undertaking," with an estimated final outlay of $1.25 billion.[4] Because of its size and complexity, it required "more than 200 licenses and permits granted by various city agencies."[5] Atlantic Improvement hoped to complete all phases of the enterprise within a dozen years. The company's sense of urgency worked to the advantage of the Breezy Point residents.

Three separate civic associations represented the different sections of the Point. Unlike their counterparts further east on the peninsula, they always worked smoothly together and, regarding the threat now posed, with unanimity. Less than a month after the official announcement that the entire Point had been sold, a joint action committee had been formed and a $75,000 defense fund raised. The committee appealed to public officials such as city councilmen, state senators, state assemblymen, and the mayor. Residents proved adept at getting the media to publish sympathetic accounts of the suffering of widows of deceased firefighters and police officers who stood to "lose their life savings."[6] More effectively, they planned to pursue a legal course. The committee's leadership consisted of lawyers from the community who agreed to take up the fight pro bono. With such resources, the residents announced their intention to hold firm until they had exhausted every possible appeal, a process that could delay all construction indefinitely. Before long, the Atlantic Improvement Corporation communicated a willingness to reach an agreement, and in August 1960 they announced that the community might buy the portion of land on which their houses stood. The corporation would keep the remainder for development.

According to the arrangement, the corporation would sell 403 acres to the Breezy Point families for $11.25 million, one-tenth of which had to be paid before the end of the year. There existed no precedents for what residents were now required to do, and they had a limited amount of time in which to do it. Forging ahead, they formed the Breezy Point Cooperative, which turned out to be the "largest single-family residential cooperative of its kind in the United States."[7] A combination of political connections and legal expertise allowed the co-op to obtain favorable tax rulings from state and federal governments; this enabled members to deduct their individual interest charges and realty taxes from their income tax returns.

The most difficult tasks the co-op faced were raising the cash for the down payment and securing the final amount in the form of approved mortgages. Appointed block captains went door-to-door over the Labor Day weekend collecting money from each family. Twenty-five hundred signed leases had to be produced by January 1961 in order to protect the sale. People borrowed chiefly by taking out first or second mortgages on their property. Urged on by persistent leaders and block captains, the co-op met the January deadline for the closing. Fewer than 10 percent of the families were not able to subscribe and had to move.[8] Those who stayed congratulated themselves for their impressive accomplishment. For its part, the Atlantic Improvement Corporation also had cause for celebration. Although its usable property had been reduced in size by slightly more than half, the purchase figure now came to only $6 million, approximately 30 cents per square foot. This constituted the cheapest price for land in all of New York City. The corporation now possessed two smaller parcels, one adjacent to Fort Tilden and the other at the western tip of the Rockaway peninsula.[9] However, the reduction in its holdings did not compromise construction plans. For the most part, the builders had avoided lengthy legal actions, and they could achieve the early start they had desired for the "city within the city."

The initial design called for the construction of two fifteen-story buildings, six more buildings of six stories each, a garden apartment complex, a shopping center, and a shore club. A few months after the Breezy Point Cooperative delivered its mortgage payments, apartment house foundations were dug. By the summer of 1962, some of the projected structures were near completion, and a few months later the two tallest ones had reached ten stories each.[10] The Board of Estimate and various city agencies continued to approve the developer's requests, including mapping the streets and providing building permits, the last of which was issued in October 1962.[11]

Regarding housing developments, Robert Moses liked to say that once you got the first stake driven, no one could stop you.[12] Breezy Point would prove him wrong. On 13 August 1962, the Regional Plan Association, a nonprofit organization that offered recommendations concerning transportation and parks to local governments in the New York area, introduced to the city planning commission a proposal to turn all of Breezy Point into a vast oceanfront park, comparable to Jones Beach. Joined with Jacob Riis Park and Fort Tilden, it would be the largest recreation facility in New York City, even larger than Central Park. In the process, all current properties, those belonging to both the Atlantic Improvement Corporation and the Breezy Point Cooperative, would be taken over. This included the summer houses, land recently purchased, and the apartment houses currently under construction.[13]

Unsolicited plans produced for the city by private groups, especially ones that required an enormous outlay of resources, usually died immediately upon delivery. Construction of a public beach at Breezy Point had been discussed before, without drawing any response from elected officials.

However, this time the agency making the proposal had the backing of some influential New Yorkers, including Mrs. Marshall Field (widow of Marshall Field III), Mellon heir Stephen Currier, Whitney North Seymour, and a member of the Rothschild family. City planning commissioners Elinor C. Guggenheim and Laurance M. Orton both promised to give the proposal a favorable hearing.[14]

The advocates made a concerted effort to achieve their goal. They set up an ad hoc organization whose title reveals their sense of urgency: the Emergency Action Campaign to Save the Beach at Breezy Point. They presented their case forcefully. The western Rockaway section was "New York's last available great natural resource," and "the last undeveloped beach front in New York City." Rather than allowing selfish economic interests to "cut off" one of the city's "most desirable beaches from public use," it should be made available for all the people, particularly the poor who could not afford transportation to Long Island's beaches. Their slogans, "A Park Where the People Are" and "For All the People or Just a Few?" demonstrate their feel for public opinion.[15]

The campaign gained the endorsement of J. Clarence Davies Jr., Mrs. Stanley Isaacs, and Eleanor Roosevelt among other well placed persons whose name recognition added to the prestige of the cause.[16] A large number of civic organizations joined in, including the Citizen's Committee for Children, the Citizen's Union, the Community Service Society, the Women's City Club, the Park Association, the Metropolitan Committee on Planning, and, with qualification, the Citizen's Housing and Planning Council.[17] Barely a month into the campaign, the *New York Times* provided editorial approval. Before the year was out, every single newspaper in the metropolitan area, as well as TV and radio stations, came out in favor of what some called "the super park." Early in 1963, the group, now called the Committee for a Park at Breezy Point, produced an expensive brochure explaining the desirability of its goal and listing its many supporters.[18]

On Breezy Point itself the reaction to the new campaign was one of shock. The Atlantic Improvement Corporation took measures to defend itself. It placed ads in newspapers and threatened legal action if the city interfered with legitimate property rights. The corporation had no wish to abandon a potentially profitable project in which it had invested time and money. While politicians began debating the issue in the fall of 1962, construction continued, and several high-rise building skeletons now graced the landscape. An immediate defense of the "city within the city" came from all the building and construction unions of New York City, followed by the AFL-CIO of New York State.[19]

The most valuable ally in the dual effort to proceed with the housing development and veto the park was the Breezy Point Cooperative. As much as the co-op had fought the Atlantic Improvement Corporation in the past, the residents now faced two unpleasant prospects if approval were given to the proposal before the city planning commission: At worst, their entire community would be eliminated, land and houses together. Even if they managed to endure while a park was built, their exclusive beach and recreation areas would be "contaminated" by central-city minorities, just the kind of visitors the gates of Breezy Point had always kept away.[20] Once again this tenacious group prepared for a difficult struggle. A first effort, the production of a co-op flyer entitled "Stop the Disaster at Breezy Point," hardly matched the public relations savvy of their powerful opponents. In fact, the arguments they made in the flyer, that a public park would bring thousands of people from other areas of New York to crowd the roads and beaches of Breezy Point, played right into the hands of the park's advocates by reminding people of the area's exclusionary practices.[21] Minority leaders in particular addressed the "type of exclusiveness" that kept blacks and Puerto Ricans out of the bungalow colony there. Even Mayor Wagner referred on occasion to the fact that land owned by the co-op "is generally restricted to non-Negroes [and] non-Jewish families."[22]

The issue of the park has to be seen in the context of the civil rights movement, which emerged nationally during the 1960s. The wealthy, white, liberal advocates of "democracy in recreation" had been active contributors to mainstream minority organizations. They encouraged the heads of twenty-two separate black and Puerto Rican groups in New York City to begin advocating the purchase of the land. National leaders such as A. Philip Randolph and Marion Anderson lent their names, while Roy Wilkins of the NAACP and Whitney Young of the Urban League became outspoken in their support. Young, in a letter to the *New York Times*, described how "Breezy Point would provide for thousands of minority and low-income citizens who live in Manhattan and Brooklyn the only outlet for their children to enjoy ocean-front beach facilities and desperately needed park and recreational resources." Black children from Harlem, accompanied by clergymen, appeared frequently at City Council and Board of Estimate meetings and spoke of how they wished to be allowed to swim in the Atlantic Ocean at Breezy Point.[23]

In its struggle to survive, the co-op effectively formed coalitions with other civic associations that opposed the plan and gained assistance from local politicians. Important New York City congressmen, including Emanuel Celler, John Lindsay (the future Mayor), and Hugh Carey (the future Governor), joined Queens Borough Presidents Clancy and, later, Cariello, in speaking out against the park, as did City Council representatives from both Queens and Brooklyn. Queens organizations, following the lead of the politicians, fell into line. Some public officials opposed the scheme on the grounds that it lacked practicality. In fact, despite the many prestigious people associated with the plan, no one had worked out essential details. The cost, as the parks commissioner Newbold Morris kept insisting, would be astronomical. He added that the city's "limited debt margin" precluded any such undertaking at this time. Abe Beame, the practical city controller, also expressed strong reservations about the burden of expenditures. Estimates approaching $60 million were frequently cited for acquiring the land, while an additional sum of between $200 and $300 million, or more, would be necessary to develop this enormous park.[24]

Secretary of the Interior Stewart Udall, after taking a helicopter flight over Breezy Point with New York's mayor in October 1962, made vague promises of federal support. But no precise figure was ever cited, and the likelihood of federal funding became even more remote as the Vietnam War began to consume domestic expenditures. Congressman Hugh Carey of Brooklyn, who happened to be a member of the House National Parks Subcommittee, maintained that "no federal aid is available for the park." Even some remarks by Udall about the federal government contributing Fort Tilden to the project proved worthless, since he had not cleared them with the Defense Department.[25]

More to the point, the argument that the new park would serve as an equivalent to Jones Beach for New York's poor, who could not afford the trip to Long Island, had little basis in reality. Subway rides to the Rockaways still cost two fares in each direction, while the stop nearest to Breezy Point, on Beach 116th Street in Rockaway Park, was several miles away, requiring an additional bus ride. The idea of extending the Rockaway subway line westward to the end of the peninsula, so that it could be used during two summer months, made little sense. The Marine Parkway Bridge tended to be overloaded during summer weekends, with mile-long lines of traffic waiting to pay tolls. To make the park accessible even to New Yorkers with cars would require the construction of a new bridge connecting

Brooklyn to the western tip of the Rockaways, a rather impractical idea. Another important factor never really considered by proponents was that Riis Park, which was to be incorporated into the larger area, had been gradually losing visitors. If the existing facility was already underutilized, who would fill the projected mammoth park?

The fight over the park at Breezy Point brought together groups on the peninsula that had never before coalesced and would not do so again. Only because its very existence was threatened did the Breezy Point Co-operative reach out to adjoining communities for assistance. Previously, its leaders had refused to involve themselves in the difficult problems faced by other parts of Rockaway, preferring to believe that their area was immune to outside influences. Nevertheless, their neighbors took up the Breezy Point struggle as if it were their own. With the exception of Neponsit and Belle Harbor, whose homeowners did not relish an enormous housing development on their doorstep, a wide range of Rockaway groups, led by the Chamber of Commerce and the Rockaway Council of Civic Associations, came to the co-op's aid.[26]

Rockaway organizations opposed the installation of a new beachfront park because it would compete with the existing ones, but the arguments they employed demonstrated a lack of political sophistication. In their statements and press releases they emphasized that the superpark would waste limited resources. Jules Michaelis, speaking for the Rockaway Council of Civic Associations in October 1962, claimed that "what Rockaway wants is better roads, sewers, flood relief, more schools, better park maintenance, relief from jet noise and real rapid transit."[27] The same kind of argument was made almost a year later, when the group issued a press release warning that the "dream park proposal . . . would divert more than $200,000,000 from essential public works to finance an unnecessary summertime facility." They constantly reiterated that "schools and transit are more important than another beach."[28] The Rockaway organizations did not seem to realize that city officials, although willing to contemplate massive funding for a park at Breezy Point, had no interest in doing the same for other urban projects, no matter how urgent. Sewer, transit, and school expenses were regarded as routine matters unworthy of special attention. It was the park that captured their interest. Alert Rockaway leaders might have shaped that issue to their advantage.

Robert Moses, who always advocated public access to recreation, opposed the Breezy Point plan. He argued that "an additional shore front park should be built in connection with further slum clearance" in Arverne, where it would do the most good.[29] Other experts on city planning, like Roger Starr, believed that the beaches throughout most of Rockaway better met the criteria for public access than did the more remote ones at the Point. He suggested that "if we are to have larger beach facilities in the Rockaways let us at least put them alongside the subway line in the Arverne–Edgemere–Far Rockaway section." Moreover, a recreation project at Rockaway Beach would be infinitely cheaper because it could take advantage of an already existing infrastructure and cause less dislocation.[30] Starr's organization, the Citizens Housing and Planning Council, called for a new proposal that would

> plan for the development of the entire Rockaway community . . . . Such a plan would ensure that no single recreational facility will be developed at the cost of sacrificing others of equal or greater potential importance.[31]

For unknown reasons, the Rockaway civic groups did not utilize the suggestions made by Moses, Starr, and the Citizens Housing and Planning Council. If, in return for joining the opposition to the Breezy Point park, they had insisted on increased support for the Rockaways, their hand might have been strengthened. They did not seize this opportunity, and the only issue on the table was deciding between a new facility at the Point or none at all. Elected officials demonstrated a willingness to spend millions on the new scheme, but very little on the existing, though deteriorating, resort. That the rest of the peninsula was not considered during these lengthy discussions reveals a great deal about the attitude of government leaders. The Rockaways, as one of the chosen repositories for New York's poor, had been "written off."

The residents of Breezy Point were also about to be written off, but they refused to accept their fate passively. The co-op continued to hold rallies, send petitions, and demonstrate at every public hearing. Elite support for the park gave their opponents considerable momentum. At one stage, the Atlantic Improvement Corporation showed a willingness to compromise. It would continue constructing those buildings already begun, but the area on the western tip would remain undeveloped for another five years. If by 1967 the city had not moved to acquire this piece of land, the corporation would resume work.[32] Because the city had reached no final decision on the park, it did not respond to the corporation's proposal.

On 25 November 1962, Mayor Wagner named a six-member task force, consisting of distinguished city officials, "to gather all pertinent information" to help his administration decide how to proceed. The task force, chaired by James Felt, was given a month to prepare a report for the mayor. It made a private recommendation that was delivered orally and never made public. This encouraged speculation that certain members had raised serious objections, mainly about the need to obtain a commitment for outside funding.[33] In March of the following year, the Board of Estimate held a public hearing on the park. Breezy Point residents used the occasion to demonstrate their fervent opposition. More than five thousand of them came by chartered bus to picket City Hall. When the hearings commenced they crowded into the building to speak against the park and to cheer or boo, depending on the speaker. So many of them spoke that the session lasted nineteen hours, one of the longest hearings in Board of Estimate history. It ended at half past five in the morning, when opponents "finally ran out of words."[34]

Politicians of various stripes joined in the struggle. Congressman Emanuel Celler told a Rockaway audience that he would oppose a park in Breezy Point with "every ounce of energy I possess."[35] In April 1963 the co-op got J. Lewis Fox, who represented the Rockaways in the New York State Legislature, to introduce a bill making it illegal to take possession of Breezy Point for the purpose of constructing a park there. The bill, which stipulated that municipalities could not build parks on lands that contained homes, easily passed both houses. Governor Rockefeller then found himself "bombarded with mail from both sides of the controversy."[36] Until then, Rockefeller had maintained a neutral stance on the issue. The *New York Times* criticized the legislature's actions on the grounds that the state would be intruding upon city "home rule policy" and called for a gubernatorial veto. Mayor Wagner then made a special appeal to the governor to follow the advice of "the paper of record." After some consideration, a veto was recorded, allowing the mayor to proceed with the project. As Wagner said after the news came down from Albany, the plan was "very much alive."[37]

On 2 June 1963, the mayor, as anticipated, announced that a Breezy Point Park "is not only desirable, but essential from the viewpoint of the long-term interests of New York City." In terms reminiscent of Robert

Moses, his opponent on this issue, Wagner added, "Parks, which provide one of the chief escapes from congestion in a city like New York, are essential for civilized living."[38] Why such a generally sensible politician allowed himself to be drawn into this costly and impractical scheme has never been fully explained. Most likely he was susceptible to the blandishments of the rich and powerful, in whose social circles he and his wife traveled.[39] Another explanation held that the mayor was persuaded by Mrs. Field's counselor, Judge Simon Rifkind, who had been the senior Wagner's law partner.[40] In response to the powerful forces backing the Breezy Point Cooperative, Wagner qualified his announcement a day later, although his statement was ambiguous. He said that while the city had no immediate plans to acquire the co-op's land, there was always a possibility "of such a need in the future."[41] The residents of the Point did not feel reassured. Antipark rallies, addressed by local politicians, were held throughout the summer months. On 2 July 1963, five hundred demonstrators formed a ring around City Hall to protest the mayor's decision. They carried a fifty-pound scroll, said to contain one hundred thousand signatures opposing the park proposal, which they presented at a public hearing called by the city planning commission to discuss the matter. At a session lasting nine hours, proponents of both positions heatedly presented their views.[42]

At this juncture, the state intervened. Laurance Rockefeller, the governor's brother and the newly installed chairman of the State Council of Parks, called for a compromise. He favored the park, but suggested that it should exclude land on which apartment construction was underway, as well as the 403 acres belonging to the co-op. The Rockefeller measure would grant the city a total of 785 acres rather than the 1,362 acres originally envisioned. While the Breezy Point residents mulled this over, the Committee for a Park at Breezy Point declared the Rockefeller proposal "totally unacceptable."[43] On 14 August, certain members of the city planning commission who were strongly committed to additional park space for New York gained approval for the creation of a public park and beach at Breezy Point by a vote of 4 to 2. Using the formula expounded by Mayor Wagner, they would give the co-op a reprieve "for a considerable number of years."[44] Again, residents faced an uncertain future.

The Board of Estimate was to make the final decision. At a public hearing, held on 26 August 1963, four thousand picketers turned out hoping to defeat the plan. Petitions were presented and speeches dragged on until half past five in the morning. The weary board reserved judgment for two weeks, when, by a vote of 20 to 2, approval was finally given to a concilia-tory solution. It resembled the Rockefeller version. The city would take over the unused land owned by the Atlantic Improvement Corporation and all beach property from Riis Park to the Point, including the private beach-es that belonged to both the corporation and the Breezy Point Cooperative. However, no attempt would be made to acquire the co-op's 403 acres, then or at any future time.[45]

The parties to the dispute reacted predictably. Although final details still remained to be worked out, Mrs. Marshall Field termed the settlement "a great victory." In January of the next year, the Committee for a Park at Breezy Point dissolved, never to be heard from again. John Hale, the lawyer for the co-op, expressed pleasure. His clients had gained security for their homes, although they would have to share their beaches with "outsiders." The most negative response came from the president of the Atlantic Improvement Corporation, who indicated that he was "shocked and dismayed" by the result.[46] Construction already in progress came to a sudden halt. The corporation considered its investment "irreparably dam-aged" because the apartment houses would be situated on an "island" in the middle of a vast public recreation area, without the stores, churches, schools, and additional services originally designed. It initiated legal pro-ceedings seeking "full consequential damages."[47]

Mayor Wagner inadvertently assisted the corporation's case for gener-ous compensation when he announced that the city would go ahead with the park:

> Breezy Point, commanding one of the most magnificent vistas avail-able anywhere within the limits of New York City and containing the only major undeveloped beachfront expanse within the limits of New York, is a precious asset incapable of duplication. . . . My only conclusion is that Breezy Point park development is not only desir-able but essential from the viewpoint of the long-term interests of New York City, despite the problems undeniably presented.[48]

The case dragged on for twelve years, with each decision reversed a num-ber of times. In the end, New York City spent almost $30 million for the land, the apartment buildings, and two private beach clubs, both of which were leased annually for private use. In 1967, $6 million was paid for land at the western tip. In 1974 the corporation was awarded $15 million. The city had already paid $5.6 million for the buildings and $4 million for the private beach clubs. In 1976 the U.S Supreme Court rejected a final appeal.[49]

Depending on one's viewpoint, $30 million for a major park site might not seem excessive, especially with the apartment houses and cabana clubs thrown in. The city had already taken possession of a good part of the Breezy Point tract by summer 1964, and more became available during the next few years.[50] However, except for two small dirt parking lots, no "great park" facility materialized. Lacking any alternative sources of funds, the city waited in vain for aid from the state and federal governments. Apparently, the Wagner administration had no real plan of action. As the *Daily News* concluded: "It turned out to be just another idea going nowhere."[51]

Structures in various stages of completion remained standing on the Breezy Point site for years. At one point, the Queens Chamber of Commerce made a request to turn the apartment buildings into middle-income cooperatives, in view of the borough's housing shortage.[52] But this proposal and similar ones garnered no response. Toward the end of his career, Robert Moses proposed a solution that appeared to be a caricature of his standard views. Shortly before his eightieth birthday in 1968, Moses suggested a massive slum-clearance program to eradicate what he termed "urban cancers." The buildings at Breezy Point, he said, should be converted into low-income cooperatives for between forty and fifty thousand inhabitants of Brooklyn's worst slum, Bedford-Stuyvesant. After this had been done, "the ghetto area vacated should be rebuilt and by repeating this process, in ten years there would be no more ghettos."[53] Needless to say, Moses's suggestion never received any support. In fact, the Lindsay administration, which did not get along with Moses, privately regarded it as a subject of "levity."[54]

The main beneficiaries of the city's ineptitude were the residents of Breezy Point. They kept their houses and their beaches and did not have to deal with unwelcome hordes invading their dominion. House valuations in the area continued to appreciate, which brought satisfaction to co-op members, although complaints were made about higher real estate taxes. A manned gate discouraged casual visitors who attempted to drive onto the Breezy Point enclave. In 1968 the co-op installed electronically operated gates for additional security across all paved streets leading off the main thoroughfare. Only members or their personal guests possessed the programmed cards that raised the gates.[55] Breezy Point continued to show its inhospitable face to the outside world.

Just when the homeowners of Breezy Point imagined that they had overcome all threats, another appeared on the horizon. In May 1969, President Nixon's secretary of the interior, Walter Hickel, flew to New York, where he unveiled a plan to establish a "Gateway National Recreation Area" in the harbor region. A crucial section, to be absorbed into the projected federal park, was Breezy Point. The Lindsay Administration, having inherited the Wagner administration's "super park" plan as well as its debts, "hailed the announcement."[56] New Yorkers would gain recreation that the financially strained city could not afford. During the congressional hearings held to work out details, Mayor Lindsay was tempted to remind the representatives of the inaccessibility of the area. He hoped to get the federal government to pay for the requisite transportation. However, advisors cautioned silence on this matter, since it might jeopardize passage of the necessary legislation.[57]

Spokespeople from the Breezy Point Cooperative testified against Gateway. As headlined in the *Daily News*, the proposal had cast a pall over the Point.[58] But the community's leaders were now experienced in organizing protests, and once again they set powerful lobbying efforts into motion. In addition, previous battles had improved their ability to manipulate the political process. They rounded up influential supporters, such as the congressman from Staten Island, John M. Murphy. Representative Murphy, who had been appointed to a subcommittee on parks, sought to insert an amendment to the Gateway legislation that would protect the property rights of Breezy Point homeowners.[59] Even more effective for the co-op was the hiring of Bill Pozen, once an assistant to the former secretary of the interior, Udall. Pozen traveled in key Washington circles, where he effectively presented the residents' viewpoint.[60] The co-op's efforts worked well. On 28 December 1972, President Nixon signed into law the Gateway National Recreation Area. It incorporated 26,172 acres, including Jamaica Bay, Broad Channel, Sandy Hook, and the beachfront owned by the Breezy Point Cooperative, for which the co-op would be compensated. The Lindsay administration turned over all acreage on the Point owned by the city to the Department of the Interior without charge. Land with homes belonging to the co-op was specifically exempted from any future government actions.[61]

While Gateway was widely celebrated at the time as a conservation and recreation breakthrough, knowledgeable people recognized its limitations. According to the Parks Council, a private New York City advisory body, the entire future of Breezy Point for mass recreation seems considerably dimmed by the low-key, largely unpublicized lobbying efforts of the Breezy Point Cooperative, which has apparently secured for itself a permanent enclave in the middle of the proposed national park, blocking development of the western tip of Breezy Point.[62]

All attempts made by the Federal Government to condemn approximately 285 acres of beach along the south shore of Breezy Point, so that the land could become part of the Gateway National Recreation Area, were contested through extensive litigation. In November 1982, a federal court in Manhattan ruled that the beach in question did, in fact, belong to the co-op and not to New York State or New York City. According to a National Park Service spokesman, condemnation was "now unlikely, because it would cost the government too much."[63]

Regarding the entire area of Breezy Point, certain positive changes did result from Gateway. Fort Tilden was finally turned over to the Park Service, and, although not much has been done with this section of the Point, a modest museum now provides general information about the fauna and flora of the Rockaways. Federal control over Jacob Riis Park has stopped the decline of the former Moses park, although it has never regained its popularity of earlier years. Most dramatically, the Gateway legislation required the U.S. Park Service, in 1978, to finally tear down the decaying structures originally built by the Atlantic Improvement Corporation, which stood for fifteen years as a reminder of past follies and possibilities never realized.

Once more the efforts of the community had secured victory against seemingly invincible forces. As far as Breezy Point was concerned, the Gateway legislation had become a dead letter. Except for small parcels of undeveloped land and the two parking lots previously mentioned, no further development took place. Despite the turmoil around them, life for residents never really changed. Seclusion and private streets, now protected by magnetic gates, remain as much a feature of life on the Point as ever. It is still difficult for outsiders to gain entry through the main gate, as the authors discovered on more than one occasion. Today Breezy Point looks much the same as it did decades ago. A few homes have been enlarged, but there have been no new buildings, since the co-op forbids them. The community is a fraction less Irish than before, with Italian Americans providing the only ethnic diversity in this solidly white enclave. The *New York Times* claims that Breezy Point, with a population approximately 98.5 percent white, is presently "the whitest neighborhood in the city."[64]

In a 1981 speech, published in a local newspaper more than ten years after the final resolution of all threats to their way of life, one of the activists recalled past events in order to draw lessons for a new generation. Her main conclusion was that unity had been the community's main asset. Then turning to what she called "the sad fate of much of the Rockaways," she bemoaned the lack of vigilance that had prevented its former (white) population from duplicating the success achieved at Breezy Point.[65]

CHAPTER 10

Divergences

The process of building numerous Rockaway housing developments during the first two decades after World War II lent itself to political influence and corruption involving construction companies, unions, lawyers, and real estate interests, among others. Democratic Party leaders steered lucrative business opportunities to certain Rockaway firms. Local politicians seem to have chosen the appraisers who evaluated the worth of condemned properties, and sometimes they even appraised real estate themselves.[1] It is generally believed that well-connected sellers of property received higher prices. Although no evidence exists of convictions for bribery, knowledgeable interviewees claimed that certain individuals received prices above market value for their properties.[2]

In March 1958, the Rockaway politician and Queens borough president, James J. Crisona, complained in a letter to Robert Moses about three separate financial awards for real estate in the Rockaways, which involved overpayments by the city for condemned land, some of them at six to ten times assessed valuation.[3] Shortly thereafter, Crisona went public with his accusations. In a report presented three months later, he specified a location known as Edgemere Park, slated to become part of the site for the new housing project in Edgemere. The owner, the New York City Waterfront Company, paid taxes on an assessed value of approximately $150,000. Nevertheless, the city appraiser, a man active in Queens Democratic politics, agreed that the city would pay the amount of $1,496,564 for the property. Adjoining land owned by New York City, one-third the size, had just been sold to private developers for $75,000. Crisona charged the city's corporation counsel with "gross negligence," and called for the appointment of a special counsel in order to set aside the agreement.[4] In response, the Waterfront Company hired a prestigious Manhattan law firm to represent them. One of its partners, future Supreme Court Justice Arthur J. Goldberg, served as their attorney. The firm's brief apparently convinced Mayor Wagner and the Board of Estimate of the propriety of the transaction, which prompted the appraiser to institute a million-dollar lawsuit against Crisona, charging libel and slander.[5] Ultimately, libel action was denied on the grounds that Crisona acted within his official capacity and was therefore "accorded absolute privilege."[6] In the process of the lengthy court battles, Crisona's accusations against the city were forgotten. Nevertheless, coming as they did from someone who knew the Rockaways intimately, they have to be taken seriously.

So many stories exist about individuals engaging in graft and corruption that they have become part of Rockaway folklore. For example, it was well known that insider information about prospective development sites enabled land purchasers, including officials of the Chamber of Commerce, to make quick profits. Real estate speculation was endemic to the Rockaways, and speculators benefited from delays in property condemnations. Because they could afford to pay for repairs or insurance, they generally could hold out longer than individual homeowners and thus received higher prices in the end. Rumors also circulated about alleged "insure and burn" schemes. Many of the decrepit, formerly popular boardwalk establishments ended in fires, some of suspicious origin.[7]

Questionable actions by local real estate brokers also affected the racial composition of Rockaway neighborhoods. Certain agencies had bad reputations, and their names invariably surface in discussions about unethical practices. In essence, they determined where people from different ethnic groups would live by steering prospective home buyers according to color. African Americans were invariably shown fewer homes from which to choose. Many of the firms also resorted to the practice of blockbusting, which followed a general pattern: Typically, they offered minority applicants a low price for a house in an all-white area. If necessary, they even helped to obtain a federally backed mortgage by having mortgage brokers inflate family income with the cooperation of corrupt public officials. Brokers would then use scare techniques to induce whites to sell out quickly, often for lower-than-market prices. They would advise homeowners to vacate before the neighborhood "tipped." Then prospective minority buyers, denied access to segregated neighborhoods elsewhere, would be encouraged to move into the still-integrated area for elevated prices. If a few of the first arrivals eventually defaulted, the companies would keep the principal and interest already received, plus the mortgage insurance from the FHA. The desired effect would have taken place: a rapid turnover in home ownership and huge profits for real estate investors.[8]

Charges were rarely filed over these practices, but in 1972 a prominent Far Rockaway real estate agency was accused of blockbusting by the chairperson of the New York City Commission on Human Rights. The firm had allegedly attempted "to induce panic selling of white owned houses" and was accused of depositing money into a minority buyer's account in order to make him eligible for an FHA mortgage. According to the allegation, brokers also spread rumors that a low-income housing project was to be built across the street.[9] Not surprisingly, no evidence of any convictions can be found. While the 1968 Fair Housing Act contained certain injunctions against blockbusting, in actuality the enforcement provisions were weak. As authorities on discrimination in housing have observed, the legislation itself "was structurally flawed and all but doomed to fail."[10]

Blockbusting laws in New York were not applied until the mid-1970s. In Rockaway, the risk of prosecution tended to be very low and the penalties minor. At most, real estate licenses of individual brokers might be suspended for a month or two, while the firm itself continued to function.[11] In the absence of significant deterrents, the practice remained a regular part of the Rockaway experience. It had started in Arverne, north of the el, and in Edgemere. Later it would spread to Far Rockaway and Bayswater. White families who were determined to remain in their homes were subjected to constant harassment. Mario Russo, a long-time resident of Arverne-Somerville, recalls receiving repeated telephone calls from brokers, even after he made it clear that he had no wish to sell. Other calls came from minority people claiming to be his new neighbors, saying they were anxious to meet him. Post cards would arrive in the mail with similar messages, including one signed "Jose Rodriguez."[12] Harassment got so bad in the early 1970s that, after a protest meeting, residents agreed to put up signs on their lawns, reading: "This house is *not* for sale."[13]

Minorities not only paid higher-than-market rates for homes in Rockaway, they had difficulty obtaining mortgages or refinancing from established lending institutions even when they had sufficient income. This happened most frequently in racially mixed neighborhoods. In desperation, they frequently turned to speculative brokers who charged usurious fees, which fostered foreclosures, rapid turnover of homes, and further deterioration of housing stock. These developments did not occur in a vacuum. They resulted from recorded instances of redlining by leading banks with branches in the Rockaways, including the Jamaica Savings Bank and the Columbia Savings & Loan Association. Investigators from the New York City Commission on Human Rights systematically documented the way in which these banks drained funds from the Rockaways by receiving local deposits and then investing them outside the community.[14]

Despite the unnaturally inflated prices and the difficulties involved in obtaining mortgages, minority families, mainly African Americans and a lesser number of Puerto Ricans, began buying homes in the changing neighborhoods of the Rockaways. Small businessmen, working people, and civil servants wishing to escape ghetto areas of New York City saw the Rockaways as a marked improvement. The first black residents in the all-white sections of Arverne north of the el tended to be families of public employees: clerical service workers, postal employees, and police.[15] They liked the openness, clean air, and greater spaciousness of the peninsula, where their children had more room to play. Just like earlier generations, they enjoyed the boardwalk and the ocean. They frequently commented on the "small town" environment, where people tended to know each other.[16] Working-class African Americans first came to the Rockaways as residents of the area's housing projects. When they were later forced to move because their earnings took them over the income limit, or because the projects had become less safe, many decided to continue residing in the community. Children did not want to leave their friends, while adults had often developed strong attachments to a particular church. Congregants of Mt. Carmel Baptist, where Rev. Joseph May presided, were particularly loath to move away.[17] These families did their best to relocate somewhere else on the peninsula.

As an additional attraction, Rockaway contained reasonable accommodations for nonaffluent minorities. Local cooperative housing, mainly built under Mitchell Lama auspices, was racially integrated. If they could afford the prices, blacks with moderate incomes could also purchase houses being abandoned by whites. A stream of newcomers, including veterans—who had less difficulty obtaining mortgages—came to Rockaway, anxious to own their first homes. On the bay side of Arverne, a considerable number of one- and two-family houses were constructed, and minority families began buying them up.

Interestingly, these working- and lower-middle-class families of color, who moved to Rockaway voluntarily, were not deterred by the community's pockets of extreme poverty, which were as bad as or worse than those they left. In effect, these African Americans came to serve as a buffer between the poor minority population and middle-class whites residing on both ends of the peninsula. Whereas whites in the United States have generally tended to "move up" to more solidly middle-class areas at a distance from the difficulties associated with urban life, middle-class blacks have had fewer choices, since their housing options have been limited by racist real estate practices. For African Americans in Rockaway and elsewhere, residential segregation proved a more significant factor than class in determining where they would live and what they would experience, confining them to neighborhoods that proved deficient in public services.[18]

Black families who chose to move to the Rockaways hoped to improve opportunities for their children. For the most part, they were leaving segregated neighborhoods with poorly performing public schools. Some of them had been sending their children to parochial schools that maintained discipline and higher expectations for students. However, in the Rockaways during the 1950s, 1960s, and even later, parochial schools were not receptive to black applicants. Several parents told us that their children had been refused admission even when, in one case, a son gave evidence that he wished to study for the priesthood. Lacking alternatives, black newcomers enrolled their children in neighborhood public schools. As the peninsula's permanent population grew in the decades after World War II, these schools rapidly became overcrowded. By the spring of 1954, the *Wave* reported that Far Rockaway High School served twice as many students as the building had been designed to contain. Starting in the fall of that year, the school instituted double sessions.[19] It would take nineteen years and several delays before a second high school began to ease the pressure. Elementary schools in the middle of the peninsula suffered similar problems. P.S. 44 in Hammels, which served children from the deteriorating adjoining neighborhood and the nearby housing project, could not adequately provide a reasonable education to the community's children. Built around 1900, by midcentury the school had become a crumbling wreck. Beyond repair, the structure was torn down, and it was replaced around 1960 by another building several blocks closer to central Hammels (P.S. 183). Before long, this new school, with a large minority enrollment, would become the most overcrowded in the Rockaways. The student body, predominantly black and poor, soon fell behind academically.[20]

For the most part, the ethnic mix of Rockaway's elementary schools reflected the neighborhoods. Belle Harbor used its political influence to keep its P.S. 114 predominantly white. The school had the best supplies and the most experienced faculty on the peninsula. All attempts by civil rights groups to fully integrate the school failed. At most, the Board of Education granted individual variances to high-performing children who sought admission, but the process was made deliberately cumbersome. Only a handful of minority children benefited. Nonetheless, these exceptions permitted administrators to claim that the school was truly integrated and that busing was not needed.[21]

When Arverne lost its Jewish population and became an overwhelmingly minority community, its local school (P.S. 42) changed as well. By 1970, it had the second highest percentage of minority students in the peninsula (67 percent). It also qualified for Title I funds.[22] A similar phenomenon occurred in the elementary and junior high schools built to serve the Arverne and Edgemere projects. Initially, these schools kept standards high. But as the nearby projects became less integrated and largely a repository for families on welfare, they began to change. A portion of the new students came from fragile families, and their problems overwhelmed the schools that served them. Maintaining discipline and even personal security within the school building became major preoccupations. Students had to be warned about random gun shots from nearby buildings. Teachers tried to arrange their own arrivals and departures in groups. The quality of learning declined precipitously.[23]

Poverty and segregation had a negative effect on learning in the Rockaways. New York State Commissioner of Education James Allen Jr. stated in 1962 that schools with more than 50 percent minority pupils failed to provide equal educational opportunities.[24] Former teachers and parents active in Rockaway PTAs have described the disparities between predominantly black and white schools in books, paper, audio-visual equipment, and art and music supplies. During the three decades after the Second World War, almost all the administrators and teachers were white. While some teachers remained dedicated, others condescended toward the minority students now filling the classrooms, and still others were unmistakably racist. In junior high schools, children were tracked according to color, with African American students placed in the lowest classes.[25]

Kenneth B. Clark has written that "the central problem" in black schools was the teachers' assumption that the children were incapable of becoming educated. He saw this as a self-fulfilling prophecy: teachers' low expectations affected students' classroom performance.[26] Black parents who had children in Rockaway schools during these years have reported how teachers' racist attitudes detrimentally impacted their children's schooling.[27] In a 1971 poll of social agency personnel serving the Rockaways, almost 70 percent believed it was of "major importance" that "there is prejudice in schools against children living in Arverne." Black families shared this view and regarded the problem as urgent.[28] In many of the Rockaway public schools, the children were simply not learning. Five out of eight elementary schools had reading levels below city norms. In four of these, the minority population was 40 percent or more.[29]

During the 1960s, the most grievous cases of mismanaged education occurred at P.S. 106 in Edgemere. Its student body, over 85 percent minority by the end of the decade, consisted mostly of transient children whose families had been deposited by the welfare department in former summer houses along the beach blocks. Because of their frequent school changes, substandard living conditions, and family problems, these children required sympathetic teachers, individual attention, and the availability of special tutoring to succeed academically. Instead, they faced overcrowded classrooms and unsympathetic teachers who rarely attempted to maintain even minimal discipline. Parents noticed that bright children were not challenged and sometimes not even given homework assignments. Rather, they and their fellow students "were treated with disrespect." The school lacked basic equipment and supplies. A former teacher spoke of never seeing unmarked books, since all materials were discards from other schools. Math and reading labs were removed and not replaced. School lunches, provided daily for children from families receiving public assistance, consisted of peanut butter sandwiches.[30] Teachers and administrators blamed their inability to educate students on the children and their families. A weak PTA put very little pressure on those responsible, and conditions continued to deteriorate.

Middle-class black families moving into the area challenged the status quo. Prominent among them was Ernest Brown, an army veteran and an employee of the New York City Housing Authority. Brown looked forward to owning a home near the shore and offering his family a more comfortable life in Rockaway than had been possible in their Manhattan project apartment. When he and his wife encountered the unacceptable state of affairs at P.S. 106, they decided to become active. In 1966, Ernest Brown was elected president of the PTA. Before long, he began to discover the origins of the school's difficulties. To begin with, Brown learned that P.S. 106 was considered an annex of P.S. 215, a well-supplied, almost all-white school in nearby Briar Place, Far Rockaway. Title I funds, which should have gone to his daughter's school to pay for reading specialists, went instead to P.S. 215. The principal there exercised ultimate control, while the Edgemere school only warranted an assistant principal. No student from the annex could ever gain admission to the superior parent school.

These conditions did not come about by chance; they had been arranged by "responsible authorities" in the early 1960s, when the local NAACP began protesting against segregation in Rockaway schools, threatening boycotts and other civil actions. The local school board at that point offered a compromise. The board, in what would become known informally as the tri-school agreement, divided the overwhelmingly black Redfern students among three Far Rockaway schools, one of which was P.S. 215.[31] (Busing to P.S. 114 in Belle Harbor was out of the question because the residents there would never tolerate more than token integration.) Perhaps because it was generally believed that urban renewal would soon eliminate the welfare population who occupied beach housing, and thus P.S. 106's main source of enrollment, the school was considered expendable. This arrangement was implemented shortly before the Brown family moved to Edgemere.

Ernest Brown insists that school integration was not his primary mission. In addition, decentralization of schools, a key issue elsewhere at this time, had little relevance for the Rockaways. District boundaries encompassed other Queens neighborhoods as well as the peninsula. Moreover, school board elections were usually won by either candidates representing the position of the teachers' union or a "parochial slate." Many Rockaway parents felt that neither faction had a genuine interest in improving peninsular public schools.[32] From the beginning, Brown realized that the only way to upgrade the quality of education for his children and his neighbors' children was to mobilize parental support. However, the principal of P.S. 215 refused to meet either with him or with any delegation from Edgemere. Nor did the revitalized PTA receive any satisfaction from either the local board or the city's central school administration at 110 Livingston Street.

Brown and his neighbors did not give up, and the struggle lasted four years. By 1970, several one-day school strikes had taken place, fully supported by parents. During these strikes, makeshift storefront schools provided temporary classes, especially important for families whose adult members worked. Some of the "militant" mothers who earned their living locally as domestics were threatened with the loss of their jobs. Brown claims that several were actually fired. Nonetheless, he believes that the final outcome justified the sacrifice. When antipoverty funding became available, the community provided job training for these mothers, enabling them to obtain employment in local health care facilities.[33] In the end the PTA won, and P.S. 106 became an independent school with its own principal. Class size was reduced. New supplies suddenly appeared, including a well-stocked library. Neglectful teachers were encouraged to transfer. A salaried person now served as permanent liaison between the parents and the school. Grades five and six from the Edgemere school were permanently assigned to P.S. 215.[34]

The one high school in Rockaway presented an additional problem. No educational institution had symbolized the former cohesiveness of the community as well as Far Rockaway High School (FRHS). Located in the middle-class section of Wavecrest, from the outset the school projected a distinctly suburban style. The Nobel Prize–winning physicist Richard Feynman was a FRHS graduate, and alumni in later years would extol its high academic standards. However, during the 1940s and early 1950s the school's social aspect often took precedence over academics. Popular students were admitted to fraternities and sororities. Teenagers from the various sections of the peninsula mixed easily, regardless of social class. Many people formed lasting friendships, and high school couples frequently married. FRHS helped promote a community spirit for the entire peninsula.

As the ethnic and economic composition of the Rockaways began to change, so did the character of the high school. The various sections of the peninsula withdrew into defensive postures, frequently in conflict with one another, and the school reflected this pattern. Youngsters from different communities became more cliquish. Students in the late 1950s and the 1960s were less likely to mix with those from different backgrounds and neighborhoods than their predecessors had been. FRHS had always had a small number of African American students. When the first housing projects were constructed, children from working-class and middle-class backgrounds assimilated readily. Academic standards were maintained and a high percentage of graduates went on to college. However, as the welfare population of the peninsula grew, and with it the number of young people from troubled families, the school had difficulty adjusting. Often these teenagers were not academically motivated. The faculty, almost exclusively white, had difficulty relating to a black student body. They had become accustomed to traditional teaching styles and compliant pupils and found themselves unable to cope with difficult behavioral problems. Some administrators tried to maintain standards, but a significant portion of the staff, either lacking empathy for minority students or harboring racist sentiments, had no desire to remain in a changing environment and transferred out.[35]

The final blow to FRHS's stature came when a second high school opened in 1973. Specializing in oceanography, Beach Channel High School (BCHS), located further west down the peninsula, started with generous funding. Students were encouraged to attend summer enrichment programs. The city supplied the school with boats to study the nearby waterways. Designated a magnet school, with an imaginative interdisciplinary curriculum, BCHS attracted the best students from the peninsula and even from other parts of New York City. FRHS suffered accordingly.[36] The establishment of a separate high school led to a loss of the sense of unity that the single school had provided. White, middle-class students from western sections, now assigned to the new school closer to their homes, had less to do with the rest of the peninsula and the people living there. Suddenly, FRHS became more of a minority school than ever before. Contacts between diverse communities became increasingly rare.

The dispensations given to the new high school did not last indefinitely. When New York's budget crisis hit in the mid-1970s, all public institutions faced drastic reductions. Forced to make choices, the Board of Education maintained adequate funding only for certain high schools. Reflecting the municipal government's attitude toward the Rockaways, the peninsula's one special school was considered expendable. Symbolically, BCHS could no longer maintain its boats. It also lost backing for the celebrated programs that appealed to gifted students. Before long, the new Rockaway high school came to resemble the older one.

The quality of an area's schools affects its demographics as well as its property values. Affluent families with young children will give up on a community if they do not believe it provides an adequate education, and, for the most part, outsiders who have other choices will not want to buy in. As local schools came to be perceived as troubled, many white middle-class families moved out of the Rockaways, frequently to adjoining Nassau County or to less expensive places further east on Long Island. Most black families did not have these options. Orthodox Jews were able to benefit from the decline of property values in the Rockaways. They bought homes at depressed prices and established Jewish parochial schools (yeshivas) that posed a new challenge to public education on the peninsula. In general, the existence of subpar public schools increases the demand for religious schools of all types. This, in turn, tends to hasten the exodus of students from public schools. A small number of secular Jewish families who chose to remain in the Rockaways also began sending their children to yeshivas. Similarly, as the Irish population declined, Catholic parochial schools slowly began accepting minority children. In 1950, there were five parochial schools in the Rockaways, four Catholic and one Jewish. In 1971, Dr. Doris Moss found an ongoing exodus from public to parochial institutions. By the end of the century, eleven Jewish and five Catholic schools were listed in the peninsula.[37]

In the postwar period, many Jews moved out of the Rockaways and a large number of other Jews moved in. During the 1960s, Jewish residents of the middle sections of the peninsula began leaving, and within a short time they were gone. With few exceptions, those who remained lived either in Belle Harbor and Neponsit to the west or Bayswater and Far Rockaway to the east. Some years earlier, a trickle of Orthodox, having found this beach community a congenial place to live, inconspicuously began settling in the southeastern part of Far Rockaway. Additional inducements included a yeshiva, the Hebrew Institute of Long Island, along with kosher butchers. Orthodox synagogues were already established.

The first Orthodox families to arrive left areas in Brooklyn, like Borough Park, that could no longer absorb their large families. Later on, religious Jews abandoned Brownsville and East New York when these Brooklyn neighborhoods underwent the transition from white to black, and they mostly settled in Far Rockaway. A little later, younger, more affluent Orthodox left Williamsburg and Crown Heights for the same reasons: they were uncomfortable with the influx of African Americans and Hispanics. Some moved to suburbs such as Monsey in Rockland County. Far Rockaway also seemed a place where they could reproduce the life they lived in Brooklyn.[38] Before long, ultra-Orthodox groups, seeking to establish their exclusive congregations, moved in and set up their own synagogues and yeshivas. Occasionally, a dynamic Rabbi would bring his followers along with him. By the 1970s, large numbers of Orthodox lived in the Rockaways along with a smattering of Hasidim.

The new Jewish section developed an identity separate from the rest of the community. Eruvs, the lines marking an area in which Orthodox Jews may conduct certain activities normally forbidden on the Sabbath, were constructed in Far Rockaway and later in Belle Harbor and Neponsit. Rabbinically supervised kosher shops closed on Friday nights and Saturdays but remained open on Sundays. New Orthodox synagogues and yeshivas were established. Mikvas, the ritual baths chiefly for women, proliferated. Reform and conservative Jews who could not function comfortably in an environment dominated by the Orthodox began to move away. Because the Jewish community of Far Rockaway bordered on the Five Towns of Nassau County, which also witnessed an increase in Orthodox families, property values eventually escalated. Not wishing to identify with a declining Rockaway, residents started calling their section "West Lawrence," emphasizing its connection with affluent Lawrence, Long Island. As this book was being written, the U.S. post office, responding to the neighborhood's political influence, was about to make their designation official.[39] Still, Far Rockaway homeowners benefited from the lower property taxes of New York City.

When rising crime rates began to affect their neighborhoods, Jewish leaders decided not to rely on the police department, which they regarded as unsympathetic to their concerns. Beginning in 1967, they formed their own security association, called the Maccabees, and began night patrols. A Jewish Defense League (JDL) chapter appeared a few years later, providing escort services for the elderly.[40] Occasionally incidents erupted between Jewish and black youths, when some of the former became overzealous in their challenges to "outsiders." As tension between the two groups increased, level heads in both the African American and Jewish communities worked out a modus vivendi.[41] Part of the informal understanding pertained to geographical demarcations. It became generally known that Beach 9th Street served as a dividing point in Far Rockaway. Jews would live to the east of that line and blacks west of it. New housing developments in the Jewish area appeared at a rapid rate to make room for an ever-expanding Orthodox population.

In the early 1970s, a Jewish Community Council of the Rockaway Peninsula appeared. Committed to Orthodox observance, it made contact with like-minded groups throughout New York City. Believing that the

best hope for rejuvenating the Rockaways was to add to the number of religious Jews on the peninsula, the council encouraged home sellers to list
property with it or with Jewish Centers. Religious Jewish buyers were
promised rapid sales and fair prices. Another successful campaign alerted
Russian Jewish refugees to the advantages of living in the Rockaways,
which resembled Brighton Beach, Brooklyn's "Little Odessa." By offering
inducements such as assistance in obtaining apartments in middle-income
high-rises near the ocean and subsidized parochial school fees, the council
brought hundreds of Russian Jews to the Wavecrest section of Far Rockaway. (In recent years the Jewish Community Council has become a more
ecumenical organization.)

Over the years, smaller Orthodox and Hasidic communities emerged
in other sections of the Rockaways, including Bayswater, Belle Harbor,
and Neponsit. They also set up synagogues, yeshivas, mikvas, and kosher
shopping facilities. The people in these enclaves share a separatist identity;
their communal and religious interests take precedence over matters involving the general good of the peninsula. They rarely mix with the diverse groups of the Rockaways, and they maintain a hostile truce with other residents that intensifies when their volunteer security forces become too
aggressive or when they protest against those who publicly interrupt observance of the sabbath or Jewish holidays. With some exceptions, the Orthodox show little interest in community-wide concerns.

Around the same time that an Orthodox population was putting down
strong roots in the Rockaways, an energized African American population
emerged, conscious of its own needs and no longer reluctant to express
them publicly. Much of the momentum came from families who had only
recently arrived. Among these newcomers were people who had been engaged in the civil rights movement in neighborhoods such as Bedford-
Stuyvesant and Harlem. Like Ernest Brown, they tended to get their start
in PTAs, since ensuring that their children received a proper education required constant vigilance. They did not depend on older organizations to
accomplish their aims. Rather, they had to create a new kind of activism.

Many of the early activists were black women. Those with domestic
responsibilities served as "block captains" or liaisons with community organizations. Church-based, almost all of them joined religious leaders such
as Rev. May in performing tasks that might be described as social work.
Their efforts were mainly voluntary, but where financial need existed, they
sometimes received nominal remuneration. They oversaw activities for the

elderly, helped with tutoring programs, and assisted pregnant women, youths in trouble, and the infirm. At a minimum, by providing transportation to church functions and voting booths, they helped people to remain attached to the institutions and goals of the black community.[42]

In the old days, politics had been monopolized by whites, with the exception of a few machine politicians such as Leonard Scarbrough. With the encouragement of leaders of the NAACP and the Council for Relocation and Slum Prevention, vigorous voter registration campaigns began. African Americans began joining Democratic Party clubs and forming coalitions with liberal whites. A number of black women assumed leadership positions in the Women's International League for Peace and Freedom and Women's Strike for Peace. African Americans began serving as poll watchers, a sign that they had gained a small measure of influence. Before long, minority candidates ran in school board elections and, eventually, for important positions on the New York City Council and the New York State Assembly. Victories did not come easily, but these early campaigns taught valuable lessons that would bear fruit in the 1980s and 1990s.[43]

Puerto Ricans constituted the other minority group that lived in the peninsula during the 1960s. Numbering just a few thousand during these years, they were later joined by immigrants from Central America and other parts of the Caribbean. By 1980, Hispanics increased to eleven percent of the total population, and this figure continues to grow every year.[44] Stores and bodegas serve their special requirements. Although Spanish-speaking churches in the peninsula favor immigration and encourage participation, Hispanics have tended to be divided and, with their relatively small numbers, do not as yet have the political impact of the other groups.

By the 1960s, most year-round Irish American residents had moved out of Seaside, although one of the last surviving summer bungalow colonies on the peninsula is in the old neighborhood of "Irishtown." Many of the people who rent for the summer are the descendants of Irish families who rented in the Rockaways for several generations.[45] The more affluent Irish Americans moved westward into Rockaway Park and Belle Harbor and remain connected to the St. Francis de Sales church. These communities, along with Breezy Point, became home to New York City firefighters, police officers, and retired civil servants. Tragically, a large contingent of the heroic firefighters who lost their lives in the World Trade Center disaster came from the Irish sections of the Rockaways. The cohesion of this community was revealed in the aftermath of 9/11, and in the second tragedy to befall them, the plane crash of 12 November 2001. Parishioners sought comfort from their local churches as they attended a seemingly endless number of funeral services.[46]

A Memorial Day parade is still held in the Rockaways, although it is more abbreviated than it was in the past. A massive parade on St. Patrick's Day, with approximately one thousand participants, is guaranteed regardless of the weather. The annual Irish Festival, which always drew huge crowds to Seaside and served as another statement of the continued Irish presence, has recently been suspended—reportedly because of the ban on outdoor alcohol consumption. There is hope that it may be resumed in the near future.[47] Only on these latter occasions do residents of gated Breezy Point come out in substantial numbers to join in a broader peninsula-wide activity. While the Irish community remains cohesive, it lacks substantial ongoing communication with other peninsular groups. On the other hand, in the mid-1980s a few liberal priests began reaching out, and an Interfaith Clergy Council was established, consisting mainly of Catholics and Reform Jews.[48] The opportunities for this kind of cooperation will probably decline, since the Jewish population has become increasingly Orthodox, and many Reform Jews have left the area.

In recent years, residents of affluent neighborhoods have tended to obfuscate their connection with the peninsula by identifying their home communities as West Lawrence, Belle Harbor, or Neponsit, instead of stating that they come from the Rockaways as their predecessors had done. People who live in Breezy Point, of course, have long had this attitude. The schisms that developed over the past decades have served to undermine the Rockaway identity that once prevailed, especially among whites. This has weakened the peninsula's ability to negotiate with the city government on matters that impact its overall quality of life. The current fragmentation did not always appear inevitable. In 1966, hope of reviving a sense of belonging for the Rockaways rose when John V. Lindsay took office as mayor. His campaign slogan had been "He is fresh and everyone else is tired,"[49] but his administration would face problems created by decades of failed policies on the peninsula. Nevertheless, his election left many in Rockaway feeling optimistic about their future.

CHAPTER 11

The 310 Acres

The election of John V. Lindsay as mayor in November 1965, after two decades of Democratic Party rule, offered a promise that politics as usual would no longer characterize municipal life. The previous three-term mayor, Robert F. Wagner Jr., had been a cautious executive who balanced various interest groups through compromise, avoiding sharp political conflicts. As a result, however, certain basic issues were given piecemeal treatment. Throughout most of his two terms in office, Mayor Lindsay initiated new projects, showing an innovative flare and a willingness to take risks. He is also credited with bringing neglected constituencies into municipal politics, including a large segment of the urban poor.[1] Unlike Wagner, Lindsay chose to make frequent trips to the Rockaways, walking the streets and mingling with the local population. Once, after dedicating a park, he played tennis on the new courts, and, during his first mayoral campaign, he visited Rockaway beach clubs and was even photographed diving into a swimming pool.[2]

Showing his disdain for the peninsula's establishment, Lindsay refused several requests from the Chamber of Commerce to contribute to the *Rockaway Review*, a formality dutifully performed every year by all of his predecessors. The mayor cited the "pressure of official duties."[3] The implication of Lindsay's refusal was clear: the chamber—whose former executive secretary, the effective George Wolpert, had retired several years earlier—had lost its political clout and would no longer be consulted on peninsular matters. The new Republican mayor preferred dealing directly with ordinary people, or at least he gave that impression. Lindsay also spoke about local control, which implied that, if they wished to exercise influence, diverse groups on the peninsula would be forced to interact. They might even have to learn to cooperate. But regarding the Rockaways, the central problem facing the new administration was the question of the 310 acres along the ocean earmarked for urban renewal by Lindsay's predecessor. The resolution of this crucial issue might well determine the next stage of Rockaway history.

Robert Moses had long had an idea about how to deal with the 310 acres, but by 1966 his influence had greatly diminished. From 1950 to 1965, under his direction, New York had managed to receive more than half the urban renewal funds in the country. During this period, the city eliminated almost one-third of its substandard housing, while "the total stock of housing units increased by almost 18 percent."[4] As already noted, the original 1949 Title I legislation permitted the U.S. government to provide money to municipalities for slum clearance and urban renewal as long as local taxpayers shared a portion of the cost, usually about one-third. In most cities the authorities condemned the slums, relocated residents, razed the area, and then turned over the abandoned property to private developers. The purchaser was then supposed to build a project that followed a comprehensive local plan for orderly future growth.[5]

In New York City, however, Moses argued that private contractors and financial institutions would be wary of such undertakings. He preferred to negotiate with prospective investors in private and to proceed only after a comprehensive agreement had been worked out. At that point the redevelopment area would be turned over to the developer, with all buildings standing and tenants continuing to pay rent. The new owner was charged with the responsibility for clearing the site and relocating families and businesses. This unique "Moses method" was responsible for the success of Title I in New York, although its creator was later blamed for relocation problems as well as corruption scandals in connection with these developments. Other municipalities throughout the country emptied high-poverty areas before completing construction arrangements and then encountered difficulties in finding interested investors.[6] As a result, large, empty tracts of land, the sites of former slums, remained vacant in St. Louis, Buffalo, and Detroit. In the 1970s, years after Moses and his distinctive approach to slum clearance had disappeared from the New York scene, the 310 acres—a two-mile-long section of Rockaway bordering the ocean—became one of the largest such undeveloped urban renewal sites in the United States.

Beginning in the early 1960s, Moses had warned about the impracticality of declaring Arverne an urban renewal area. Wagner administration officials ignored him. When Lindsay came to power, his administration rejected the Moses method as symptomatic of top-down, undemocratic machine politics. But Moses did not give up easily. As late as 1967 and 1968, the diminished Power Broker again advocated his previous plan of building an extension of the Shore Parkway along the beach all the way to Far Rockaway and the Atlantic Beach Bridge and then proceeding with housing redevelopment. This time Albany was willing to allocate funding as part of the state arterial system; nevertheless, the project still required city approval. Moses argued that the new road would make the eastern sections of the Rockaways more accessible to the public; he proposed expanding the beach, adding new playgrounds, rest areas, and parking fields. An inportant aspect of his plan was the initiation of slum clearance. In a special appeal made in 1967 to the new commissioner of parks, August Heckscher, Moses reminded his successor: "You have the responsibility to give our citizens the best possible recreational facilities."[7] However, these arguments failed to impress those who now exercised power in New York City.

Mayor Wagner had bequeathed to the Lindsay administration Arverne's designation (along with the beach blocks of Edgemere) as an Urban Renewal District. His administration had done virtually nothing in the intervening year to improve the area's terrible living conditions, which continued to deteriorate. Lindsay officials believed that they had no alternative but to follow the urban renewal initiative set in motion by their predecessors. As Don Elliot, the city planning commissioner under Lindsay, recalled, "Nobody could figure out what else to do."[8] Arverne had some of the most deplorable housing stock in New York. In 1966, district attorney Nat H. Hentel called it "the worst part of our city." The chief inspector for the Queens Office of Buildings described the area as "a near hopeless case."[9] Clearly, something had to be done. The original Wagner report on urban renewal offered vague guidelines for receiving federal financing to make this section viable again, as both "a residential community" and as a resort with fully realized "recreational value." Few specifics had ever been spelled out, although the November 1964 statement did mention "a renewal plan" that was to be used.[10]

When the new municipal administration took over in January 1966, everyone concerned about the Rockaways agreed that a plan of action needed to be devised before proceeding further. Lindsay, wishing to establish a fresh intellectual impetus in urban affairs, welcomed the development of such a plan. Business groups in Rockaway fully concurred.[11] Shortly after taking office, the mayor named a Resort Amusement Advisory Committee to look into ways of "achieving the best possible year round economy" for the Rockaways and Coney Island. New York had just received a federal grant of $800,000 "for planning and surveying the Arverne urban renewal area."[12] In turn, the new City Planning Commission set in motion an agenda for all of New York City that contained an extensive section on the Rockaways and the Arverne Urban Renewal Project. It specifically referred to "preliminary proposals and plans [for Arverne] which now are being reviewed by several city agencies, including the City Planning Commission."[13] A few years later the Department of City Planning produced another report, dealing exclusively with the Rockaways, "to set the tone for future action."[14] These municipal publications complemented elaborate reports commissioned by the office of the Borough President of Queens.[15] In addressing the problems that beset the peninsula, these studies set similar goals:

1. To eliminate the slums and then offer adequate housing for low- and middle-income tenants, primarily on-site residents
2. To develop the recreational potential of the peninsula for year-round use
3. To involve tenant and community participation in planning the renewal project

This last point was especially relevant to the Lindsay approach to governing, but few specifics were offered.[16]

Concerned parties soon recognized the absence of particulars. In February 1967, Governor Nelson Rockefeller held up a bill calling for acquisition of slum property in Rockaway on the grounds that "the urban renewal plans were indefinite."[17] More than three years later, when details of urban renewal for Arverne were finally published, editorials in the *Wave* complained about their vagueness, indicating that—even at this late date—the planners did not have a precise blueprint for carrying out the renewal scheme. "It seems unbelievable," the same paper lamented after three more months had passed, that "local residents have not yet seen a plan showing what the project will look like."[18] Of the plethora of expensive and time consuming reports produced every few years, none contained an agenda for action. Although Arverne was officially given "priority status" a few months after Lindsay assumed office in January 1966, nothing happened for more than a year. The Board of Estimate approved Arverne as "an early action site" in April 1967, giving the government a green light to proceed.[19] The following month, Lindsay applied for initial federal funding for the project.[20] All these official plans and reports disappeared from view shortly after being completed; none of them had any lasting consequences. In the meantime, the situation in the Rockaways continued to go downhill.

The delays in setting urban renewal in motion indicated that, despite their many public statements, Lindsay administration officials did not consider Rockaway a priority. Many years later, former officials admitted as much, acknowledging that even Coney Island came before the Rockaways in their estimation.[21] Whenever funds became available, they found better reasons to target places like the South Bronx or Brownsville.[22] For them, Arverne represented a situation out of control, without a viable solution. They rejected Moses's approach, which had its own set of problems, but all the alternatives they could think of seemed equally bad. Even when construction companies were willing to start the development process on their own, the administration resisted on the grounds that such an operation resembled the undemocratic Moses method. Among other things, Lindsay feared the repetition of relocation horror stories that had turned public opinion against other slum clearance projects.[23] While his officials wanted their administration to be more responsible and humane, they realized that the public housing projected for Rockaway did not contain enough apartments for all the site tenants. Moreover, almost all were welfare recipients who faced eligibility restrictions. Plans might call for "standard housing in good neighborhoods," but where in New York could poor minorities find such apartments? And what kinds of buildings would replace the derelict summer rookeries? Title I guidelines mandated low-income housing for Arverne, along with middle-income and even some luxury dwellings. Would affluent or middle-class renters care to reside in close proximity to poor people of color? Schools would be needed, but given the exodus of white families from the public school system in the Rockaways, would these new ones immediately become segregated? New services would be required, but where would the money be found to pay for these in addition to the schools?

An official land use plan released in 1968 called for "provision of as many units as feasible of new housing for low and moderate income families, built to high standards of construction and design," as well as "creation of an overall environment of the highest possible quality to meet the needs of the Arverne development area."[24] This statement illustrates the amorphousness of the stated goals for Arverne. The fuzziness of the guidelines, along with the delays, fed into the conflicting desires of Rockaway organizations and neighborhood clubs that had grown over time. While civil rights advocates wanted more low-income projects for the minority poor, white business groups wished to remove this population from the peninsula in order to clear the way for luxury buildings. One attempt by the Housing and Redevelopment Board to hold an open community meeting in February 1967, for discussion of urban renewal, ended in chaos. A *Long Island Press* headline, "Meeting Shatters Arverne Project United Front," summed it up.[25] Subsequently, a community advisory council was appointed, but it operated under a "gag rule" and does not seem to have been privy to any official information.[26] Community participation ironically became the first casualty of the Lindsay approach in the Rockaways.

Meanwhile, the tragic fate of Hammels was visited on Arverne. The number of derelict summer houses occupied year-round grew in number. By 1969, approximately 1,700 families were officially listed as living in the 310 acres scheduled for urban renewal. It was estimated that 89 percent were black and 10 percent Puerto Rican. Almost all of them received regular welfare payments.[27] With few exceptions, the shacks lacked minimum amenities, including adequate heat. The extensive delays only made things worse, since no incentive existed to repair buildings awaiting condemnation. Many landlords stopped paying taxes, enabling the city to quickly acquire these properties. Scores of boarded-up homes began to appear throughout the area. On the average, twenty antiquated boilers broke down each week in 1970, according to one report.[28] The creation of an on-site urban renewal office had little effect. As far as the community was concerned, its most important function was to serve as a focal point for various protest demonstrations.

Jason R. Nathan, the administrator of the Housing and Development Administration, visited Arverne in the fall of 1967 and spoke of "the ugliness of block after block of crumbling houses." He found it "almost impossible to tell which of the buildings with broken or boarded windows, sagging porches and sinking foundations are occupied or abandoned." Nathan went on to describe what happened to Holiday House, a former luxury hotel:

> Now it is a rooming house for the poor, as are so many other hous-
> es in the community. It is a display case for almost every violation
> on the books: cracked walls, falling plaster, sagging floors, dan-
> gerous wiring, deteriorated plumbing, and a sinking foundation. It
> was vacated this year by order of the Fire department. The story
> of Holiday House is not unusual in Arverne.[29]

In this instance, residents were removed from the premises, a rare occurrence. All too often, fires broke out before inspectors declared buildings unsafe, accelerating deterioration and sometimes causing injuries and deaths.[30] Fires became such a regular feature of the Arverne scene during the late 1960s that firefighters responsible for the district could find little time for rest while on duty. Assignment to the Rockaways was said to be a punishment for those who had trouble with superiors at other stations. Offenders found themselves shipped off to what firemen called "Siberia," a label given by mainlanders (and Arthur Miller's police officer in "The Price") to this remote community with its unpleasant reputation.[31]

Many Arverne children suffered from lead poisoning. In 1970 alone there were two hundred cases, sixty-three serious enough to require hospitalization.[32] Most of these children returned to their contaminated apartments after treatment. Other diseases began afflicting neighborhood children as well. A *Long Island Press* headline in late 1969 read: "Rats and Garbage Where Children Play." The story described how "litter of every sort lines the streets where youngsters play in garbage strewn and rat infested lots."[33] Crime was endemic to the area, victimizing chiefly the poor and helpless. And still the Lindsay administration delayed.

Mayor Lindsay came out to the Rockaways on several occasions. He was always at his best walking the streets, talking to people, and listening to their concerns. His presence impressed members of the minority community, since no previous mayor had ever shown the slightest interest in them. Some Lindsay admirers argue that his visibility helped to prevent race riots in New York during the late 1960s, when they were erupting in other parts of the country.[34] Rockaway was actually pinpointed by the mayor's troubleshooters as one of the New York City neighborhoods likely to have a riot during the summer of 1967, but nothing happened. Unfortunately, aside from his expressions of interest in the community, which temporarily helped to lift morale, Lindsay's visits had no practical effect on the burning questions affecting the peninsula, including the fate of the 310 acres.

Previous New York City Title I projects, including the one in Hammels, encountered major relocation difficulties.[35] This time officials did not wish to rehouse tenants off-site. However, their approach caused its own set of problems. Minority spokespeople, alarmed by the decay of Arverne, protested the failure to ensure proper heating, the high incidence of lead poisoning, and the lack of minimum services. African American organizations conducted frequent sit-ins at the project office.[36] Business leaders began to speak out as well. They worried that the terrible conditions in Arverne reflected badly on the entire community, and they publicly condemned Lindsay for making a bad situation worse.[37] The Lindsay administration, for its part, feared that urban redevelopment would once again create new slums. "We are determined to avoid shifting families from one site to another," spokesmen told reporters in 1966.[38] With the support of Queens Borough President Cariello, who had given his approval as early as 1964, officials planned a new federally financed low-income project to be built on the peninsula. For various reasons, however, including a late completion date, occupancy of the Beach 41st Street Houses did not begin until 1973, and the project housed only a handful of Arverne families.[39]

The Lindsay administration did offer one innovation: it divided the large Arverne-Edgemere renewal area into three separate and approximately equal sections, labeled Arverne I, Arverne II East, and Arverne II West. Stages of development were to be staggered, with acquisition of land beginning in one section at a time. Buildings would be evaluated, and those deemed viable would be rehabilitated, thus permitting displaced families to be rehoused in them temporarily. The rest of the buildings would be demolished. New housing would be constructed to provide permanent accommodations for the original residents. In the second section the cycle would be repeated.[40] However, New York City did not begin acquiring the property until the autumn of 1967, three years after the urban renewal designation. Final acquisition of all the land did not take place until January 1970.[41] The various postponements ensured that only a handful of existing structures would ever be salvaged.

As they attempted the process of rehabilitation, city engineers found few precedents for the improvement of such old structures, and work dragged on. The chairman of the Housing Authority, Al Walsh, had to constantly circumvent the restrictive regulations set down by civil service unions. Whenever a rehabilitated building received approval, as many families as possible would be moved into the repaired structure, while the condemned buildings were torn down.[42] However, drug addicts in the area began stealing fixtures such as pipes and wiring from the new dwellings. Within a short time, the renovated residences reverted to their former state, or they became even worse.[43] Rehabilitation clearly did not work in such circumstances. Critics accused the Lindsay administration, now in its second term, of failing to keep its promises. They maintained that "not a single building has been rehabilitated anywhere in Arverne."[44]

In a last-ditch effort, the planners proposed the use of prefabricated mobile homes. This policy, first suggested in November 1970, was adopted by the Housing Development Office at the beginning of March 1971. Within a few days, the sanitation department started clearing a five-block area near the beach.[45] For the first time, administration spokesmen acknowledged that "tenants are suffering" and "need help now" and that "nothing could be worse than present living conditions." Preference for the trailers would be given to site residents who had large numbers of children and presently lived in the most derelict buildings.[46] Except for Rockaway's business leaders, the new plan won immediate approval. The mayor spoke in favor of it. Influential Queens politicians, such as the future borough president Donald Manes, quickly joined in with their applause. The proposal gained the support of Rev. May and other local civil rights leaders, on the grounds that no other alternative existed. The Rockaway Health Council, condemning the "drastically unhealthy conditions" existing on the site, signed on as well. When the City Planning Commission voted by a large margin to change zoning rules, thereby permitting mobile homes to be placed in Arverne, all paths seemed clear.[47]

Just as the Housing Development Office was making preparations for the mobile homes, they were stopped short by the dominant African American leader in New York City politics, Manhattan Borough President Percy Sutton. In a prepared statement delivered in April 1971, Sutton began by acknowledging the tragic situation in the Rockaways, admitting that "there is probably no area in the city where residents live under more desperate conditions than in the Arverne Renewal Area." Nonetheless, he contended that relocating families into trailers set "a dangerous precedent" because in New York City temporary arrangements have a way of becoming permanent. Unwilling to oppose Sutton, the Board of Estimate killed the mobile homes policy a month later.[48] Neither Sutton nor the Board of Estimate offered any other plan to help the Arverne site's families. The board members, mainly Democrats voting with Sutton, ignored a petition signed by residents urging mobile homes because "another winter in these houses would seriously threaten the health of our children."[49] This setback to municipal housing policy in the far-off Rockaways received scant public notice and caused the Lindsay administration no political embarrassment. But the suffering of site tenants continued unabated.

The late 1960s and early 1970s witnessed a growing exodus of working- and lower-middle-class families from low-income projects, including those in Rockaway, thereby providing space for others.[50] A certain number of the Arverne tenants had been on waiting lists for public housing, and a few hundred managed to fill vacancies as these became available. Likewise, a handful of residents were eligible for Mitchell Lama buildings that mandated a percentage of low-income families. However, most of those who left the site found housing on their own, generally in substandard dwellings. By the spring of 1971, when the Board of Estimate rejected the mobile homes plan, approximately 550 families still resided in the area.[51] The rest of the 1,700 originally tabulated had simply moved away. Those who stayed behind in 1971 now occupied a deserted landscape, and soon they were forced out as well. Once more, converted rooming houses and bungalows became the chief resource for those needing to be rehoused. The effort to find alternatives to the much-assailed Moses method never produced any viable solutions. The Lindsay policies had merely repeated the familiar cycle of expanding blight.

The percentage of families on welfare living in the eastern sections of the peninsula multiplied at this time. Not all of them had been displaced from Arverne. Many came from crowded neighborhoods outside the community, and, as was frequently the case, a relatively high proportion of those consisted of individuals and families hard to place elsewhere. In October 1971, a *Wave* headline read: "Start of New Slum Area in Far Rockaway Feared." The accompanying story reported instances of "finders fees" paid by the welfare department.[52] The next year, the Borough President's office claimed that a total of 7,800 welfare clients lived in the Rockaways. Residents came to believe that Lindsay's Human Resources Administration, despite the name change, repeated practices associated with Wagner's welfare department and its predecessors.[53]

By the early 1970s, only a small amount of housing stock for summer visitors remained. It stood close to the ocean in Wavecrest and Far Rockaway and along the bay in Edgemere. More substantial year-round homes nearby lost their white, middle-class tenants and began renting to poorer people, chiefly African Americans and Puerto Ricans. The peninsula's minority population expanded rapidly in the 1970s, when the total number of people living in the Rockaways approached 100,000. (This figure remained fairly constant for decades, although in recent years it has increased.) The major change during the 1970s occurred in the growing ratio of black to white and in family income. By 1990, almost 55 percent of residents were either African American or Puerto Rican. In the same year, more than 40 percent of those in three Rockaway census tracts lived below the poverty line.[54]

The increase in poor people toward the eastern end of Rockaway had an impact on its businesses. Despite the peninsula's permanent population more than doubling since World War II, the purchasing power of customers declined. With the end of the peninsula's resort function, the profits derived from an enlarged summer clientele disappeared along with the tourists. Local businesses also suffered from high rents, New York City taxes, and competition from new malls. Many shops on Central Avenue (Beach 20th St.) in Far Rockaway and on B. 116th St. in Rockaway Park simply closed their doors, while those that remained sold cheaper goods. Clothing and appliance stores, along with car dealerships, shut down around this time. One after another, Far Rockaway's three movie theatres closed, as did the others on the peninsula.[55] One of the reasons for diminishing business was the reduction or elimination of evening store hours in Far Rockaway's main business district. Safety considerations forced shoppers and shop owners to exercise caution. Scare headlines in the local press from the late 1960s on—"Crime Here on Increase," "New Patrolmen Ordered to Control Night Muggings," "New Crime Wave Causing Concern"—reinforced public apprehension and hastened the middle-class exodus from certain adjoining streets.[56] Superficial remedies, such as repaved sidewalks, improved lighting, and talk of a volunteer anticrime patrol, had little effect. Fear also took its toll on what remained of Rockaway's status as a resort.[57] The elimination of the double subway fare in 1975 did not have any noticeable impact on either tourism or business. The Off Track Betting

(OTB) office in Far Rockaway closed in the early 1980s. Its closure symbolized that this area of New York had become poorer than poor. Outsiders talked about the "wreckage" of Rockaway as a viable neighborhood.[58]

The early 1970s were difficult years for the Rockaways. Bad storms during the winter of 1970–71 led to severe beach erosion. By 1973 at least fourteen blocks of beach had completely disappeared, and the oceanfront had to be closed to the public. The boardwalk, now rotting away, had become a dangerous wreck.[59] Beach restoration, along with promised boardwalk repair, was minimal. Two separate articles in the *Long Island Press* suggested the improbability of reviving recreation in Rockaway. One, in November 1974, reported that "Mayor Beame called on President Ford to restore $2 million in impounded funds for beach sand replenishment in the Rockaways." This was less than a year before Ford sent his notorious "Drop Dead" message to New York City. A year later, the newspaper's headline proclaimed, "Redecking of Boardwalk Halted Due to City's Serious Fiscal Situation."[60]

The area with the worst erosion and broken walkways bordered on the now abandoned Arverne Renewal District. Demolished structures and burned out hulks dominated the landscape. Some deserted buildings became squats for drug addicts and the homeless. Debris left by demolition contractors created an enormous dump. Broken-down appliances and rusted-out automobiles were junked amid streets strewn with garbage. Scavengers picked their way across rubbish heaps where rats roamed freely. Much of the debris was ultimately removed. But in later years the homeless would continue to create makeshift shelters among the ruins, while packs of wild dogs roamed around, occasionally attacking people as they walked or jogged on the nearby boardwalk. Many believed that homeless people used these dogs for protection.[61]

At the end of 1966, the federal government provided close to $10.5 million for acquisition of property, demonstrating a serious commitment to the Arverne project.[62] City fathers regularly promised decent accommodations for thousands of local families, along with schools, parks, shopping, and employment opportunities, and the local media reported all these hopeful statements.[63] However, the 10,000 units of housing originally projected kept shrinking, eventually to 4,500. Similarly, design plans changed. First the emphasis was on high density, a bit later on a mixture of high-rise and low-rise, and finally garden apartments and single-family dwellings were mentioned.[64] In 1971 the New York State Urban Development Corporation announced that it would construct apartment houses containing approximately one thousand rental units for moderate- and subsidized low-income families. Ocean Village, consisting of eleven buildings ranging from one to nineteen stories, in the middle of the area, was completed in 1974. Some time later, a private developer built a small number of one- and two-family homes nearby. All together, only 30 acres of the 310 were redeveloped.[65]

The numerous delays that beset Lindsay's "plans" for Arverne turned out to be disastrous. In January 1973, shortly after the beginning of an abbreviated second term, the Nixon administration announced a moratorium on all federal housing subsidies for low- and middle-income housing construction.[66] Local people hoped that this drastic action would only be temporary. But in a public statement later that month, President Nixon spoke disparagingly about government-supported urban development projects. The results had been disappointing, he announced.[67] In the Rockaways, it took quite a while for the significance of the Nixon order to sink in. The initial reaction was disbelief. The Chamber of Commerce president in his 1973 message spoke about "a temporary standstill," adding, "yet *we know* the area cannot be permitted to remain as it is."[68] Every so often a report of a new development for the renewal site attracted attention. Such rumors invariably exacerbated disagreements between different constituencies. The chamber and the various civic organizations continued to disapprove of building new housing for low-income families on the grounds that the Rockaways "were already burdened with large numbers of poor and troubled people."[69]

In the years following the moratorium, business interests called for the private development of recreational facilities, motels, and a convention center. Some proposed bringing in gambling casinos that would enable the Rockaways to compete with Atlantic City, and a study was commissioned by Queens County in the mid-1970s to explore this option.[70] All of these projects provoked considerable opposition because they violated stipulations concerning the use of government urban renewal property and long-standing parks department principles. Rockaway civil rights advocates also joined in the protest. None of these schemes went beyond the discussion phase.

Nixon's ban on federal housing subsidies had the strongest impact on the poor. Despite a decade of promises, displaced residents from Arverne understood that they would never be provided with decent accommodations. Rev. May and his supporters held out hope that a humane solution could still be found for the many minority families living in Rockaway's destitute neighborhoods.[71] Yet aside from protesting Chamber of Commerce luxury housing designs and calling for more low-income projects at Board of Estimate public hearings, they could do little to influence the situation. Well-publicized disputes regarding announced construction projects were often cited as the reason for the failure to do anything with the 310 acres. But in truth, Rockaway fell victim to the economic downturn of the 1970s. The recessions of these years, according to one reliable account, "devastated New York City more than any other city, with the possible exception of Detroit."[72] New York's fiscal crisis of the middle of the decade, leading to a dramatic bailout followed by austerity, should have removed any illusions that the municipal government would continue to finance generous social programs or low-income housing. New York State subsidies for such construction had already begun to dry up by 1965.[73]

As the budget for New York City decreased in the years after 1975, so did city services, gradually affecting every aspect of community life. Significant cuts were made in schools, libraries, hospitals, parks, sanitation, and the police and fire departments. The city's infrastructure began to decay. The City University, defying tradition, began charging tuition in 1976. Many of the War on Poverty jobs that had survived the Vietnam-era cuts now disappeared. Paraprofessionals in various capacities were laid off. Youth programs, summer jobs, and senior citizen programs went by the wayside. While the entire city suffered and bled from these reductions, declining neighborhoods such as the Rockaways hemorrhaged.[74] The 1970s proved to be a particularly hard time for the poor. During this decade, ghetto poverty nearly tripled and barrio poverty doubled.[75] When prosperity began to return in the following years, conservative mayors such as Ed Koch seemed more interested in promoting private investment and supporting real estate interests than in restoring services to low-income communities. Predictably, "poverty and the rent burden on poor families rose substantially over this period."[76]

Changing attitudes toward social reform always seem to coincide with periods of financial constraint. Domestic upheavals during the 1960s, including urban riots, reinforced conservatives' attacks on public housing. Low-income projects were seen as repositories for crime and drugs. That by the end of the decade they contained a predominantly minority population contributed to a popular perception that such housing should not be expanded. Attacks on the Moses model of large-scale slum clearance and massive high-rise projects also influenced public opinion. City planners and architects declared such an approach bankrupt as early as the late 1950s and early 1960s. By the next decade, traditional visions of urban renewal could find few defenders among housing experts.[77] In the country at large, Nixon's moratorium engendered little protest.[78]

Of the many New York City projects at different stages of completion, the one in Arverne-Edgemere was by far the largest. Land that had been cleared with such difficulty remained vacant, and the new apartments were not built. Rockaway's "great wasteland," often described as "an atomic bomb site," remained a shameful reminder of failed policies and indifference to the poor. Everyone who observed the desolation of the Rockaways confronted the same question: how could oceanfront property with such potential be allowed to lie fallow? Former city administrators spoke about the vulnerability of the area, implying that its fate was inevitable. Old-timers debated whether Robert Moses could have remedied the situation. Among the local population, whites saw the barren land as a symbol of neglect and stupidity. They tended to blame various public officials and politicians. African Americans called the failure to find a solution racist. Surely, they reasoned, if the Rockaways were a predominantly white community, builders would have invested eagerly, and government agencies would have encouraged these projects.

In the meantime, the forsaken land remained. Since other empty areas could be found in cities elsewhere in the country, clearly Rockaway was not singled out for special treatment. But observers found something particularly disturbing about this space bordering the beach and the ocean. Its presence served as a depressing reminder that a place once associated with pleasure for millions of people no longer existed. It felt like a defilement of nature. In addition, the largely vacant 310-acre tract exemplified changes in public policy and public attitudes that led to the neglect of mass recreation during the last decades of the twentieth century. For well over thirty years, this loss has affected the quality of life of Rockaway residents and all New Yorkers.

CHAPTER 12

The Reckoning

Physically, Rockaway at the millenium, shaped by the events that followed the Second World War, looks much the same as it did in 1975. Despite certain changes, many of the trends observed at that time persist. Older residents remain skeptical about the future, even though local officials sound an optimistic note.[1] The famed resort of an earlier era, with its amusement parks, bungalow colonies, and hotels, like Humpty Dumpty could not be put back together. The elimination of the two-fare subway zone, which for residents constituted perhaps the most notable improvement of the mid-1970s, failed to have a broader impact. The promised increase in tourism never materialized. In 1985 Rockaway's famed Playland was dismantled, leaving not one carousel, ferris wheel, or children's ride to be found anywhere on the peninsula.

Population figures in Rockaway have steadily increased, reaching approximately 105,000 in 2002, with a greater percentage of minorities than ever before. If it were possible to document all of the residents, this figure might be even larger. Many of today's residents are poor, and unemployment figures remain high. A number of immigrants from the Caribbean, the former Soviet Union, and elsewhere have moved to the peninsula.[2] While the Rockaways contain ample space, including the still-empty 310 acres, no new low-rent apartment houses have been built because federal, state, and local governments have ceased to provide money for such construction. The large concentration of housing projects already built has helped to discourage substantial private investment.

Given the inflation in New York's real estate market and Rockaway's spaciousness, some small, privately financed developments have appeared, such as the one on the former Playland site and another in the Somerville section of Arverne, once a marshland. The rest of the New York metropolitan area has begun to run out of available space for new housing, and empty Rockaway may therefore benefit from further construction. The general reduction in crime associated with Rudolph Giuliani's two terms as mayor has led to improved security on the peninsula, which should offer an additional inducement. However, no one can say with confidence whether such trends will continue.

Additional nursing homes dot the landscape, lending a geriatric character to certain beach neighborhoods, despite the Rockaways' containing a higher proportion of children than any other area in New York City. Mental patients continue to be placed in for-profit group homes near the shore and in family homes in other parts of the peninsula. Natives have long since become accustomed to the noise of jet planes from John F. Kennedy Airport. It takes newcomers somewhat longer to adjust to the high decibel levels.

Increasing numbers of students attend parochial schools, while more affluent secular families send their children to magnet schools on the other side of the Marine Parkway Bridge (newly named for famed baseball player and manager, Gil Hodges) in Brooklyn.[3] Most families have to rely on standard public education. But public schools in the Rockaways, like those in many other parts of New York City and urban areas elsewhere, are clearly overburdened and unable to provide an adequate learning environment for their students. Attendance rates are now the lowest in Queens. By the 1990s, academic performance at Rockaway schools ranked close to the bottom of all the schools in the borough, with only 46 percent of students reading at or above grade level.[4]

Communities located at the western end of the peninsula continue to go their separate ways, protected from the kinds of changes that affected the eastern and middle sections. The old shopping district of Far Rockaway never recovered its former vitality. Once, the area around Central Avenue (Beach 20th St.) contained three movie theatres and boasted upscale clothing and appliance stores, numerous shops, and restaurants. Today, it appears shoddy and run-down, with check-cashing establishments, bargain stores, storefront churches, and empty buildings. No movie houses or automobile dealerships can be found anywhere in the Rockaways (see figures 9–12). Locals have to do their major shopping in malls or stores elsewhere.

At the same time, large portions of this same Far Rockaway are thriving as Orthodox Jewish enclaves, now including ultra-Orthodox and Hassidim. Indeed, they continue to expand. While an active Community Board (# 14) takes a peninsula-wide outlook, white religious groups and the more affluent have continued to turn inward. The foremost among earlier Rockaway unifiers, the Chamber of Commerce, still represents real estate interests by advocating for market-rate housing, but it long ago lost its credibility as the sole voice of the Rockaways. The *Rockaway Review*, the chamber's house organ, which appeared several times a year until the 1970s, is now limited to an annual edition.

Despite all the conflicting evidence, optimism persists that a way will ultimately be found to revive the area's economic viability. Every once in a while, a revitalizing scheme has been floated for the 310 acres, such as legalized gambling or the creation of a mammoth recreation center, but none of these schemes have materialized. Several announced housing developments have fallen through, although as of this writing another ambitious construction plan, for one-third of the abandoned oceanfront area, has been announced. "Arverne by the Sea" is to be built under the auspices of a private construction firm. It remains to be seen whether this latest proposal will come to fruition or whether it will suffer the fate of all the others.[5]

From the vantage point of Manhattan, Rockaway seems far away, a place of no great importance where little of consequence takes place. The events of 11 September 2001, followed by the terrible plane crash two months later, briefly brought the peninsula to public attention, but it soon faded from view once again. Natives seem to prefer it this way because, generally speaking, news stories about the Rockaways over the years have been unflattering.[6]

Rockaway bears only superficial resemblance to the place that existed during the immediate postwar period, so fondly remembered by people of an earlier generation. It is not unique in this regard; rather, its fate resembles that of urban areas throughout the United States. Current inhabitants, many of whom are members of minority groups, occupy apartments and houses abandoned by middle-class whites who have gone to live elsewhere. People have a tendency to see a direct relationship between these trends, and the newly arrived are often scapegoated. In reality, other explanations can be found. Suburbanization occurred nationally. After World War II, middle-class people gravitated to neighborhoods with new single-family houses, garages, and manicured lawns. The younger generation was ready to cut its ties to the past and move to the suburbs. That this happened, to a certain extent, even to all-white, affluent Belle Harbor and Neponsit indicates that other causal factors were at work besides the racial ones.[7]

Research for this book revealed different perspectives on the "Rockaway reality." Old-timers bemoaned the loss of their special place, a common refrain in a nation that experienced so much change after the Second World War. They see that new groups, with different values and priorities, have replaced them. A largely cohesive community has fragmented into a number of distinct ones that rarely act in unison. But those who romanticize a previous age ignore the negative features of their dominant culture. Minorities view the past differently, remembering the injustices that existed in "the good old days." Undoubtedly, the majority culture paints the entire peninsula in bleak terms because large sections have become predominantly African American. Many people, including former residents, view today's Rockaway as an undesirable "slum," a term that has come to have racist connotations.[8] It implies, without close examination, that an area populated by minorities must by definition be a site of urban decay and distress. At the outset of our research for this project, we found an obscure article written in 1974 by Richard Geist, a former owner of the Playland amusement park. Its title, "The Wreck of the Rockaways," revealed his personal feeling that the area had become "depressed."[9] Media coverage takes a similar approach; twenty-five years after Geist's article, in 1999, a *New York Times* piece on released mental patients described the peninsula as follows: "Rockaway, Queens is a shabby seaside resort of old boarding houses and for-profit adult homes."[10] Such descriptions, while true for some parts of the peninsula, ignore the affluent western sections. They also fail to do justice to the heterogeneity of the black community, now containing a growing working- and middle-class contingent. These are the families who own well-kept homes or co-op apartments, hold down responsible jobs, and care about their children's education and future prospects.

In the course of our investigations, Rockaway residents throughout the peninsula told us of their contentment with the quality of their lives, often describing their reasons for living in the Rockaways in terms that echo previous generations. They enjoy the relatively peaceful environment, with beach, ocean, and bay right at hand, and find walking on the boardwalk in all seasons as invigorating as ever. They insist that the air is superior to that in any other part of the city. They believe in the small-town atmosphere, despite the presence of high-rise buildings. Local churches and synagogues continue to play a vital role in the lives of today's multiethnic population. For various reasons, these are more important to residents than ever before. This religious connection is another factor frequently cited by those who remain in the area. Provinciality appears to be a feature of Rockaway existence now as before, and a sense that life in such an environment has its own special flavor persists. A recent novel by a native, *From Rockaway*, describes young people whose worldview does not extend beyond the connecting bridges.[11] Various places located across Jamaica Bay are still referred to as "the mainland."

Many members of minority groups have found advantages in changed circumstances in the Rockaways. Clearly, opportunities on the peninsula for the large number of young people without skills remain scarce, and idle youth without hope represent Rockaway's major problem—one for which our society has yet to find a solution. At the same time, minority men and women hold civil service, hospital, nursing home, and group home positions, often with social security and health benefits. Local schools now have teachers as well as administrative personnel who are African American and Latino. Among other advantages, they serve as role models for their students. Despite the difficulties that undoubtedly exist, people of color who have lived in the Rockaways for a while often assert that life is better for them now than previously.

Rockaway after the war represented a challenge. It was only a matter of time before the ancient summer houses that dominated its shorefront would deteriorate. The changing vacation requirements of urban America were rapidly rendering them obsolete. The community itself did not have the resources to undertake the necessary remedies. Unless outside authorities took constructive measures to bring about a revival, the resort would inevitably self-destruct. Once this occurred, opportunistic forces filled the resulting vacuum. Successive New York City administrations shared a lack of concern for the maintenance of an important recreational asset. They also had no regard for the well-being of Rockaway's citizens and ignored the impact of their harsh policies. This held true for both Democratic and Republican administrations, liberal and conservative alike. Their attitude indicates that they never really had any plans to make the most of this ocean community.

Robert Moses, who believed that the area's resort feature should be cherished, was unique among city officials. It became evident during the research on this book that the time has come to reassess Moses's role over a thirty-five-year period, for his actions in the Rockaways do not completely match standard interpretations of him and his legacy. His personal arrogance and disregard for most urban communities cannot be denied. Yet he was the only official who actually did have a plan for Rockaway, and the only one who seems to have appreciated its function as a resource for New York City's people. Recognizing early on that the peninsula's flimsy summer houses were going to decay, Moses tried against considerable odds to rectify the situation. He first started to improve the Rockaways in the mid-1930s, and the very last undertaking of his career was the rebuilding of the Cross Bay Bridge in 1970. Our account detailed the number of separate housing developments for which he was responsible. The support that he gave to integrated low- and middle-income projects undercuts the view that he always pursued racist policies, notwithstanding the ills connected with relocation.

Moses's refusal to allow private interests to exercise control over public spaces is a major theme recurring throughout his career, exemplified by his endeavors in Rockaway. His desire to both establish parkland and make it accessible refutes widely held views that he had no interest in the masses. The elimination of pollution in Jamaica Bay and the creation of the Jamaica Bay Wildlife Refuge, the largest of its kind within any U.S. urban center, demonstrate that Moses was interested in ecology long before it became fashionable. This is an aspect of his career that is usually ignored. His commitment to bringing the subway to the peninsula in 1950 is at odds with the generalization that Moses always promoted automobile transportation to the exclusion of mass transit. Moreover, in the Rockaways public transit actually competed with two of his own TBTA toll bridges. Yet despite his "Power Broker" reputation, he did not always have the final word. If he had stayed in power a little longer, it is possible that he could have found a solution to those aspects of urban decay that did the Rockaway community so much harm. We will never know.

Former and present residents tend to blame outside forces for the problems that beset the Rockaways, with much justification. The exporting of urban problems into this peripheral area began after the war and continues to this day, although on a reduced scale.[12] For at least half a century, New York City officials cynically brought poor people into an inconveniently located area with no job opportunities that offered little hope for adults and children. In fact, officials selected those whom they deemed unlikely to become employable, responsible citizens. They undoubtedly realized that some of these transferred people would cause trouble in their new environment. But this does not appear to have concerned them.

Similarly, officialdom steadily constructed multiple low-income housing projects in Rockaway because few other neighborhoods would accept them. For the same reason, they permitted nursing homes and group homes for mental patients in greater numbers than anywhere else in New York. While these facilities provided an outlet for the city at large, and even jobs for locals, they detracted from the recreational appeal of this former resort and contributed to the community's negative image. Rockaway, now very much an urban community, manifests urban problems. It also suffers from insufficient resources and a lack of services. The decline in public education decreases the opportunities of many of the peninsula's children. Limited access to medical care for the poor detrimentally affects their health and that of their families.

The forces shaping the Rockaways produced similar results elsewhere in the nation. After World War II, the migration of poor minorities from the American south, Puerto Rico, and Mexico led to crowding in many cities, compounding housing shortages. Government and banking decisions determined that white suburbs would thrive, while communities of color would be redlined and denied financing. Urban redevelopment programs like Title I succeeded at the expense of the poor all over the country. No municipality successfully dealt with the inequities of relocation. What is special about the postwar period is that government agencies on every level played an active role in designing and implementing policies that increased racial segregation and the suffering of minorities.[13]

To be sure, influential individuals within the community also contributed to the events that unfolded in the Rockaways. Established local leaders and politicians failed to mount an adequate campaign to prevent the cycle of deterioration. Borough presidents, who might have defended one of Queens's key areas, helped undermine it by allowing the city to unload its most serious problems on the peninsula. Certain well-placed inhabitants, especially those connected with real estate, got rich as large sections of their own neighborhoods declined, and then they literally moved away from the problems they helped create. Speculators bought up land that they knew would later be purchased by government agencies at higher prices. Individual landlords who made quick profits at the expense of poor families must also be held accountable. Paid high rentals by the welfare department, despite the inadequacy of the buildings they provided, some made small fortunes. Rockaway lawyers served these property owners at every turn, and, too frequently, inspectors accepted bribes to overlook abuses. Finally, the local real estate firms that practiced blockbusting and the local banks that redlined must take their share of the blame.

Breezy Point offers an enlightening contrast, since the residents of this small area of the Rockaways successfully came together and defended their community from threats that would have altered its special character. The forces wishing to change it were formidable indeed. Yet the citizens mobilized, and they eventually took their fight out of Rockaway and into larger power centers. No opposition of such dimension ever emerged in the other parts of the peninsula that the city saw fit to exploit. Public officials took advantage of both the vulnerability and the lack of resistance in most of Rockaway. Poor people, mainly African American, whom they were unwilling to place elsewhere, ended up in almost all sections of the peninsula, save Breezy Point, Neponsit, and Belle Harbor. Racism played a key role in this process because white communities throughout New York City would not accept an influx of black residents. Municipal leaders and administrators of city agencies accepted this as a given when they steered blacks to declining areas, thus reinforcing residential segregation. Our study demonstrates how impoverished minorities were mistreated in Rockaway, probably more than in any other part of the city. Families with young children were relocated from one destroyed neighborhood to another within a short period of time. Some were moved as many as three or four times in ten years, and the squalor kept getting worse as additional people were brought in. They were evicted repeatedly, without consideration for their well-being, and invariably placed in dangerously inadequate accommodations. Few, if any, services were made available to them.

Encouraging the segregation of poor minorities in the Rockaways has had an additional stifling effect. Scholars have pointed out that African Americans living in segregated enclaves find themselves cut off from "the culture, norms and behavior of the rest of American society." As a result, they become "among the most isolated people on earth."[14] Antisocial behavior patterns are reinforced by a lack of contact with countervailing forces. In Rockaway, the area's remoteness compounded this sense of isolation from the mainstream. A variety of government agencies helped perpetuate conditions associated with the worst forms of deprivation. They thereby ensured the perpetuation of the "estranged poor"—the so-called "underclass"—whose existence the respectable members of society then proceeded to deplore.[15]

The relocated people had no way of protecting themselves from the pain that was being inflicted on them and little chance of improving their own lives or those of their children. Their story ranks with some of the most terrible episodes of the recent past. It is difficult to believe that whites would have received such treatment, and in fact they did not. Except for the very poor and elderly among them, displaced Jews managed to make other arrangements. While many of the Irish who were forced to leave Seaside against their will because of Title I were inconvenienced, most of them wound up in equivalent and sometimes better conditions than before. Those responsible for the inhumane relocation of impoverished minorities in Rockaway have yet to receive the opprobrium that they deserve.

Not all locals stood by passively. Starting in the 1930s, African American self-help groups protected otherwise defenseless domestic workers. Civil rights organizations led the fight for better housing, jobs, education, health care, and human services. Leaders such as Eleanor Hull, Reverend Joseph H. May, Lena Cook, Helen Rausnitz, and Ernest Brown stand out in this regard. Concerned parents and dedicated teachers did their best to improve the schools. Various organizations highlighted public health concerns and called for improved living conditions and health provisions for all residents. Life would have been worse for poor people if these advocacy groups had not played an active role.

Some writers on ghetto life have written about working- and middle-class African Americans abandoning their communities, leaving them bereft of leaders and role models. For example, in *The Truly Disadvantaged*, William Julius Wilson argued that blacks of better means benefited from the civil rights movement and affirmative action programs by taking their gains and going to live in better circumstances, away from their former segregated neighborhoods. They left behind weakened institutions (e.g., churches and recreational facilities) and a population less able to cope with economic dislocation and structural unemployment. The result, Wilson believed, was a concentration of the exclusively poor, who manifested the pathologies of inner cities: "low aspirations, poor education, family instability, illegitimacy, unemployment, crime, drug addiction, alcoholism, frequent illness and early death."[16] While Wilson's heralded thesis may apply in certain circumstances, it has little relevance to the Rockaways. For despite the presence of low-income projects and neighborhoods that ranked among the poorest anywhere, working- and middle-class African Americans continued to move to the peninsula voluntarily. Moreover, many of them became community activists in order to improve the lives of their families and their neighbors. Although some activists were secular, many derived a commitment to help others from a strong church affiliation. Their example suggests that the Wilson thesis needs to be reexamined.

With regard to politics as well, developments in the Rockaways force us to modify generalizations about the black experience. Craig Steven Wilder makes a standard argument when he concludes that what ghettos have in common is "the lack of power that allows their residents to be physically concentrated and socially targeted."[17] This statement accurately describes what happened to the poor people who were shifted around from one Rockaway housing disaster to another. But it does not do justice to the political involvement of its black population, which has achieved a great measure of success in recent years. Initially, Rockaway's African Americans supported white candidates who recognized the special needs of their community. Starting in the early 1970s, blacks themselves began running for political office. By the late 1980s, minority representatives had been elected to positions of importance in the New York State Assembly and the New York City Council. In 1998, Gregory W. Meeks of Far Rockaway was elected to Congress. The changing demographics of the peninsula made this possible. But without the voter registration campaigns and the learning process derived from earlier defeats, numbers alone would not have made the difference. Current elected officials have shown their appreciation for the efforts and inspiration of their forerunners. Congressman Meeks has spoken of the encouragement given to him early in his career by Rev. Joseph H. May.[18] As a symbol of the black community's strength, the Arverne and Edgemere sections of a major Rockaway thoroughfare, Beach Channel Drive, were renamed Rev. Joseph H. May Drive in October 1996, nine years after his death. Mayor Rudolph Giuliani signed the bill making the new designation official in a ceremony at Mt. Carmel Baptist Church.[19]

Despite some successes, serious problems remain. Statistics presented throughout this book indicate that the health, education, and welfare of the peninsula's inhabitants have ranked in the lowest possible categories. To cite one further example: "About 19 percent of residents of the Rockaways received public assistance in 1993, higher than in Queens and New York City (8 percent and 15 percent respectively)."[20] Although recent figures show some decline in the numbers on welfare, this probably reflects a similar phenomenon throughout New York City resulting from the new welfare law's restrictive regulations. However, changes in the law do not necessarily eradicate poverty. The ills of the inner city enumerated by William Julius Wilson still describe several parts of the peninsula only too accurately. In spite of evidence that these conditions resulted largely from the city's actions in the

Rockaways, there is little indication that governmental authorities will undertake to undo the damage that their predecessors inflicted.

A society based upon an individualistic ethos may not concern itself with its most vulnerable citizens, or it may blame the victim. In addition, racism helps to erase feelings of empathy. The initial developments in the Rockaways occurred during a time of relative prosperity. The financial constraints of the mid-1970s only made conditions worse. The negligible political fallout from the warehouse approach to poverty on this isolated peninsula led politicians and bureaucrats to conclude that they could make decisions with impunity in peripheral areas involving people who were invisible to the larger population. Shipping problems off to a distant place was the equivalent of sweeping them under the carpet. From the perspective of city officials, it did not matter that the carpet grew bulky. The Rockaways became a convenient disposal outlet for inconvenient individuals and families.

Because these opportunistic policies eventually increased antipathy toward the poor, they served to discredit the liberal administrative state. This process undermined liberalism itself, eventually leading to the enactment of still harsher policies. Starting with politicians such as Mayor Ed Koch, the city dropped any pretense that government agencies cared for the less fortunate. In fact, Koch's trajectory from left to right marked on a local level the withdrawal of government responsibility for human welfare that characterized the Reagan administration on the national level. Even with the return of New York's prosperity during the Giuliani years, advocacy for the less fortunate was not restored. In fact, quite the opposite came to pass. It can be argued that the events that unfolded in Rockaway during the three decades after World War II served as a harbinger of the way in which the poor would be treated in the future. For example, the fate of the homeless in contemporary urban America is a subject few choose to examine closely.

Elected officials and their administrative associates who made decisions about the Rockaways clearly gave little thought to the consequences of their actions. They ignored their complicity in destroying a public resource and refused to be deterred by the human suffering that their decisions caused. Thus, we are forced to conclude that the fate of the Rockaways after World War II reveals unpleasant truths about our society. What we have described is not a history to feel proud of. The 310 acres along the beach in Arverne-Edgemere, allowed to remain empty for so many years, have come to symbolize the greed, opportunism, racism, indifference to the poor, and public policy failures that prevailed in the United States during the postwar decades.

1. Turbulent seas in Rockaway (Courtesy of Vincent Seyfried)

2. Jacob Riis Park on a summer day, 1937 (Metropolitan Transit authority)

3. Chamber of Commerce
Executive Secretary George
Wolpert with Commissioner
Robert Moses, ca. late 1940s
(*Rockaway Review*)

4. A suburban-style scene in Arverne, winter 1951. Note flooded streets
(Photo: Stanley Smolin)

5. Children standing in front of condemned houses, ca. 1959
(Courtesy of Rev. Joseph H. May Dedication Committee)

6. Edgemere Houses, the largest low-income project in the Rockaways
(Photo by Miguel Mercado)

7. Voter registration, Mt. Carmel Baptist Church. Rev. Joseph H. May, Helen Rausnitz, and a voter, ca. 1963 (Courtesy of Rev. Joseph H. May Dedication Committee)

8. Playland's Roller Coaster, near the beach, in the process of being torn down. Hammels low-income project is rear left, Dayton middle-income houses rear right, and a portion of Seaside in the foreground; ca. 1985 (Long Island Collection, Queensborough Public Library)

CENTRAL AVENUE   FAR ROCKAWAY. N. Y.

9. Beach 20th St. (Central Ave.) in Far Rockaway, ca. 1940 (Courtesy of Vincent Seyfried)

10. A shop on the corner of Beach 20th St. (Central Ave.) and Cornaga Ave. in 2002 (Photo by Miguel Mercado)

11. The Strand movie theater on Beach 20th St. (Central Ave.) at its opening in 1919 (Courtesy of Vincent Seyfried)

Strand Theatre, *Far Rockaway, N. Y.*

12. The Strand theater in 2002 (Photo by Miguel Mercado)

13. Sands and weeds on a section of the 310 acres, 2002 (Photo by Miguel Mercado)

14. The Jamaica Bay Wildlife Refuge (Photo by Denis Macrae)

15. New housing on the former Playland site, 2002 (Photo by Miguel Mercado)

Notes

Introduction

1. Vincent Seyfried and William Asadorian, *Old Rockaway, New York, in Early Photographs* (Mineola, N.Y.: Dover, 2000), p. vii.

2. *Rockaway Review*, August 1950.

3. We owe this observation to Jay Greenfield.

4. Kenneth T. Jackson, *Crabgrass Frontier* (New York: Oxford University Press, 1985).

5. Thomas J. Sugrue, *The Origins of the Urban Crisis: Race and Inequality in Postwar Detroit* (Princeton: Princeton University Press, 1996), p. 3.

6. Hillel Levine and Lawrence Harmon, *The Death of an American Jewish Community: A Tragedy of Good Intentions* (New York: The Free Press, 1993).

7. See William Serrin, *Homestead: The Glory and Tragedy of an American Steel Town* (New York: Times Books, 1992).

8. Jeanie Wylie, *Poletown: Community Betrayed* (Urbana: University of Illinois Press, 1989).

9. Robert Caro, *The Power Broker: Robert Moses and the Fall of New York* (New York: Vintage Books, 1975)

10. Wendell Pritchett, *Brownsville, Brooklyn: Blacks, Jews, and the Changing Face of the Ghetto* (Chicago: University of Chicago Press, 2002), p. 121.

1. The Resort in Summer and Winter

1. *New York Times*, 26 May 1986.

2. See chapter 2.

3. Robert Caro, *The Power Broker: Robert Moses and the Fall of New York* (New York: Vintage Books, 1975), pp. 851–94; Marshall Berman, *All That Is Solid Melts into Air* (New York: Simon and Schuster, 1988), pp. 290–312.

4. Herbert Gans, *The Urban Villages* (New York: The Free Press, 1962).

5. Thomas J. Sugrue, *The Origins of the Urban Crisis: Race and Inequality in Postwar Detroit* (Princeton: Princeton University Press, 1996); Hillel Levine and Lawrence Harmon, *The Death of an American Jewish Community: A Tragedy of Good Intentions* (New York: The Free Press, 1993).

6. Roger Waldinger, *Still the Promised City? African Americans and New Immigrants in Postindustrial New York* (Cambridge: Harvard University Press, 1996), p. 43.

7. *The WPA Guide to New York City: The Federal Writers' Project Guide to the 1930s* (New York: Random House, 1992), p. 591.

8. Vincent Seyfried and William Asadorian, *Old Rockaway, New York, in Early Photographs* (Mineola, N.Y.: Dover, 2000), p. viii.

9. "Rockaway Hot to Secede," *Sunday Daily News*, 19 August 2001.

10. *WPA Guide to NYC*, p. 591.

11. *Rockaway Review*, December 1950; J. Clarence Davies III, *Neighborhood Groups and Urban Renewal* (New York: Columbia University Press, 1966), pp. 35–36.

12. 1947 letter to prospective members; *Rockaway Review*, December, 1950.

13. Caro, *The Power Broker*, passim.

14. See New York City Department of Parks, *The Rockaway Improvement* (1939); "Remarks of Robert Moses at Marine Park, Brooklyn," 12 August 1963, Moses Papers, Metropolitan Transportation Authority, Box 613-2.

15. See chapter 6.

16. *Newsday*, 4 December 1988.

17. *The Livable City*, (New York: The Municipal Art Society, 1988).

18. Andrew Garvin, *The American City: What Works, What Doesn't* (New York: McGraw Hill, 1996), p. 37.

19. *Newsday*, 4 December 1988.

20. Ibid.

21. We owe this term to Robert Twombly.

22. New York City Department of Parks, *The Improvement of Coney Island* (1939).

23. New York City Department of Parks, *The Future of Jamaica Bay* (1938).

24. See for example, New York City Department of Parks, *The Improvement of Coney Island, Rockaway, and South Beach* (1937). The term "slum" was used by Moses and his contemporaries for physically run-down neighborhoods. In later years it came to have racist connotations.

25. *Rockaway Review*, October 1958.

26. *The Improvement of Coney Island*.

27. *Newsday*, 4 December 1988.

28. *The Improvement of Coney Island.*

29. *Rockaway Review*, June, July 1939.

30. See chapter 5 for a more detailed account of Jamaica Bay.

31. *Rockaway Review*, August 1950.

32. *The Rockaway Improvement.*

33. An exception is Jeffrey A. Kroessler, "Robert Moses and the New Deal in Queens," in *Robert Moses: Single-Minded Genius*, ed. Joann P. Krieg (Interlocken, N.Y.: Heart of Lakes, 1989), pp. 101–8. Also see the unpublished dissertation by Jeffrey A. Kroessler, "Building Queens: The Urbanization of New York's Largest Borough" (Ph.D. diss., City University of New York, 1991).

34. *Rockaway Review*, December 1937.

35. *New York Journal American*, n.d., Moses files, 1938, MTA.

36. See letter from the president of the LIRR to Robert Moses, 15 July 1939 in *The Rockaway Improvement*; *Rockaway Review*, October 1950.

37. *Newsday*, 6 June 1970; *The Rockaway Improvement*; *Rockaway Review*, July, August 1939.

38. *Newsday*, 20 June 1970.

2. Race and Real Estate

1. The historical information comes mainly from Vincent Seyfried and William Asadorian, *Old Rockaway, New York, in Early Photographs* (Mineola, N.Y.: Dover, 2000); Marion R. Casey, "From the East Side to the Seaside," in *The New York Irish*, ed. Ronald H. Baylor and Timothy J. Meagher (Baltimore: Johns Hopkins University Press, 1996), p. 407; Kenneth T. Jackson, ed., *The Encyclopedia of New York* (New Haven: Yale University Press, 1995), passim.

2. Babian, Elaine, interview, New York, 12 May 1999; Rausnitz, Helen and William, interview, Rockaway, N.Y., 7 July 1999; Lerner, Ray, interview, Rockaway, N.Y., 18 July, 2001.

3. *Rockaway Review*, February 1945; Municipal Archives, O'd Box 76, file 793.

4. Interviews at Mt. Carmel Baptist Church, Rockaway, N.Y., 12 December 1998 and 24 February 1999; Barbara Blumberg, *The New Deal and the Unemployed: The View from New York City* (Lewisburg, Pa.: Bucknell University Press, 1979), pp. 82–83.

5. Craig Steven Wilder, *A Covenant with Color: Race and Social Power in Brooklyn* (New York: Columbia University Press, 2000), p. 168.

6. Olivia P. Frost et. al., *Aspects of Negro Life in the Borough of Queens, New York City* (New York: Urban League, 1947), p. 7.

7. Ibid; Blumberg, *New Deal and the Unemployed*, p. 268.

8. Information about the League comes from their *65th Anniversary Papers* (1996) and from Dennis, Josie, and Mae Thomas, interview, Rockaway, N.Y., 13 March, 1999.

9. Gilbert Osofsky, *Harlem: The Making of a Ghetto* (New York: Harper and Row, 1966) p. 56.

10. "Ghetto" is defined as areas of high black poverty. See Kenneth B. Clark, *Dark Ghettos: Dilemmas of Social Power*, 2nd ed. (Middletown, Conn.: Wesleyan University Press, 1965).

11. Frost et al., *Aspects of Negro Life*, p. 45.

12. William O'Dwyer, General Correspondence, Municipal Archives, Box 76, Folder 793; *Rockaway Review*, February 1945.

13. *Rockaway Review*, February 1945.

14. McCarthy, Henry L., "Memoir" (Oral History Office, Columbia University). McCarthy witnessed corruption in the Buildings Department during these years.

15. For the best discussion of appraisals by the HOLC see Kenneth T. Jackson, *Crabgrass Frontier* (New York: Oxford University Press, 1985), pp. 197–99. The actual surveys are housed in the National Archives, College Park, Md.

16. The Rockaway material is in the National Archives, RG 195, Box 76.

17. Jackson, *Crabgrass Frontier*, pp. 197–99. "Redlining" is the practice by banks of denying loans to particular areas.

18. Charles Abrams, *Forbidden Neighbors: A Study of Prejudice in Housing* (New York: Harper and Row, 1955), p. 161.

19. *Rockaway Review*, February 1945.

20. The best treatment of Moses's role in housing remains the book by Joel Schwartz, *The New York Approach: Robert Moses, Urban Liberals, and Redevelopment of the Inner City* (Columbus, Ohio: Ohio State University Press, 1993).

21. Robert Moses, *Housing and Recreation* (New York: New York City Department of Parks, 1938); also see J. Clarence Davies III, *Neighborhood Groups and Urban Renewal* (New York: Columbia University Press, 1966), pp. 39–40.

22. Women's Industrial Service League, *65th Anniversary Papers*.

23. *Rockaway Review*, November 1940.

24. Ibid., February 1945, December 1945.

25. See, for example, Thomas J. Sugrue, *The Origins of the Urban Crisis: Race and Inequality in Postwar Detroit* (Princeton: Princeton University Press, 1996), pp. 58, 72, 82; Arnold R. Hirsch, *Making the Second Ghetto: Race and Housing in Chicago, 1940–1960* (New York: Cambridge University Press, 1983), p. 226.

26. See chapter 3.

27. See Wendell Pritchett, *Brownsville, Brooklyn: Blacks, Jews, and the Changing Face of the Ghetto* (Chicago: University of Chicago Press, 2002), pp. 63, 100; Schwartz, *New York Approach*, pp. 119–20.

28. Rockaway Chamber of Commerce, Service Bulletin, 1945.

29. See chapter 3.

30. Schwartz, *New York Approach*, pp. 68, 77, 86–87, 108.

31. New York City Housing Authority, Files, Series 06, Box 0068c2, Folder 01, LaGuardia Community College.

32. *Rockaway Review*, November 1945.

33. Ibid., January 1946.

34. Rockaway Chamber of Commerce, News Bulletin, 15 November 1946.

35. O'Dwyer, General Correspondence, Municipal Archives, Box 107880, Folder 019; *Rockaway Review*, November 1946.

36. *Rockaway Review*, October 1946; Bulletin of the Rockaway Chamber of Commerce, 1947.

37. See the interesting discussion of Rockaway exemptions by Leon Schneider, *Rockaway Review*, June–July 1963.

38. O'Dwyer, General Correspondence, Municipal Archives, Box 107893, Folder 41.

39. News Bulletin to Members of Chamber of Commerce, 15 January 1946 and 15 November 1946; O'Dwyer, General Correspondence, Box 107880, Folder 019, Municipal Archives.

40. *Rockaway Review*, November 1948.

41. Ibid., December 1947; also see chapter 1.

3. The Trestle Burns and the Projects Begin

1. For example, from the *Rockaway Review*, October 1947: "Construction Co-ordinator Robert Moses has given assurance that the city has not abandoned the idea of replacing the wooden railroad trestle over Jamaica Bay."

2. Ibid., July 1949, September 1950, October 1951, October 1952; *New York Herald Tribune*, 17 July 1963.

3. William O'Dwyer, General Correspondence, Box 265, Municipal Archives.

4. Robert Moses, *Housing and Recreation* (New York: New York City Department of Parks, 1938); *Rockaway Review*, June 1939

5. *New York Times*, 6 June 1950; Robert Moses Files, Boxes 175-2 and 613-1, Metropolitan Transportation Authority.

6. Moses Files, Box 613-2, MTA.

7. Ibid.

8. *Wave*, 28 June 1956.

9. Interview with Leon Locke, former publisher of the *Wave*, who called the subway link's completion the "death knell." Interview, Rockaway, N.Y., 5 October 1998. Many former residents make the same point.

10. *Rockaway Review*, September 1951, February 1957.

11. Ibid., March 1960.

12. Ibid.; *Herald Tribune*, 17 July 1963.

13. *Long Island Press*, 26 June 1958; *Rockaway Review*, October 1961.

14. Vincent Impelliteri, General Correspondence, 27 March 1951, 14 June 1951, Municipal Archives.

15. *Rockaway Review*, August 1956, February 1957.

16. See chapter 5.

17. See chapter 4.

18. Kenneth T. Jackson, *Crabgrass Frontier* (New York: Oxford University Press, 1985), p. 221.

19. *Rockaway Review*, June, July 1959.

20. Lawrence Friedman, *Government and Slum Housing* (Chicago: Rand McNally, 1968), p. 109; Roger Starr, "Easing the Housing Crisis," in Peter D. Salins, ed., *New York Unbound* (New York: Basil Blackwell, 1988), p. 179; Ira S. Lowry, "Where Should the Poor Live?" in Salins, pp. 94–95.

21. *Rockaway Review*, March 1950.

22. *New York Sun*, 21 September 1945.

23. *Rockaway Review*, February 1948.

24. Ibid., February 1949.

25. New York City Housing Authority, Files, Summary of Project Data, 1955, MTA.

26. *Rockaway Review*, September 1949, December 1949.

27. Ibid., December 1950.

28. See below and also Friedman, *Slum Housing*, p. 111

29. NYC Housing Authority, Summary of Project Data, Files, LaGuardia Community College, 31 March 1955.

30. Many of these observations are based on interviews with former residents during 1998 and 1999.

31. Dennis, Josie, and Mae Thomas, interview, Rockaway, N.Y., 13 March 1998.

32. *Rockaway Review*, April 1938.

33. *Wave*, 10 February 1949.

34. See statement by Chairman Thomas F. Farrell of the NYC Housing Authority about the coming Hammels project, *Rockaway Review*, December 1949.

35. *Wave*, 18 September 1949.

36. *Long Island Press*, 11 May 1950.

37. Ibid., 24 May 1950.

38. *Wave*, 24 April 1950, 19 August 1954.

39. J. Clarence Davies III, *Neighborhood Groups and Urban Renewal* (New York, Columbia University Press, 1966), p. 38. See also the *Long Island Press*, 11 May 1950. Fox also did legal work for a number of Hammels real estate brokers.

40. *Long Island Press*, 3 November 1958.

41. Ibid., 25 March 1954. A fuller description of this new site will be given in chapter 4.

42. *Wave*, 19 August 1954.

43. NYC Housing Authority, Summary of Project Data, Moses Files, 1956, MTA.

44. See numerous articles about growing crime rates in the *Wave* from 1954 onward.

45. *Rockaway Review*, June and July 1953.

46. Norman I. Fainstein and Susan S. Fainstein, "Governing Regimes and the Political Economy of Development in New York City, 1946–1984," in *Power, Culture, and Place*, ed. John H. Mollenkopf (New York: Russell Sage Foundation, 1988), p. 165.

47. See chapter 4 for a discussion of welfare issues in Rockaway.

48. *Wave*, 6 June 1957.

49. *Long Island Press*, 2 August 1954.

4. Rockaway's Welfare

1. *Wave*, 15 February 1969.

2. *Rockaway Review* complained about this problem regularly, e.g., May 1953.

3. Ibid., December 1955.

4. Robert Halpern, *Fragile Families, Fragile Solutions* (New York: Columbia University Press, 1999), pp. 98, 106.

5. Winifred Bell, *Aid to Dependent Children* (New York: Columbia University Press, 1965), pp. 20, 21, 25, 80.

6. Kenneth T. Jackson, ed., *The Encyclopedia of New York City* (New Haven: Yale University Press, 1995); Martin Shefter, *Political Crises, Fiscal Crises* (New York: Basic Books, 1985), p. 107.

7. James T. Patterson, *America's Struggle Against Poverty, 1900–1980* (Cambridge: Harvard University Press, 1981), p. 86.

8. Ibid., p. 88.

9. See the discussion in Bell, *Dependent Children*, pp. 62–65.

10. Henry L. McCarthy, "Memoir," (Oral History Office, Columbia University), passim.

11. Ellen Schrecker, *Many are the Crimes: McCarthyism in America* (Boston: Little, Brown, 1998), pp. 384–85. Thomas Sugrue, in *The Origins of the Urban Crisis: Race and Inequality in Postwar Detroit* (Princeton: Princeton University Press, 1996), p.7, makes a similar point. See also the favorable article by Jerome Beatty about Hilliard in the conservative *American Mercury*, 1 September 1950.

12. Bell, *Dependent Children*, p. 90; Daniel Walkowitz, *Working with Class* (Chapel Hill: University of North Carolina Press, 1999), p. 222.

13. Walkowitz, *Working*, p. 237.

14. Dumpson, (former commissioner) James R., interview, New York, 19 April 1999.

15. Doris Moss, "A Study of Attitudes Toward Community Problems in Arverne, Queens," (master's thesis, Brooklyn College, 1965), pp. 33–34.

16. *Rockaway Review*, June 1949.

17. *Wave*, 12 June 1958, 28 August 1952.

18. *Rockaway Review*, June 1949.

19. J. Clarence Davies III, *Neighborhood Groups and Urban Renewal* (New York, Columbia University Press, 1966), p. 33. Also see below in this chapter.

20. *Rockaway Review*, June 1950.

21. Ibid.

22. Ibid.

23. Wendell Pritchett, *Brownsville, Brooklyn: Blacks, Jews, and the Changing Face of the Ghetto* (Chicago: University of Chicago Press, 2002), pp. 143–44.

24. Arnold R. Hirsch, *Making the Second Ghetto: Race and Housing in Chicago, 1940–1960* (New York: Cambridge University Press, 1983); Sugrue, *Urban Crisis*; Jonathan Rieder, *Canarsie: The Jews and Italians of Brooklyn Against Liberalism* (Cambridge; Harvard University Press. 1985); George J. Sanchez, *Becoming Mexican American* (New York: Oxford University Press, 1993); Gilbert Osofsky, *Harlem: The Making of a Ghetto* (New York: Harper and Row, 1968).

25. Davies, *Neighborhood Groups*, p. 33.

26. *Rockaway Review*, June 1950, June 1951.

27. McCarthy, "Oral History," passim.

28. William O'Dwyer, Vincent Impelliteri, and Robert F. Wagner, Departmental Files, Department of Welfare, Municipal Archives.

29. *Long Island Press*, 12 August 1958.

30. Roger Starr, *The Rise and Fall of New York City* (New York: Basic Books, 1985), p. 97.

31. Ibid.

32. William O'Dwyer, Departmental Letters, Municipal Archives, Box 64, 5 May 1950.

33. *Wave*, 2 September 1967; see also 27 January 1972.

34. *Rockaway Review*, October 1953; *Wave*, 24 April 1952.

35. Grace Hewell, "Neighborhood Health Improvement Through Functional Organizing" (Ph.D. diss., Columbia Teachers College, 1958), p. 73.

36. See chapter 6.

37. *Rockaway Review*, August 1952: *Wave*, 24 April 1952; *Rockaway Journal*, 17 March 1953.

38. *Wave*, 21 May 1953.

39. *Long Island Press*, 25 March 1954.

40. *Wave*, 2 July 1952, 10 July 1952.

41. *Long Island Press*, 25 March 1954.

42. Ibid.; Hewell, "Neighborhood Health," p. 8.

43. See e.g., *Wave*, 10 February 1949; Hewell, "Neighborhood Health," p. 8.

44. Hewell, "Neighborhood Health," pp. 15, 23, 24.

45. Ibid., pp. 23–24, 29.

46. *Long Island Press*, 25 March 1954.

47. Ibid., 9 June 1954.

48. *Rockaway Review*, December 1957.

49. See chapter 2.

50. *Long Island Press*, 27 March 1954.

51. *Rockaway Review*, August 1952.

52. *Wave*, 24 April 1952, 10 July 1952, 12 March 1953.

53. *New York Daily News*, 10 May 1953.

54. *Rockaway Review*, October 1953.

55. *Wave*, 17 September 1952; Hewell, "Neighborhood Health," p. 42.

56. Charles Abrams, *Forbidden Neighbors: A Study of Prejudice in Housing* (New York: Harper and Row, 1955), pp. 181–82; Sugrue, *Urban Crisis*, p. 214

57. See Wolpert's letter to Moses, *Wave*, 10 July 1952.

58. *Rockaway Review*, June, July 1952. Emphasis added.

59. *Wave*, 21 May 1953.

60. Ibid., 2 July 1953.

61. *Daily News*, 10 May 1953.

62. *Wave*, 12 June 1958; also see *Long Island Press*, 11 November 1958.

63. *Rockaway Review*, October 1958.

64. *Wave*, 4 September 1958.

65. As quoted by Davies in *Neighborhood Groups*, pp. 59–60, from New York Housing and Redevelopment files.

66. *Wave*, e.g., 28 October 1958.

67. James J. Crisona to the Board of Estimate, Moses Papers, Box 1260-3, 2 October 1958, MTA.

68. Gorelick, Sol (formerly of the Brownsville Welfare Center), phone interview, 25 April 1999.

69. E.g., *Long Island Press*, 2 August 1954.

70. Ibid., 25 March 1954.

71. E.g., *Wave*, 25 March 1954, 21 March 1957.

72. *Long Island Press*, 14 August 1958.

73. Ibid., 8 November 1958; *Wave*, 13 November 1958, 20 November 1958.

74. *Long Island Press*, 15 November 1958.

5. Robert Moses and the End of a Resort

1. *The WPA Guide to New York City: The Federal Writers' Project Guide to the 1930s* (New York: Random House, 1992), p. 591.

2. Ibid.

3. The historical information comes from Kenneth T. Jackson, ed., *The Encyclopedia of New York City* (New Haven: Yale University Press, 1995) and Vincent Seyfried and William Asadorian, *Old Rockaway, New York, in Early Photographs* (Mineola, N.Y.: Dover, 2000), passim.

4. *Rockaway Review*, October 1950. This refers to the total number of beachgoers who were tabulated each day for the entire summer, not to forty-eight million different individuals.

5. Ibid., February 1958.

6. Ibid., June, July 1959.

7. See, e.g., Seyfried and Asadorian, *Old Rockaway*, "Introduction."

8. *Rockaway Review*, October 1958.

9. Lena Lencek and Gideon Bosker, *The Beach: The History of Paradise on Earth* (New York: Viking, 1998), passim.

10. All figures supplied by U.S. Census Reports.

11. *Rockaway Review*, December 1959.

12. Robert Moses, *Housing and Recreation* (New York: New York City Department of Parks, 1938).

13. *Rockaway Review*, October 1958.

14. Ibid., June 1946, October 1948.

15. Ibid., August 1948.

16. New York City Department of Parks, Files, Box 107888, Folder 125, Municipal Archives.

17. *Rockaway Review*, September 1949.

18. Alexander Garvin, *The American City: What Works, What Doesn't* (New York: McGraw Hill, 1966), p. 68.

19. *Long Island Press*, 13 October 1957, 23 September 1959.

20. Robert F. Wagner, General Correspondence, 1961, Municipal Archives.

21. *Rockaway Review*, September 1938.

22. See chapter 1.

23. New York City Department of Parks, *The Future of Jamaica Bay* (1938).

24. Samuel P. Hays, *Conservation and the Gospel of Efficiency: The Progressive Conservation Movement, 1890–1920* (New York: Atheneum, 1969).

25. *Rockaway Review*, October 1958; See also October 1944, April 1945.

26. *The Future of Jamaica Bay.*

27. *Rockaway Review*, April 1945.

28. *Long Island Press*, 18 June 1948.

29. *The Urban Audubon*, August–September 1987; also see chapter 3.

30. *New York Times*, 7 May 1955; Jackson, ed., *Encyclopedia of New York City.*

31. *Newsday*, 20 June 1970.

32. Jeffrey A. Kroessler, "Building Queens: The Urbanization of New York City's Largest Borough" (Ph.D. diss, City University of New York, 1991), p. 435.

33. *Rockaway Review*, October 1958; *Long Island Press*, 10 October 1958.

34. *Rockaway Review*, June, July 1954.

35. Moses Files, Box 1260-3, 13 October 1961, MTA.

36. Symbolic of the changing character of the Rockaways, since 1996 certain bayside parks and ball fields have been used by immigrants for playing cricket.

37. *Rockaway Review*, August 1951.

38. Ibid., February 1949.

39. Crisona's involvement was indicated by Assemblywoman Audrey Pfeffer. Interview, 27 June 2000.

40. Department of Parks, Files, Box 107902, Folder 62, Municipal Archives.

41. *Long Island Press*, 11 May 1958.

42. New York City Department of Parks, Files, Box 107902, Folder 62, Municipal Archives.

43. Ibid.

44. Wagner, General Correspondence, 8 July 1955, Municipal Archives.

45. *Long Island Press*, 11 May 1958; *Rockaway Review*, October 1958.

46. See chapter 6 for details.

47. Moses Papers, Box 116, 22 October 1957, New York Public Library.

6. Storms over Title I

1. Mauss, Evelyn, phone interview, 29 April 1999.

2. Michael Harrington, *The Other America: Poverty in the United States* (New York: Macmillan, 1962).

3. Grace Hewell, "Neighborhood Health Improvement Through Functional Organization" (Ph.D. diss., Columbia Teachers College, 1958). p. 181.

4. See, e.g., *Wave*, 9 November 1967.

5. J. Clarence Davies III, *Neighborhood Groups and Urban Renewal* (New York: Columbia University Press, 1966), p. 38; See Kenneth L. Kusmer, *A Ghetto Takes Place: Black Cleveland, 1870–1970* (Urbana: University of Illinois Press, 1976), pp. 245–47; Arnold R. Hirsch, *Making the Second Ghetto: Race and Housing in Chicago, 1940–1960* (New York: Cambridge University Press, 1983), p. 129.

6. Davies reaches a similar conclusion. See *Neighborhood Groups*, pp. 33–34.

7. Robert A. Caro, *The Power Broker: Robert Moses and the Fall of New York* (New York: Vintage Books, 1975), pp. 318–19, 513–14, 557, 1086–87; *Newsday*, 4 December 1988.

8. Martin Anderson, *The Federal Bulldozer: A Critical Analysis of Urban Renewal* (Cambridge: M.I.T. Press, 1964), p. 42.

9. Norman I. Fainstein and Susan S. Fainstein, "Governing Regimes and the Political Economy of Development in New York City, 1946–1984," in *Power, Culture, and Place*, ed. John Hull Mollenkopf, (New York: Russell Sage Foundation, 1980), p. 165.

10. NYC Housing Authority, Files, Series 06, Box 068c2, Folder 2, La-Guardia Community College.

11. Ibid.

12. Robert Moses, *Public Works: A Dangerous Trade* (New York: McGraw Hill, 1970), pp. 454–56.

13. Letter to James J. Crisona, 28 October 1958, Moses Papers, Box 117, New York Public Library.

14. Kenneth T. Jackson, ed., *Encyclopedia of New York City* (New Haven: Yale University Press, 1995); Moses Papers, Box 116, New York Public Library.

15. Caro, *Power Broker*, p. 965.

16. *Newsday*, 14 December 1988.

17. Ibid., 13 October 1974.

18. NYC Housing Authority, Files, Series 06, Boxes 068C2 and 068C3, Folder 2, 2 December 1953, 2 and 18 October 1954, LaGuardia Community College.

19. *Wave: 100th Anniversary Collector's Edition* 24 July, 1993, p. 66.

20. Alice McDermott, *Charming Billy*, (New York: Delta, 1998), p. 54.

21. *Wave*, 25 February 1954, 4 March 1954.

22. Ibid., 18 February 1954.

23. Hewell, "Neighborhood Health," p. 52.

24. As quoted by Davies, *Neighborhood Groups*, p. 43.

25. Caro, *Power Broker*, p. 277.

26. *Long Island Press*, 17 February 1955, 28 July 1955.

27. See chapter 7.

28. *Wave*, 18 March 1954, 15 April 1954, 20 April 1954, 18 March 1954, 27 May 1954.

29. NYC Housing Authority, Files, Box 068C1, Folder 4, 3 June 1954, La-Guardia Community College.

30. *Wave*, 3 June 1954.

31. *New York Times*, 17 June 1954.

32. Moses, *Public Works*, p. 455.

33. Ibid.

34. See, e.g., *Wave*, 12 June 1958, 6 November 1958.

35. Moses, *Public Works*, p. 455.

36. Davies, *Neighborhood Groups*, p.47.

37. New York City Board of Estimate, Papers, 18 December 1958, Municipal Archives.

38. Moses Papers, Box 117, 29 September 1958, New York Public Library.

39. See chapter 5.

40. Caro, *Power Broker* p. 746.

41. Ibid., pp. 749–51.

42. *Long Island Press*, 5 April 1958, 2 July 1959.

43. Ibid., 30 September 1959; Moses, *Public Works*, p. 455.

44. *Long Island Press*, 3 November 1959; Moses, *Public Works*, p. 455.

45. Davies, *Neighborhood Groups*, pp. 56–58.

46. Moses, *Public Works*, p. 456; Davies, *Neighborhood Groups*, pp. 51–56. We have generally followed their treatments, as well as information obtained from interviews.

47. See chapter 7.

48. Moses, *Public Works*, p. 456.

49. Caro, *Power Broker*, p. 1065.

50. Ibid., pp. 1047–59; Davies, *Neighborhood Groups*, pp. 17–19. Mollen, Milton,

interview, New York, 2 October 1998; Winnick, Louis D., interview, New York, 14 September, 1998. These interviews helped clarify the way in which Moses was eased out of power in city housing matters.

51. Davies, *Neighborhood Groups*, pp. 19–23.

7. Where They Live

1. *Long Island Press*, 12 December 1959.

2. Ibid., 15 December 1960, *The New York Post*, 29 June 1961, 30 June 1961; Doris Moss, "A Study of Attitudes Towards Community Problems in Arverne, Queens" (master's thesis, Brooklyn College, 1965), p. 27.

3. Moss, "Study of Attitudes," p. 27.

4. *Long Island Press*, 17 December 1959.

5. Moses Files, Box 1262-2, 30 September 1959, MTA.

6. *Long Island Press*, 12 August 1958; *New York Post*, 28 June 1961.

7. *Long Island Press*, 9 April 1961, *New York Post*, 28 June 1961; J. Clarence Davies III, *Neighborhood Groups and Urban Renewal* (New York: Columbia University Press, 1966), p. 59.

8. Davies, *Neighborhood Groups*, p. 59.

9. Moss, "Study of Attitudes," pp. 24–25.

10. *Long Island Press*, 17 December 1959.

11. Ibid., 9 April 1961.

12. Ibid. A Title I commissioner said that 500 of the 664 Hammels site families who had moved out as of 9 April 1961 were presumed to be living in the Rockaways.

13. Norman I. Fainstein and Susan S. Fainstein, "Governing Regimes and the Political Economy of Development in New York City, 1946–1984," in *Power, Culture, and Place*, ed. John Hull Mollenkopf (New York: Russell Sage Foundation, 1980), p. 167.

14. Moses Files, Box 1262-4, 6 August 1958, MTA; *Long Island Press*, 10 October 1958.

15. Moses Files, Box 1262-4, December 1958, MTA; Moses Papers, Box 116, New York Public Library.

16. Moses Files, Box 1262-2, MTA.

17. Moses Papers, Box 117, New York Public Library.

18. *Long Island Press*, 4 April 1961.

19. Green, Rev. Moses and Louidell, interview, Rockaway, N.Y., 6 April 1999.

20. *New York Post*, 30 June 1961.

21. Moses Files, Box 1259-1, 1957, MTA.

22. *Long Island Press*, 11 August 1958; *Rockaway Review*, August, September 1962.

23. Moss, "Study of Attitudes," p. 25.

24. *New York Times*, 19 November 1959; Davies, *Neighborhood Groups*, pp. 40–41.

25. Zipkin, Norman, phone interview, 8 May 1999.

26. NYC Housing Authority, Files, Box 0070Ef, LaGuardia Community College.

27. *Long Island Press*, 18 November 1958; *Rockaway Review*, October 1959.

28. *Rockaway Review*, January 1956.

29. *Long Island Press*, 12 February 1959.

30. Moses Files, Box 1262-3, 17 September 1958, MTA; *Long Island Press*, 21 February 1959.

31. *Long Island Press*, 9 April 1961.

32. Ibid., 17 December 1959.

33. Moses Papers, Box 117, 15 December 1958, New York Public Library.

34. *Long Island Press*, 13 April 1960.

35. Ibid., 23 March 1961.

36. *Rockaway Review*, December 1960.

37. Vincent J. Cannato, *The Ungovernable City: John Lindsay and His Struggle to Save New York* (New York: Basic Books, 2001), p. 113.

38. *Long Island Press*, 11 February 1960, 12 April 1960.

39. *New York Post*, 29 June 1961.

40. Ibid., 28 June 1961.

41. *Rockaway Review*, December 1960. Emphasis added.

42. Davies, *Neighborhood Groups*, p. 66.

43. See letters in Robert F. Wagner, General Correspondence, 1960, Municipal Archives.

44. *New York Times*, 11 November 1959.

45. *Wave*, 26 November 1959.

46. As quoted by Davies, *Neighborhood Groups*, p. 62.

47. *New York Post*, 30 June 1961.

48. Information about Rev. May comes from Robinson, Dr. Ann E. G., interview, New Haven, Conn., 27 March 1999; and members of Mount Carmel Church, interview, Rockaway, N.Y., 18 December 1998. Also see Margo Janet McKenzie and Julia Mae Blair, *Reverend Joseph H. May: Pastor, Humanitarian, Community Activist* (Arverne, N.Y.: May Book Dedication Committee, 2001).

49. Rausnitz, Helen and William, interviews, Rockaway, N.Y., 10 December 1998.

50. *Long Island Press*, 21 January 1960.

51. Davies, *Neighborhood Groups*, pp. 65–66.

52. *Long Island Press*, 9 April 1961.

53. Davies, *Neighborhood Groups*, p. 66.

54. *Wave*, 3 April 1962.

55. Rausnitz, Helen and William, interviews.

56. Nathan Glazer, "Housing Problems and Housing Policies," *Public Interest* 7 (spring 1967): 21–51; Jane Jacobs, *The Death and Life of Great American Cities* (New York: Modern Library, 1993).

57. Glasgow, Lovette, interview, Rockaway, N.Y., 22 January 1999; Maple, Goldie, interview, Rockaway, N.Y., 22 January 1999; Klein, Julie, interview, West New York, N.J., 4 October 2001.

58. Robinson, interview.

59. Davies, *Neighborhood Groups*, p. 63.

60. *Long Island Press*, 6 September 1961.

61. Ibid., 17 September 1961.

62. *Wave*, 19 April 1962.

63. *Daily News*, 15 October 1961; Davies, *Neighborhood Groups*, p. 67.

64. *Long Island Press*, 14 March 1962.

65. *Amsterdam News*, 30 December 1961.

66. *Wave*, 15 March 1962.

67. *Rockaway Journal*, 8 October 1974.

8. Trends of the Sixties

1. See his letter to a Rockaway correspondent, Moses Files, Box 1262-3, 15 December 1958, MTA.

2. Moses Papers, Box 117, 17 December 1959, New York Public Library.

3. Ibid.

4. Moses Files, Box 1260-3, 31 October 1961, MTA.

5. Moses Papers, Box 117, 17 December 1959, New York Public Library.

6. Moses Files, Box 1260-3, 28 December 1961, MTA.

7. Ibid.

8. Ibid.

9. Moses Files, Box 1260-3, 27 November 1961, 21 May 1962, MTA; DeMatteis, Fred, interview, Rockaway, N.Y., 14 July 1999.

10. Moses Files, Box 1260-3, 12 December 1961, MTA.

11. *New York Times*, 4 September 1962.

12. J. Clarence Davies III, *Neighborhood Groups and Urban Renewal* (New York: Columbia University Press, 1966), pp. 17–18; see also chapter 5.

13. Moses Files, Box 1260-3, 21 December 1961, 18 May 1962, MTA.

14. *Newsday*, 4 December 1988.

15. Moses Files, Box 1260-3, 2 November 1961, 19 March 1962, MTA.

16. Ibid., 3 April 1962, 18 May 1962.

17. Ibid., 27 August 1962.

18. Ibid.

19. Ibid., 5 September 1962.

20. Robert A. Caro, *The Power Broker: Robert Moses and the Fall of New York*

(New York: Vintage Books, 1975), pp. 1073–76; "Public Papers of Nelson Rockefeller" (New York: State of New York, 1963), p. 280.

21. New York Department of City Planning, Newsletters, September, October 1963; Moses Files, 1260-3, 27 August 1962, MTA.

22. New York Department of City Planning, Newsletters, April, May 1964.

23. Ibid., November 1964.

24. *Rockaway Review*, June, July 1963.

25. Davies, *Neighborhood Groups*, p. 68.

26. *Rockaway Review*, December 1963.

27. Doris Moss, "A Study of Attitudes Towards Community Problems in
Arverne, Queens" (master's thesis, Brooklyn College, 1965), p. 93.

28. *Long Island Star Journal*, 16 March 1966.

29. Moss, "Study of Attitudes," pp. 60–61.

30. *New York Times*, 23 May 1980.

31. Doris Moss, "Arverne Revisited: The Relative Importance of Community Problems" (Ph.D. diss., New York University School of Education, 1972), pp.
99, 186–87.

32. *New York Times*, 9 December 1966.

33. "Comprehensive Pediatric Care for Rockaway," paper submitted to New
York Department of Health, Education, and Welfare, 1966; Klein, Julie, interview, West New York, N.J., 4 October 2001.

34. *Wave*, 19 October 1967, 9 September 1971; Moss, "Arverne Revisited,"
pp. 71, 196.

35. *New York Times*, 13 January 1972.

36. "Comprehensive Pediatric Care."

37. Moss, "Arverne Revisited," pp. 192, 196.

38. Ann Braden Johnson, *Out of Bedlam: The Truth About Deinstitutionalization* (New York: Basic Books, 1980), pp. 37, 93, 120, 125; *New York Times*, 13 December 2001, 28 April 2002.

39. Michael Winerip, "Bedlam on the Streets," *New York Times Magazine* (23
May 1999).

40. *Sunday Daily News*, 21 July 1974; *The New York Times Magazine* article emphasizes the dangers to the community of unsupervised released mental
patients.

41. *Long Island Press*, 8 June 1974.

42. United Way of New York City, *Neighborhood Profile No. 3: The Rocka-
ways/Broad Channel Community District 12, Queens*, (New York: United Way,
1994), p. 9.

43. Rausnitz, Helen and William, interviews, Rockaway, N.Y., 10 December
1998 and 7 July 1999; Pfeffer, Audrey, interview, Rockaway, N.Y., 27 June 2000;
Locke, Leon, interview, Rockaway, N.Y., 5 October 1998.

44. Klein, Julie, interview.

45. Moss, "Arverne Revisited," pp. 71, 216; *Daily News*, 3 May 1970; Klein,

Julie, interview; Green, Rev. Moses and Louidell, interview, Rockaway, N.Y., 6 April 1999.

46. Babian, Elaine, Goldie Maple, and Lovette Glasgow, interviews, New York, 20 September 2001.

47. *Wave*, 17 March 1969; "Profile: Lena Cook," prepared by the Committee for the Reelection of Lena Cook, 1970.

48. Mauss, Evelyn, phone interview, 29 April, 1999; Schwach, Howard, interview, Rockaway, N.Y., 1 April 2002; Maple, interview.

49. Green, Rev. Moses, interview.

50. Margo Janet McKenzie and Julia Mae Blair, *Reverend Joseph H. May: Pastor, Humanitarian, Community Activist* (Arverne, N.Y.: The Reverend H. May Book Dedication Committee, 2001).

51. *Wave*, 6 September 1962; *Long Island Press*, 17 May 1962, 28 June 1962.

52. Wagner, General Correspondence, 7 July 1962, 12 July 1962, Municipal Archives.

53. *Long Island Press*, 28 November 1964.

54. Wagner, General Correspondence, 6 June 1963, Municipal Archives.

55. Glasgow and Maple, interviews.

56. *Wave*, 10 January 1963.

57. Jewel Bellush, "Housing: The Scattered Site Controversy," in *Race and Politics*, ed. Jewel Bellush and Stephen M. David (New York: Prager, 1971) p. 110.

58. *Long Island Press*, 30 November 1964; Wagner, General Correspondence, 6 June 1963, Municipal Archives.

59. *Long Island Press*, 16 June 1963.

60. See chapter 10.

61. Interviews with Goldie Maple and residents, former and present.

62. There is a good discussion of this process in Alexander Garvin, *The American City: What Works, What Doesn't* (New York: McGraw Hill, 1966), pp. 169–70.

63. Elizabeth Wood, *The Small Hard Core: The Housing of Problem Families in New York City* (New York: Citizens Housing and Planning Council, 1957); Nicholas Lemann, *The Promised Land* (New York: Knopf, 1991) p. 233.

64. Kenneth T. Jackson, *Crabgrass Frontier* (New York: Oxford University Press, 1985), p. 227; Norman I. Fainstein and Susan S. Fainstein, "Governing Regimes and the Political Economy of Development in New York City, 1946–1984," in *Power, Culture, and Place*, ed. John Hull Mollenkopf (New York: Russell Sage Foundation, 1980), p. 75.

65. Gaska, (District Manager) Jonathan L., interview, Rockaway, N.Y., 16 April 2002.

66. Pfeffer, interview.

67. Barry Gotteher, *The Mayor's Man* (New York: Doubleday, 1975), p. 298.

68. *Long Island Press*, 9 May 1975.

69. United Way, *Neighborhood Profile No. 3*, p. 24.

70. *Sunday Daily News*, 29 July 1984.

71. Roger Starr, "Easing the Housing Crisis," in *New York Unbound*, ed. Peter D. Salins (New York: Basil Blackwell, 1988) p. 179; Garvin, *The American City*, p. 170.

72. Muñoz, Glenn, phone interview, 5 April 2000; Glenn Muñoz lived in the Grant Houses from 1958 to 1977.

73. *Wave*, 28 March 1968.

9. The Whitest Neighborhood in New York City

1. Vincent Seyfried and William Asadorian. *Old Rockaway, New York, in Early Photographs* (Mineola, N.Y.: Dover, 2000), p. 94.

2. *Rockaway News*, 20 July 1995.

3. *Long Island Press*, 14 March 1960.

4. Ibid.; *Long Island Star Journal*, 14 March 1960.

5. Atlantic Improvement Corporation, Annual Report, 1963, Breezy Point Files, Municipal Archives.

6. *Long Island Press*, 17 March 1960; *Long Island Star Journal*, 18 March 1960.

7. *Sunday Daily News*, 30 September 1973.

8. *Rockaway News*, 20 July 1995; *Long Island Press*, 11 November 1960.

9. *New York Herald Tribune*, 19 April 1966.

10. *Newsday*, 17 September 1966; *Herald Tribune*, 31 May 1963.

11. See advertisement in the *New York Times*, 26 July 1963.

12. Robert A. Caro, *The Power Broker: Robert Moses and the Fall of New York* (New York: Vintage, 1975), p. 779.

13. *New York Times*, 15 August 1962.

14. See Robert Paul Gregory, "Parks and People, Values and Decisions: Proposals for the Breezy Point Park, New York City" (Ph.D. diss., Cornell University, 1980).

15. *Long Island Press*, 10 April 1962; *New York Times*, 24 July 1963; *Herald Tribune*, 19 April 1965.

16. *New York Times*, 5 October 1962.

17. *World Telegram and Sun*, 20 September 1962.

18. Breezy Point Files, Municipal Archives.

19. *Long Island Press*, 29 November 1962.

20. *New York Times*, 26 August 1962.

21. Gregory, "Parks and People," p. 14.

22. *Herald Tribune*, 6 June 1963; *New York Times*, 23 July 1963.

23. *New York Times*, 4 April 1963, 22 July 1962; Starr, Roger, interview, New York, 5 May, 1999.

24. *New York Times*, 19 October 1962; *Herald Tribune*, 7 July 1963; *Long Island Press*, 27 March 1963.

25. *New York Times*, 3 October 1962, 5 October 1962; *Herald Tribune*, 11 October 1962.

26. See list compiled by Breezy Point Cooperative, Breezy Point Files, 20 December 1962, Municipal Archives.

27. *Long Island Press*, 31 October 1962.

28. Breezy Point Files, 22 August 1963, Municipal Archives; *New York Journal-American*, 29 October 1962.

29. *New York Times*, 11 October 1961; *Herald Tribune*, 25 November 1962.

30. *New York Times*, 6 August 1963.

31. Newsletter, Citizens Housing and Planning Council, 16 July 1963.

32. Gregory, "Parks and People," p. 19.

33. *New York Times*, 26 November 1962; *Herald Tribune*, 16 December 1962. Newbold Morris was one of the members and this was his reservation.

34. *Long Island Press*, 27 March 1963.

35. Ibid., 1 November 1962.

36. Ibid., 4 April 1963; *Herald Tribune*, 14 April 1963.

37. *New York Times*, 5 April 1963, 20 April 1963, 23 April 1963.

38. Ibid., 3 June 1963.

39. This was suggested by Roger Starr, interview.

40. *Herald Tribune*, 19 April 1965.

41. Ibid., 4 June 1963.

42. Ibid., 23 July 1963; *New York Times*, 22 July 1963.

43. *New York Times*, 24 July 1963.

44. Newsletter, Citizens Housing and Planning Council, August 1963.

45. *Herald Tribune*, 13 September 1963; *New York Times*, 16 September 1963.

46. *Long Island Press*, 13 September 1963; Gregory, "Parks and People," p. 32.

47. Atlantic Improvement Corporation, Annual Report, 1963, Breezy Point Files, Municipal Archives.

48. Ibid.

49. *New York Times*, 3 December 1974; *Long Island Press*, 2 July 1976; *New York Post*, 16 June 1967.

50. *Long Island Star Journal*, 8 August 1964.

51. *Daily News*, 30 September 1973.

52. "Statement on Breezy Point," Queens Chamber of Commerce, Queensborough Public Library, 14 August 1962.

53. Moses's words, *New York Times*, 3 February 1969.

54. Nat Hentoff, *A Political Life: The Education of John Lindsay*, (New York: Knopf, 1969) p. 297.

55. *New York Times*, 4 July 1968.

56. Ibid., 14 May 1969.

57. Ibid., 29 December 1972.

58. *Daily News*, 30 April 1969.

59. *New York Times*, 15 December 1969.

60. Gregory, "Parks and People," p. 39.

61. *New York Times*, 29 December 1972.

62. Parks Council Newsletter, December 1971, Municipal Archives.

63. *Newsday*, 17 November 1982.

64. *New York Times*, 18 June 2001.

65. *Rockaway News*, 20 July 1995.

10. Divergences

1. Vann, Sid, interview, Lawrence, N.Y., 25 August 1998.

2. Cirker, Heywood, interview, Mineola, N.Y., 7 July 1998; Locke, Leon, interview, Rockaway, N.Y., 5 October 1998; and others.

3. Moses Papers, Box 117, 24 March 1958, New York Public Library.

4. *New York Times*, 6 June 1958, 14 June 1958.

5. Ibid., 18 June 1958; also see the brief prepared by Karelsen & Karelsen law firm and sent to the Rockaway Chamber of Commerce, 14 June 1958, kindly provided to the authors by Emil Lucev.

6. *Sheridan v. Crisona*, New York State Court of Appeals, 2 April 1964.

7. Locke, interview.

8. Samuel G. Freedman describes this practice in Brooklyn in *Upon This Rock: The Miracles of a Black Church* (New York: Harper Collins, 1993), p. 104.

9. *Wave*, 27 April 1972.

10. Douglas S. Massey and Nancy A. Denton, *American Apartheid: Segregation and the Making of the Underclass* (Cambridge: Harvard University Press, 1993), pp. 14, 179.

11. *Long Island Press*, 9 March 1975.

12. *Daily News*, 1 August 1971; Russo, Mario, interview, Rockaway, N.Y., 1 February 1999.

13. *Wave*, 17 February 1972. Emphasis in the original.

14. New York City Commission on Human Rights, Neighborhood Stabilization Program, *Redlining in Rockaway*, (New York, 1978).

15. Zipkin, Norman, phone interview, 8 May 1999; Brodbar, Norman, interview, Hackensack, N.J., 17 September 2001. Also see Craig Steven Wilder, *A Covenant with Color: Race and Social Power in Brooklyn* (New York: Columbia University Press, 2000), pp. 227, 229.

16. This paragraph and the next are based on several interviews conducted over a four year period.

17. Glasgow, Lovette, and Goldie Maple, interview, Rockaway, N.Y., 22 January, 1999.

18. Mary Pattillo-McCoy, *Black Picket Fences: Privilege and Peril Among the Black Middle Class* (Chicago: University of Chicago Press, 1999), pp. 6, 38, 215.

19. *Wave*, 25 March 1954.

20. Doris Moss, "Arverne Revisited: The Relative Importance of Community Problems" (Ph.D. diss. New York University School of Education, 1972), p. 91; New York City Board of Education Utilization Handbook, 1971.

21. Babian, Elaine, interview, New York, 12 May 1999; Rausnitz, Helen, interview, Rockaway, N.Y., 10 December 1998 and 7 July 1999.

22. *Wave*, 18 January 1968.

23. Oakes, Sonya, phone interview, 1 June 2000; Liebling, Brenda, phone interview, 22 May 2000.

24. Diane Ravitch, *The Great School Wars* (New York: Basic Books, 1974), p. 268.

25. Interviews with Elaine Babian and Brenda Liebling.

26. Kenneth B. Clark, *Dark Ghetto: Dilemmas of Social Power*, 2nd ed. (Middletown, Conn.: Wesleyan University Press, 1965), pp. 127–28.

27. Green, Rev. Moses and Louidell, interviews, Rockaway, N.Y., 6 April 1999.

28. Moss, "Arverne Revisited," pp. 131, 182.

29. Ibid., p. 194.

30. Brown, Ernest, interview, Rockaway, N.Y., 2 July 2000; Babian, interview.

31. *Wave*, 6 February 1964.

32. Ibid., 1 March 1973.

33. Brown and Maple, interviews.

34. Babian, interview.

35. Cohen, Mickey, phone interview, 29 May 2000; Lerner, Ray, interview, Rockaway, N.Y., 18 July 2001.

36. Cohen, interview; Goldschmidt, Bridget, interview, New York, 23 April 2000.

37. Moss "Arverne Revisited," pp. 72–75; *Rockaway Review*, September 1950; Community Board #14, *Resource Directory*, July 1998.

38. George Kranzler, *Williamsburg: A Jewish Community in Transition*, (New York: Philipp Feldheim, 1961), pp. 15, 206; Egon Mayer, *From Suburb to Shtetl: The Jews of Boro Park* (Philadelphia: Temple University Press, 1979), pp. 24, 35, 83.

39. Interviews with Howard Schwach (Rockaway, N.Y., 1 April 2002) and some members of the Orthodox community who preferred to remain anonymous.

40. *Wave*, 14 December 1967; *Daily News*, 27 November 1971.

41. Pfeffer, Audrey, interview, Rockaway, N.Y., 27 June 2000.

42. Stephen Gregory has noted similar activities among black women in Corona. See *Black Corona: Race and the Politics of Place in an Urban Community* (Princeton: Princeton University Press, 1998), p. 54.

43. Maple and Glasgow, interviews.

44. United Way of New York City, *Neighborhood Profile No. 3: The Rockaways/Broad Channel Community District 12, Queens* (New York: United Way, 1994).

45. *New York Times*, 19 August 2001.

46. *Boston Globe*, 19 September 2001; *New York Times*, 18 November 2001.

47. *The Wave: 100th Anniversary Collector's Edition*; Schwach, interview.

48. Rauch, Stuart, phone interview, 15 January 2002.

49. Vincent J. Cannato, *The Ungovernable City: John Lindsay and His Struggle to Save New York* (New York: Basic Books, 2001), p. 41.

11. The 310 Acres

1. Douglas Yates, *The Ungovernable City* (Cambridge: MIT Press, 1977), p. 153.

2. Vincent J. Cannato, *The Ungovernable City: John Lindsay and His Struggle to Save New York* (New York: Basic Books, 2001), p.43.

3. Governor Rockefeller continued to send in his articles. See Lindsay, General Correspondence, 1 May 1971, 19 June 1972, Municipal Archives.

4. Charles R. Morris, *The Cost of Good Intentions: New York City and the Liberal Experiment, 1965–1975* (New York: W. W. Norton, 1980), pp. 17–18.

5. Moses Files, Box 1258-3, 1949, MTA.

6. Alexander Garvin, *The American City: What Works, What Doesn't* (New York: McGraw Hill, 1966), pp. 134–35.

7. Moses Files, Box 1260-14, June 1967, MTA.

8. Elliot, Don, interview, 29 September 1998.

9. *Long Island Press*, 22 July 1966, 29 October 1966.

10. Department of City Planning, Newsletter, November 1964.

11. *Rockaway Review*, December 1964, February, March 1965.

12. *Long Island Press*, 3 August 1966.

13. New York City Planning Commision, *Plan for New York City: Queens, a Proposal* (New York, 1969).

14. New York City Planning Commission, *The Rockaways: A Report to the Community* (New York, 1973).

15. E.g., Borough of Queens, *The Rockaway Plan*, February 1973; Queens Borough President, "Study and Recommendation for the Development of the Recreational Resources & Parklands of the Rockaway Penninsula & Broad Channel" (New York, 1975).

16. Planning Commission, *Queens: A Proposal*; Planning Commission, *The Rockaways*.

17. *Long Island Press*, 19 February 1967.

18. *Wave*, 11 May 1970, 6 August 1970.

19. *Long Island Press*, 21 April 1967.

20. *New York Times*, 8 December 1966; Lindsay, Subject Files, Box 11, 26 May 1967, Municipal Archives.

21. Walsh, Al, interview, New York, 28 April 2000; Elliot, Don, interview, New York, 29 September 1998.

22. Garvin, Alexander, phone interview, 24 June 1999.

23. DeMatteis, Fred. interview, Rockaway, N.Y., 14 July 1999.

24. Moses Files, Box 1261-4, 2 December 1968, MTA.

25. *Long Island Press*, 5 February 1967.

26. Ibid., 20 May 1967.

27. *Sunday Daily News*, 2 May 1971; *The Village Voice*, 19 August 1971.

28. Village Voice, 19 August 1971.

29. *Rockaway Review*, "Holiday Issue," 1967.

30. E.g., *Wave*, 20 March 1969, 8 January 1970.

31. Ibid., 24 July 1969; also see above, chapter 4.

32. *Wave*, 7 January 1971; *Village Voice*, 19 August 1971.

33. *Long Island Press*, 23 November 1969.

34. Gottehrer, Barry. *The Mayor's Man* (New York: Doubleday, 1975), pp. 41, 71.

35. See chapter 6.

36. *Long Island Press*, 13 January 1970.

37. Ibid., 20 May 1967; *Rockaway Review*, Summer 1968.

38. *Long Island Press*, 13 September 1966.

39. Planning Commission, *The Rockaways*; also see chapter 8.

40. *Village Voice*, 19 August 1971; Moses Files, Box 1261-4, 2 December 1968, MTA.

41. *Long Island Press*, 6 December 1967; *Daily News*, 11 January 1970.

42. Walsh, interview.

43. *Long Island Press*, 22 March 1970.

44. *Village Voice*, 19 August 1971.

45. *Long Island Press*, 14 November 1970, 1 March 1971, 18 March 1971.

46. Ibid., 18 March 1971.

47. Ibid., 4 March 1971; *Daily News*, 18 March 1971.

48. *Long Island Press*, 2 April 1971, 11 May 1971.

49. Lindsay, General Correspondence, 1971, Municipal Archives.

50. See chapter 8.

51. *Long Island Press*, 2 May 1971; *Village Voice*, 19 August 1971.

52. *Wave*, 12 October 1971.

53. *New York Times*, 13 January 1972; *Rockaway Review*, 1974.

54. *New York Times*, 26 May 1986; Queens County, "The Rockaway Resort Casino Study," January 1979; United Way of New York City, *Neighborhood Profile No. 3: The Rockaways/Broad Channel Community District 12, Queens* (New York: United Way, 1994).

55. *Rockaway Review*, 1973, 1974.

56. *Wave*, 24 July 1969, 20 August 1970, 4 January 1973.

57. Ibid., 9 March 1972.

58. Cannato, *Ungovernable City*, p. 509; Locke, Leon, interview, Rockaway, N.Y., 5 October 1998.

59. *Long Island Press*, 16 April 1970, 23 April 1973.

60. Ibid., 7 November 1974, 19 November 1975.

61. *New York Times*, 28 December 2001.

62. Ibid., 9 December 1966, 9 August 1967.

63. *Rockaway Review*, summer 1968.

64. Ibid., "Holiday Issue," 1967; Planning Commission, *The Rockaways*.

65. *Rockaway Journal*, 4 May 1971; Queens County, "Casino Study."

66. *New York Times*, 9 January 1973.

67. Ibid., 30 January 1973.

68. *Rockaway Review*, 1973, our emphasis.

69. *New York Times*, 18 July 1987.

70. *Daily News*, 28 November 1974; *Long Island Press*, 26 October 1975.

71. *Long Island Press*, 5 December 1975.

72. John H. Mollenkopf, *A Phoenix in the Ashes: The Rise and Fall of the Koch Coalition in New York City Politics* (Princeton: Princeton University Press, 1992), p. 13.

73. Norman I. Fainstein and Susan S. Fainstein, "Governing Regimes and the Political Economy of Development in New York City, 1946–1984," in *Power, Culture, and Place*, ed. John Hull Mollenkopf (New York: Russell Sage Foundation, 1980), p. 180.

74. For an excellent account of these cuts on one Queens neighborhood, see Roger Sanjek, *The Future of Us All: Race and Neighborhood Politics in New York City* (Ithaca, N.Y.: Cornell University Press, 2000), pp. 93–94.

75. Paul A. Jargowsky, *Poverty and Place: Ghettos, Barrios, and the American City* (New York: Russell Sage Foundation, 1997), pp. 46–47. "Barrio" is defined as an area of high Hispanic poverty. See chapter 2, note 10, for a definition of "ghetto."

76. Mollenkopf, *Phoenix*, p. 133.

77. *New York Times*, 18 July 1987. There is a sizeable literature here; see e.g., Jane Jacobs, *The Death and Life of Great American Cities* (New York: Modern Library, 1993); Martin Anderson, *The Federal Bulldozer: A Critical Analysis of Urban Renewal* (Cambridge: MIT Press, 1964); Richard Plunz, *A History of Housing in New York City* (New York: Columbia University Press,1990).

78. George Sternlieb and David Listokin, "A Review of National Housing Policy," in *Housing America's Poor*, ed. Peter D. Salins (Chapel Hill: University of North Carolina Press, 1987), p. 30.

12. The Reckoning

1. District Manager James Gaska always seems upbeat. Interview, Rockaway, N.Y., 16 April 2002. But see the headline in the *New York Times*, "Out Here [the Rockaways] Doubt Springs Eternal," 4 February 2002.

2. United Way of New York City, *Neighborhood Profile No. 3: The Rockaways/Broad Channel Community District 12, Queens* (New York: United Way, 1994).

3. Rauch, Stuart, phone interview, 15 January, 2002.

4. United Way, *Neighborhood Profile*.

5. *New York Times*, 4 December 2001.

6. Locke, Leon, interview, Rockaway, N.Y., 5 October 1998. Schwach, Howard, interview, Rockaway, N.Y., 1 April 2002.

7. Jonathan Rieder makes a similar point regarding Canarsie. See his *Canarsie: The Jews and Italians of Brooklyn Against Liberalism* (Cambridge: Harvard University Press, 1985), p. 23.

8. For a discussion of terminology, see Jennifer L. Hochschild, *Facing Up to the American Dream* (Princeton: Princeton University Press, 1995).

9. Richard Geist, "The Wreck of the Rockaways," *New York Affairs* 2 (1974): 92.

10. Michael Winerip, "Bedlam on the Streets," *New York Times Magazine* (23 May 1999).

11. Jill Eisenstadt, *From Rockaway* (New York: Vintage, 1988).

12. Gaska, interview.

13. See especially Kenneth T. Jackson, *Crabgrass Frontier* (New York: Oxford University Press, 1985), and Douglas S. Massey and Nancy A. Denton, *American Apartheid: Segregation and the Making of an Underclass* (Cambridge: Harvard University Press, 1963).

14. Massey and Denton, *American Apartheid*, p. 77.

15. Hochschild, *Facing Up* , p. 6.

16. William Julius Wilson, *The Truly Disadvantaged: The Inner City, the Underclass, and Public Policy* (Chicago: University of Chicago Press, 1987), pp. 4, 7, 8, 56–58.

17. Craig Steven Wilder, *A Covenant with Color: Race and Social Power in Brooklyn* (New York: Columbia University Press, 2000.), p. 234.

18. Congressman Gregory W. Meeks, speech at Arverne Library, 17 September 2001.

19. *Wave*, 31 August 1996.

20. United Way, *Neighborhood Profile*.

Bibliography

Official Publications and Documents

Arverne Urban Renewal Project. *Cultural Resources Survey*. New York, 1986.

Borough of Queens. *The Rockaway Plan*. New York, 1973.

Breezy Point Files. Municipal Archives.

Citizens Housing and Planing Council. Newsletters.

Community Board #14. *Resource Directory*. New York, 1998.

"Comprehensive Pediatric Care for Rockaway," Paper submitted to New York Department of Health, Education, and Welfare, 1966.

Home Owners' Loan Corporation. City Survey Files. RG 195. National Archives.

Impelliteri, Vincent. Departmental Files. Municipal Archives.

————. General Correspondence. Municipal Archives

Lindsay, John V. Departmental Files. Municipal Archives.

————. General Correspondence. Municipal Archives.

————. Subject Files. Municipal Archives.

Moses, Robert. Files. Metropolitan Transportation Authority.

————. Papers. New York Public Library.

National Park Service. "Gateway, National Recreation Area." New York and New Jersey, n.d.

New York City Board of Education. Utilization Handbooks.

New York City Board of Estimate. Papers. Municipal Archives.

New York City Commission on Human Rights. *Redlining in Rockaway*. New York, 1978.

New York City Department of City Planning. Newsletters.

New York City Department of Parks. Files. Municipal Archives.

————. *Cross Bay Boulevard Improvement*. 1941.

————. *The Future of Jamaica Bay*. 1938.

————. *The Improvement of Coney Island.* 1939.

————. *The Improvement of Coney Island, Rockaway, and South Beach.* 1937.

————. *The Rockaway Improvement.* 1939.

New York City Housing Authority. Files. LaGuardia Community College.

New York City Parks Council. Newsletter. Municipal Archives.

New York City Planning Commission. *Plan for New York City: Queens, A Proposal.* 1969.

————. *The Rockaways: A Report to the Community.* New York, 1973.

O'Dwyer, William. Departmental Files. Municipal Archives.

————. General Correspondence. Municipal Archives.

Queens Borough President. "Study and Recommendation for the Development of the Recreational Resources & Parklands of the Rockaway Penninsula & Broad Channel." New York, 1975.

Queens County. "The Rockaway Resort Casino Study." January, 1979.

Rockaway Review. Chamber of Commerce of the Rockaways.

Rockefeller, Nelson A. Public Papers. State of New York.

Urban Action Task Force. Office of Mayor John V. Lindsay. "Report on the Rockaways." New York, 1971.

U.S. Bureau of the Census. Census Reports. 1950, 1960, 1970, 1980, 1990.

Wagner, Robert F. Departmental Files. Municipal Archives.

————. General Correspondence. Municipal Archives.

Newspapers

Amsterdam News
Boston Globe
Long Island Press
Long Island Star Journal.
Newsday
New York Daily Mirror
New York Daily News
New York Herald Tribune
New York Journal American
New York Post
New York Sun
New York Times
New York World Telegram and Sun
Rockaway Journal
Rockaway News
Sunday Daily News
Village Voice
Wave

Secondary Works

Adams, Charles. *The City is the Frontier*. New York: Harper and Row, 1965.
———. *Forbidden Neighbors: A Study in Housing*. New York: Harper and Row, 1955.
Anderson, Martin, *The Federal Bulldozer: A Critical Analysis of Urban Renewal*. Cambridge: MIT Press, 1964.
Beatty, Jerome. "The Most Hated Man in Town." *American Mercury* (1 September, 1950): 24–25, 116–20.
Bell, Winifred. *Aid to Dependent Children*. New York: Columbia University Press, 1965.
Bellush, Jewel. "Housing: The Scattered-Site Controversy." In *Race and Politics in New York City*, edited by Jewel Bellush and Stephen M. David, pp. 98–133. New York: Praeger, 1971.
Berman, Marshall. *All That is Solid Melts into Air*. New York: Simon and Schuster, 1988.
Blau, Joel. *The Visible Poor: Homelessness in the United States*. New York: Oxford University Press, 1992.
Blumberg, Barbara. *The New Deal and the Unemployed: The View from New York City*. Lewisburg, Pa.: Bucknell University Press, 1979.
Cannato, Vincent J. *The Ungovernable City: John Lindsay and His Struggle to Save New York*. New York: Basic Books, 2001.
Caro, Robert A. *The Power Broker: Robert Moses and the Fall of New York*. New York: Vintage Books, 1975.
Casey, Marion R. "From the East Side to the Seaside." In *The New York Irish*, edited by Ronald H. Baylor and Timothy J. Meager, pp. 395–415. Baltimore: Johns Hopkins Press, 1996.
Clark, Kenneth B. *Dark Ghetto: Dilemmas of Social Power*. 2nd ed. Middletown, Conn.: Wesleyan University Press, 1965.
Davies, J. Clarence III. *Neighborhood Groups and Urban Renewal*. New York: Columbia University Press, 1966.
Eisenstadt, Jill. *From Rockaway*. New York: Vintage Books, 1988.
Fainstein, Norman I., and Susan S. Fainstein, "Governing Regimes and the Political Economy of Development in New York City, 1946–1984." In *Power, Culture, and Place*, edited by John Hull Mollenkopf, pp. 161–199. New York: Russell Sage Foundation, 1980.
Friedman, Lawrence M. *Government and Slum Housing*. Chicago: Rand McNally, 1968.
Friedman, Samuel G. *Upon this Rock: The Miracles of a Black Church*. New York: Harper Collins, 1993.
Frost, Olivia P., et al. *Aspects of Negro Life in the Borough of Queens, New York City*. New York: Urban League of Greater New York City, 1947.
Gans, Herbert J. *The Urban Villages*. New York: Free Press, 1962.

Garvin, Alexander. *The American City: What Works, What Doesn't*. New York: McGraw Hill, 1966.

Geist, Richard. "The Wreck of the Rockaways." *New York Affairs* 2 (1974): 90–103.

Glazer, Nathan. "Housing Problems and Housing Policies." *The Public Interest* 7, (Spring 1967): 21–51.

Gottehrer, Barry. *The Mayor's Man*. New York: Doubleday, 1975.

Gregory, Robert Paul. "Parks and People, Values and Decisions: Proposals for the Breezy Point Park, New York City." Ph.D. diss., Cornell University, 1980.

Gregory, Steven. *Black Corona: Race and the Politics of Place in an Urban Community*. Princeton: Princeton University Press, 1998.

Halpern, Robert. *Fragile Families, Fragile Solutions*. New York: Columbia University Press, 1999

Harrington, Michael. *The Other America: Poverty in the United States*. New York: Macmillan, 1962.

Hays, Samuel P. *Conservation and the Gospel of Efficiency: The Progressive Conservation Movement, 1890–1920*. New York: Atheneum, 1969.

Helper, Rose. *Racial Policies and Practices of Real Estate Brokers*. Minneapolis: University of Minneapolis Press, 1969.

Hentoff, Nat. *A Political Life: The Education of John V. Lindsay*. New York: Knopf, 1969.

Hewell, Grace. "Neighborhood Health Improvement Through Functional Organization." Ph.D. diss., Columbia Teachers College, 1958.

Hirsch, Arnold R. *Making the Second Ghetto: Race and Housing in Chicago, 1940–1960*. New York: Cambridge University Press, 1983.

Hochschild, Jennifer L. *Facing Up to the American Dream*. Princeton: Princeton University Press, 1995.

Jackson, Kenneth T. *Crabgrass Frontier*. New York: Oxford University Press, 1985.

———., ed. *The Encyclopedia of New York City*. New Haven: Yale University Press, 1995.

Jacobs, Jane. *The Death and Life of Great American Cities*. New York: Modern Library, 1993

Jargowsky, Paul A. *Poverty and Place: Ghettos, Barrios, and the American City*. New York: Russell Sage Foundation, 1997.

Jencks, Christopher, and Paul E. Peterson, eds. *The Urban Underclass*. Washington, D.C.: The Brookings Institution, 1991.

Johnson, Ann Braden. *Out of Bedlam: The Truth About Deinstitutionalization*. New York: Basic Books, 1990.

Kranzler, George. *Williamsburg: A Jewish Community in Transition*. New York: Philipp Feldheim, 1961.

Kroessler, Jeffrey A. "Building Queens: The Urbanization of New York City's Largest Borough." Ph.D. diss., City University of New York, 1991.

———. "Robert Moses and the New Deal in Queens." In *Robert Moses: Single-*

Minded Genius, edited by Joann P. Krieg, 101–108. Interlocken, N.Y.: Heart of Lakes, 1989.

Kusmer, Kenneth L. *A Ghetto Takes Shape: Black Cleveland, 1870–1970.* Urbana: University of Illinois Press, 1976.

Lemann, Nicholas. *The Promise Land.* New York: Knopf, 1991.

Lencek, Lena, and Gideon Bosker. *The Beach: The History of Paradise on Earth.* New York: Viking, 1998.

Levine, Hillel, and Lawrence Harmon. *The Death of an American Jewish Community: A Tragedy of Good Intentions.* New York: The Free Press, 1992.

The Livable City. New York: Municipal Art Society, 1998.

Lowry, Ira S. "Where Should the Poor Live?" In *New York Unbound*, edited by Peter D. Salins. New York: Basil Blackwell, 1988.

Massey, Douglas S., and Nancy A. Denton, *American Apartheid: Segregation and the Making of an Underclass.* Cambridge: Harvard University Press, 1963.

Mayer, Egon. *From Suburb to Shtetl: The Jews of Boro Park.* Philadelphia: Temple University Press, 1979.

McCarthy, Henry L. "Memoir." Oral History Office, Columbia University.

McDermott, Alice. *Charming Billy.* New York: Delta, 1998

McKenzie, Margo Janet, and Julia Mae Blair. *Reverend Joseph H. May: Pastor, Humanitarian, Community Activist.* Arverne, N.Y.: The Reverend Joseph H. May Book Dedication Committee, 2001.

Mendelson, Mary Adelaide. *Tender Loving Greed: How the Incredibly Lucrative Nursing Home 'Industry' is Exploiting America's Old People and Defrauding Us All.* New York: Knopf, 1974.

Mollenkopf, John H. *A Phoenix in the Ashes: The Rise and Fall of the Koch Coalition in New York City Politics.* Princeton: Princeton University Press, 1992.

Morris, Charles R. *The Cost of Good Intentions: New York City and the Liberal Experiment, 1960–1975.* New York: W. W. Norton and Company, 1980.

Moses, Robert. *Housing and Recreation.* New York: New York City Department of Parks, 1938.

———. *Public Works: A Dangerous Trade.* New York: McGraw Hill, 1970.

Moss, Doris, "Arverne Revisited: The Relative Importance of Community Problems." Ph.D. diss., New York University School of Education, 1972.

———. "A Study of Attitudes Towards Community Problems in Arverne, Queens." Master's thesis, Brooklyn College, 1965.

Osofsky, Gilbert. *Harlem: The Making of a Ghetto.* New York: Harper and Row, 1968.

Patterson, James T. *America's Struggle Against Poverty, 1900–1980.* Cambridge: Harvard University Press, 1981.

Pattillo-McCoy, Mary. *Black Picket Fences: Privilege and Peril Among the Black Middle Class.* Chicago: University of Chicago Press, 2000.

Plunz, Richard A. *A History of Housing in New York City.* New York: Columbia University Press, 1990.

Pritchett, Wendell. *Brownsville, Brooklyn: Blacks, Jews, and the Changing Face of the Ghetto*. Chicago: University of Chicago Press, 2002.

Queens Chamber of Commerce. "Statement on Breezy Point." 14 August 1962. Queensborough Public Library.

Ravitch, Diane. *The Great School Wars*. New York: Basic Books, 1974.

Rieder, Jonathan. *Canarsie: The Jews and Italians of Brooklyn Against Liberalism*. Cambridge: Harvard University Press, 1985.

Sanchez, George J. *Becoming Mexican American*. New York: Oxford University Press, 1993.

Sanjek, Roger. *The Future of Us All: Race and Neighborhood Politics in New York City*. Ithaca: Cornell University Press, 1998.

Schrecker, Ellen. *Many Are the Crimes: McCarthyism in America*. Boston: Little, Brown and Company, 1998.

Schwartz, Joel. *The New York Approach: Robert Moses, Urban Liberals, and Redevelopment of the Inner City*. Columbus, Ohio: Ohio State University Press, 1993.

Serrin, William. *Homestead: The Glory and Tragedy of an American Steel Town*. New York: Times Books, 1992.

Seyfried, Vincent, and William Asadorian. *Old Rockaway, New York, in Early Photographs*. Mineola, N.Y.: Dover Publications, 2000.

Shefter, Martin. *Political Crisis, Fiscal Crisis*. New York: Basic Books, 1985.

Starr, Roger. "Easing the Housing Crisis." In *New York Unbound*, edited by Peter D. Salins, 170–86. New York: Basil Blackwell, 1988.

———. *The Rise and Fall of New York City*. New York: Basic Books, 1985.

Steinlieb, George, and David Listokin. "A Review of National Housing Policy." In *Housing America's Poor*, edited by Peter Salins, 14–44. Chapel Hill: University of North Carolina Press, 1987.

Sugrue, Thomas J. *The Origins of the Urban Crisis: Race and Inequality in Postwar Detroit*. Princeton: Princeton University Press, 1996.

Tobier, Emanuel. *The Changing Face of Poverty: Trends in New York City's Population in Poverty, 1960–1990*. New York: Community Service Society, 1984.

United Way of New York City. *Neighborhood Profile No. 3: The Rockaways/Broad Channel Community District 12, Queens*. New York: United Way, 1994.

The Urban Audubon (August–September 1987).

Waldinger, Roger. *Still the Promised Land? African Americans and New Immigrants in Postindustrial New York*. Cambridge: Harvard University Press, 1996.

Walkowitz, Daniel. *Working with Class*. Chapel Hill: University of North Carolina Press, 1999.

Waters, Mary C. *Black Identities: West Indian Dreams and American Realities*. Cambridge: Harvard University Press, 1999.

Wave: 100th Anniversary Collector's Edition. 24 July, 1993.

Wilder, Craig Steven. *A Covenant with Color: Race and Social Power in Brooklyn*. New York: Columbia University Press, 2000.

Wilson, William Julius. *The Truly Disadvantaged: The Inner City, the Underclass, and Public Policy*. Chicago: University of Chicago Press, 1987.

Winerip, Michael. "Bedlam on the Streets." *New York Times Magazine* (23 May 1999).

Winnick, Louis. *New People in Old Neighborhoods*. New York: Russell Sage Foundation, 1990.

Women's Industrial Service League. *65th Anniversary Papers*. 1996.

Wood, Elizabeth. *The Small Hard Core: The Housing of Problem Families in New York City*. New York: Citizens' Housing and Planning Council of New York, 1957.

The WPA Guide to New York City: The Federal Writers' Project Guide to the 1930s. Reprint. New York: Random House, 1992.

Wylie, Jeanie. *Poletown: Community Betrayed*. Urbana: University of Illinois Press, 1989.

Yates, Douglas. *The Ungovernable City*. Cambridge: MIT Press, 1977.

Index